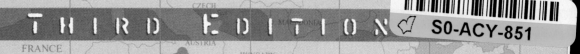

THIRD EDITION

THE CAREER ADVENTURE

YOUR GUIDE TO PERSONAL ASSESSMENT, CAREER EXPLORATION, AND DECISION MAKING

Susan M. Johnston

SINCLAIR COMMUNITY COLLEGE

Prentice
Hall

Upper Saddle River, New Jersey
Columbus, Ohio

Library of Congress Cataloging-in-Publication Data

Johnston, Susan M.
    The career adventure : your guide to personal assessment, career exploration, and
decision making / Susan M. Johnston.—3rd ed.
        p. cm.
    Includes bibliographical references and index.
    ISBN 0-13-093833-5
    1. Vocational guidance.   2. Vocational interests.   3. Self-evaluation.   4. Job hunting.   5.
College students—Employment.   I. Title.

HF5381 .J574 2002
650.14—dc21   2001028750

Vice President and Publisher: Jeffery W. Johnston
Acquisitions Editor: Sande Johnson
Assistant Editor: Cecilia Johnson
Production Editor: Holcomb Hathaway
Design Coordinator: Diane C. Lorenzo
Cover Designer: Andrew Lundberg
Cover Art: Lisa Zador/Artville
Production Manager: Pamela D. Bennett
Director of Marketing: Kevin Flanagan
Marketing Manager: Christina Quadhamer
Marketing Assistant: Barbara Koontz

This book was set in Goudy by Aerocraft Charter Art Service. It was printed and bound by Banta Book
Group. The cover was printed by Banta Book Group.

Prentice-Hall International (UK) Limited, *London*
Prentice-Hall of Australia Pty. Limited, *Sydney*
Prentice-Hall Canada Inc., *Toronto*
Prentice-Hall Hispanoamericana, S.A., *Mexico*
Prentice-Hall of India Private Limited, *New Delhi*
Prentice-Hall of Japan, Inc., *Tokyo*
Pearson Education Singapore Pte. Ltd.
Editora Prentice-Hall do Brasil, Ltda., *Rio de Janeiro*

10 9 8 7 6 5

ISBN 0-13-093833-5

CONTENTS

PART II CAREER EXPLORATION 45

LEARNING ABOUT THE WORLD OF WORK

4 Exploring the World of Work 47

5 Networking 71

Establishing Contacts and Support

6 Decision Making and Goal Setting   89

PART III THE JOB CAMPAIGN   103

ORGANIZING YOUR SEARCH

7 Designing Your Resume and Cover Letters   105

8 Interviewing with Confidence   139

9 Developing Job Leads   157

10 Trying Out a Career   173

11 Continuing Your Adventure   185

APPENDIX

1 Sample Resumes and Cover Letters   189

APPENDIX

2 Additional Resources   195

DEDICATION

To my husband Jack, and my sons, Charlie, Mitch, and Russ . . .
My deepest gratitude for your love and support.

PREFACE

Choosing a career is an exciting process of self-discovery. It draws you out into the world to explore careers, and sets your path with decisions that will result in insight, growth, and reward. This journey is most fulfilling when undertaken with a belief in yourself, a willingness to risk, and a sense of humor! The adventure does not end when a career is chosen—the career is always a work in progress and continues to change as the adventurer grows and changes.

The most important resource in any career adventure is you—the person who explores new vistas and makes the career choice. *The Career Adventure: Your Guide to Personal Assessment, Career Exploration, and Decision Making, Third Edition*, is designed to actively engage readers in planning their own careers. The exercises and activities found throughout the book make the adventure an interactive one; you are encouraged to consider thoughtfully each step of the journey, building confidence as you see your decisions yield results.

The book is divided into three parts. Part I, "Self-Assessment: Learning About Yourself," focuses on self-knowledge and discovery. Students explore career dreams, motivations, values, life stages, abilities and skills, personality, and interests. Examining these areas begins the process of discernment that is critical to making a meaningful career choice.

Part II, "Career Exploration: Learning About the World of Work," guides you through the career market and trends and investigates government resources and other publications. Important discussions of networking and decision making, accompanied by practical exercises, help readers set goals and then formulate plans and develop skills to achieve those goals.

Part III, "The Job Campaign: Organizing Your Search," looks at the job search, examining the details of resume writing, interviewing and marketing skills, and how to gain hands-on experience through internships and volunteer work. You will have an immediate opportunity to apply new skills when working through the exercises. Even students who do not plan to enter the full-time job market immediately will benefit greatly from the information in Part III.

This third edition of *The Career Adventure* takes a fresh look at the adventure of career planning and the influence of information technology on the process and landscape of career development. Perhaps no field has been influenced as profoundly by the explosion of information as has career planning. Finding information is easy. Indeed, we're buried in data. Chapter 4, *Exploring the World of Work*, seeks to simplify and focus the process of gathering data by offering guidelines for productive use of the Internet. Along with Web sites of proven value (at the end of each chapter and in Appendix 2), I recommend search techniques that minimize "Web wandering." These techniques make the Internet the valued tool it should be, instead of a maze of career cul-de-sacs.

Additionally, the infusion of technology into the workplace spurred explosive growth during the 1990s. While growth has leveled, we are still likely to find ourselves on an ecomonic roller coaster as we cope with energy needs and extend the infrastructure of technology to every corner of our culture. This edition emphasizes steady, step-by-step progression toward goals that flow from your growth and your ability to calmly go with that flow, without being at the mercy of economic trends.

Suggestions for group discussions appear throughout the book, giving you the opportunity to interact with peers, instructors, administrators, and the community. Internet resources and pertinent Web sites are offered throughout the book to expand your information base and help you become familiar with using electronic resources, necessary skills in today's career/job marketplace. This real-world exchange connects the classroom to the larger world, in preparation for the actual job campaign.

The world around us plays a dramatic and constantly changing role in our career adventures. However, it is the adventurer who guides the journey and determines the outcome. Recognizing what information is needed, knowing how and where it can be found, and understanding what can be done with it are the keys to achieving any and every goal. *The Career Adventure* was written to help you acquire the skill and confidence to see the goal and achieve it!

ACKNOWLEDGMENTS

This book could not have become a reality without the generous support and encouragement of the following people. I would like to thank them for their efforts.

Dr. Lamarr Reese, Terry Maiwurm, and Leonard Banks supported my growth and development as a career counselor. They were exceptional resources in the development of particular ideas for the book and in helping me to better understand cooperative education and its value to students. Brenda Krueger and M. L. Smith shared with me their ideas about personality development and cooperative education. I would also like to extend my appreciation to Tony Allen, who was invaluable in helping me more fully understand the significance of diversity in career issues. A big thank you to Bruce Anderson for guidance on electronic transmission of resumes. My thanks also go to Jon Sergeant, the Bureau of Labor Statistics, for assistance with labor trends data.

Karen Witt, Ann Hall, and Dodie Munn allowed me to enjoy the special relationship that comes from shepherding students through career decision making in the Adult Re-Entry classes. The staff members of the Career Planning and Placement Center, the Experience-Based Education Department, and the Learning Resources Center of Sinclair Community College aided me in locating materials and helped me to understand more fully the challenges that students encounter when making career decisions in a college setting. Their help was invaluable.

My thanks to Dr. Priscilla Mutter, who taught me about letting go and finding balance. My special thanks to Del Vaughan for the opportunity he gave me to work with students under his leadership—a peak experience as a career professional. I would also like to extend my gratitude to Dr. Jean Cook for her active promotion and support of my goals and dreams and her continuing belief in my ability to make them a reality.

I am very grateful to the following reviewers, who read this material in various stages of its development and offered ideas as to how it might be improved: Mikel J. Johnson, Emporia State University; Carole J. Wentzel, Orange County Community College; Jan L. Brakefield, University of Alabama; Pat Joachim Kitzman, Central College; Eve Madigan, Los Angeles Trade Technical College; Dave Sonenberg, Southeast Community College; Pablo Cardona, Milwaukee Area Technical College; Katy Kemeny, Lansing Community College; Cliff Nelson, Hinds Community College; and Maria Mitchell, Reading Area Community College. Students will find the book more readable and more helpful as a result of their efforts.

I would also like to thank Sande Johnson, Cecilia Johnson, Pam Bennett, JoEllen Gohr, and Gay Pauley for their guidance and support as editors and production coordinators of this book.

Finally, I would like to thank my parents, Claude and Marcia Kelnhofer, for instilling in me a strong work ethic and a basic respect for all types of work. Their influence led me to a deeper understanding of the meaning of work and career in our growth and development as human beings.

Indian
Ocean

of
Carpentaria

Coral
Sea

VANUAT

AUSTRALIA

NEW CALEDONIA

ABOUT THE AUTHOR

With approximately 20 years of experience in career development and counseling, Susan M. Johnston has had the opportunity to work closely with hundreds of students and clients who have chosen to take on the challenge of career planning. As an instructor in career planning and a private practice career advisor, she has guided individuals through the process of self-assessment, career exploration, and decision making to achieve their career goals. Prior to her classroom and private practice experience, she held positions at Sinclair Community College in the area of Cooperative Education and with the Career Planning and Placement Center. In addition to her teaching and counseling services, she is currently providing career planning consulting services to secondary schools seeking to update and implement career development programs.

Susan graduated summa cum laude from Wright State University with a B. A. in Communications and holds an M. S. Ed. in Counseling from the University of Dayton. In past positions, she has been on assignment with the State Department in India for the U. S. Information Agency, and prior to her experience as an educator, she was a contract negotiator for the U. S. Air Force. She is an active member of the American Counseling Association, the National Career Development Association, and the Ohio Counseling Association. She also has written a number of articles and presented workshops in the areas of career planning and balancing roles.

Susan is married to Jack W. Johnston, a man who is regularly mistaken for Paul McCartney. Unfortunately, when she was growing up, Susan's favorite Beatle was Ringo; fortunately, as Jack has aged, he has begun to look more like Ringo. He is the CEO of DAPSCO, a business services corporation.

Susan is a pacifist whose oldest son, Charles, is a U. S. Marine of whom she is insufferably proud. He is also a student at The Ohio State University. Susan's middle son, Mitch, is a varsity soccer player and co-captain of his high school soccer team. She and Mitch took swing dance lessons two years ago and were a hit at the Mother–Son Dance. Her youngest son, Russ, is a total football monster as the offensive guard for his championship team.

INTRODUCTION

Welcome to the exciting, chaotic process of career decision making! We are all involved in our own real-life career adventure. We are constantly challenged to understand more deeply who we are and what we are looking for in our lives and our careers. This process of choosing a career is an adventure—a discovery of *who you are*. Understanding yourself is an important aspect of growing and becoming an adult in our culture. The real you has a voice that seeks expression in a variety of ways, one of which is through your career.

A career is a primary path for personal growth, a way to define and expand yourself at the same time. It is a source of economic support, emotional strength, and a means for self-discovery. Making a career choice involves finding an arena that will meet your needs and offer you opportunities for genuine growth.

This book offers a model for career development. It will guide you through the process of career decision making and start you on the path toward a satisfying career. The steps in this process are summarized below:

- *Self-Assessment:* Learning about you, your motivations, values, skills, interests. You are the starting point in your career development.
- *Career Exploration:* Finding out about the world of work and how you might fit into careers that interest you. This step involves taking a look at careers and the job market.
- *The Job Campaign:* Preparing yourself for available opportunities and the challenges of entering the world of work.

Achieving your career goals requires organization and preparation. Let's start by taking a closer look at the process you will use as you begin your journey.

SELF-ASSESSMENT

In the first three chapters you will begin the exciting and challenging process of self-assessment. The self-assessment process is similar to exploring a room in which there are a huge number of interesting objects, all related to one another, like pieces of a puzzle. As you wander through the room, you see that each object represents some aspect of your life and experience. You may recognize many of the objects from past experiences. Some of them may prompt memories of joy, sorrow, satisfaction, or any number of emotions. Some may evoke no feelings at all, but may simply reflect something about yourself that you have always known and accepted. Whatever your reaction, you realize that each of these things is a part of you and has contributed to who you are now and to what you may eventually become.

Making career decisions begins in almost the same fashion. You examine aspects of your life, values, personality, motivations, interests, and skills, in order to understand yourself better. Once you have assessed your needs and interests, you will then identify occupations and careers that correspond with those needs and interests. Finding out more about potential occupations and careers is the next phase of career decision making.

CAREER EXPLORATION

After discovering what careers most appeal to you, the next step is to learn as much as you can about them. In Chapters 4, 5, and 6, you will learn how to research the career market and explore available jobs. Some of the information you gather will be drawn from written materials. New career information resources are becoming available daily through information technology. You will also obtain much useful information by talking with people who have firsthand knowledge of the field—a process known as *networking*.

Networking gives you an inside look at a career and the people who have chosen that discipline before you have to make a commitment to that career. In addition, through networking you begin to develop your own set of contacts, some of whom may remain a valuable resource throughout your work life.

At this point in a career adventure, you will be ready to make concrete decisions about your career and begin to commit more formally to your career goal.

YOUR JOB CAMPAIGN

Chapters 7, 8, and 9 cover the tools and techniques for organizing a job-search campaign that will lead you to the career of your choice. Having knowledge and skills in a particular field is only one component of career success. In addition, you will learn how to showcase your abilities so that when you begin your job search, you will have a competitive edge. A well-written resume, an organized marketing campaign taking advantage of conventional and electronic search tools, and a comfortable interviewing style all are proven methods for job marketability.

The final two chapters discuss ways to "try out" a career before making a final decision and to develop a clear sense of the importance of the career in your continuing development.

Finding your career is a lifelong process—increased self-awareness allows you to grow, learn, gain insights, and make satisfying decisions as your career unfolds.

BEGINNING THE ADVENTURE

Learning about yourself and the work world, researching options, and making decisions—all of these steps are challenging and may create anxiety for many people. It may feel at times as if you are about to leap off a cliff into the unknown. Make up your mind that you are *ready* to jump into your career adventure. As you do, your strength and confidence will increase because you know:

■ *You will be doing everything possible to ensure a soft landing.* You will do the homework and the research, and you will feel secure with the information that you gain. You are a bright person who is learning to make the right choices. You are ready and well prepared.

■ *Even if your worst fears become reality and you are not satisfied with your choice, you can always change your mind.* You will be prepared to handle any obstacle that comes along. Besides, you have plenty of time to "wiggle your way" toward your ultimate goal. Your effort now will put you ahead of the game later.

And remember . . . this is an adventure! The freedom to examine who you are, the world in which you live, and then move toward a personal goal is a precious privilege—one that countless people around the world would risk everything to have. Ever since we were children, we've all been asked "What do you want to be when you grow up?" That question presumes free choice and its accompanying responsibilities. Cherish the freedom and excitement that this discovery process offers you. Whether you are 18 or 50, the career choices you make are the living reflections of who you are. Yes, the process may be chaotic and confusing at times. But it is the adventure of your lifetime. Go after it and enjoy the freedom and fun of **your** career!

PART ONE

SELF-ASSESSMENT

LEARNING ABOUT YOURSELF

The only place to start the career adventure is with *you*. Knowing as much as possible about yourself is critical to the decisions you make in the future. This is your chance to discover and appreciate the things that make you a unique individual.

The adventure begins by examining different areas of your life and experiences, with the goal of making any fuzzy and vague aspects more real and concrete. These components of who you are will gain meaning as you learn to relate them to your everyday life and translate them into possible career choices. Self-assessment reveals who you are more clearly. Then you can connect with a career that brings you meaning and fulfillment.

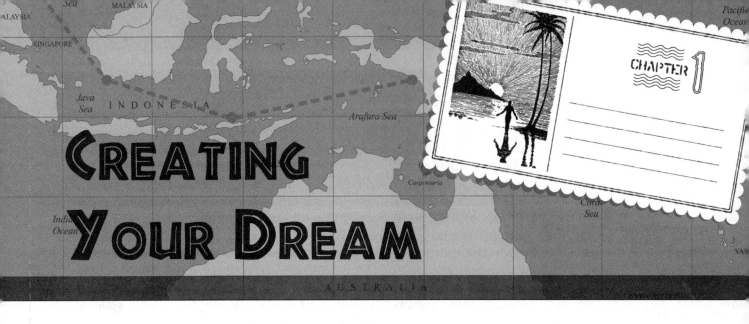

CREATING YOUR DREAM

To start, let's dream a bit . . .

Your dreams, fantasies, hopes, or whatever you wish to call them, are essential elements in career decision making. You may have met people who say "I've wanted to be a nurse (teacher, doctor, writer, and so on) ever since I was a child and here I am, and I love every minute of it." Sometimes it's that simple. Some lucky people have a dream or a vision of what they want to be. They pursue it and make it happen.

Think back for a minute about the dreams you had as a child. What did you see yourself doing as an adult? What did you dream about?

Jot down the idea(s) that you recall. How does it feel to think back to a time when anything seemed possible—a time before other responsibilities and obstacles may have eclipsed your dreams and made them unrealistic?

Do those dreams still appeal to you? Do they hold the same promise and excitement that they did when you were younger? Are they still possible as career choices? Or have you lost interest in the career that at one time seemed like the right one? Have you changed? Has the career you dreamt of changed?

WHO ARE YOU? WHO WOULD YOU LIKE TO BE?

A few years ago I worked with Jack, a young man who was struggling to decide whether to attend college or to find a job after high school. Jack had many interests and could not zero in on one specific career area. Finally I asked him just to imagine what he would do if he could do *anything at all*. He kind of snorted and said, "That's easy. I'd like to be a baseball player for the Cincinnati Reds." His natural response revealed that he enjoyed athletics and competition. Now we had to identify some options that might utilize those strengths in the unglamorous world of everyday life. "Well," I ventured, "if you couldn't do that, then what else do you think you might like?" He said, "I could play basketball for the Chicago Bulls."

Jack's dreams were understandable but probably unrealistic. He was focused on an idealized vision of himself, which made it hard for him to translate that vision into real-life terms.

Dreams allow us to see all the possibilities that exist within us. They give us insights into our true selves and what we want to be. Although it is enjoyable to imagine ourselves as superheroes, using our unique gifts to bring ourselves and others fulfillment, it is perhaps more important to identify realistic goals that encompass at least a *piece* of the dream. If you can't be Tiger Woods, perhaps you can coach or perform in another athletic setting and still find satisfaction. You might discover that being a recreation manager or a trainer for a professional team would satisfy some aspects of your dream.

Figure 1.1 shows that at age 18, with luck, you can look forward to a career that may extend to the ripe old age of 70, allowing you over 50 years to get in touch with your true self. Inherent in that process is having time to make choices, rethink those choices, and possibly change them to achieve more satisfying outcomes—living and learning. The trick is to keep your eye on the dream while learning and working with it so that it reflects your evolving identity.

I have also worked with people in their forties or fifties. People in this age range can expect to work for 20 to 30 more years. Older workers also have an advantage over 18-year-olds. They have lived long enough to have developed a sense of themselves, which helps them understand their needs, interests, and goals if they wish to seek a new career.

Sometimes, however, their insight may be clouded. Many people who look for new careers later in life have often spent a great deal of time putting other people's needs first. Single parents, homemakers, adults with dependents, and people who were raised to be model children frequently struggle to discern what they want and how they feel, because they are unaccustomed to putting their *own* feelings first.

It may be difficult for you, too, to put aside the needs of those you love for the moment, but it is crucial, at least for the initial phase of the career decision-making process, that you allow yourself to be as free as possible to consider every option and every dream. Throughout the book, you will have ample opportunity to identify obstacles and to develop strategies for overcoming them. For now, your primary task is to look honestly at your needs and hopes and translate those into goals that will help you achieve self-expression and fulfillment.

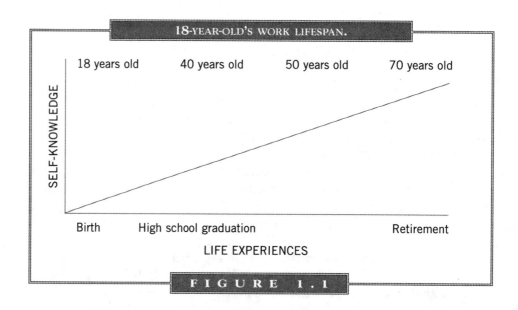

FIGURE 1.1

One final word. Now is not the time to start tallying your limitations and numbering the obstacles. Psychologists tell us that success and well-being are derived from a host of qualities unrelated to intelligence and physical capability. These qualities, referred to as "emotional intelligence," allow people to excel in the real world beyond the classroom. Daniel Goleman, author of the book *Emotional Intelligence*, identifies a number of qualities associated with emotional intelligence:

- *self-awareness*: the ability to recognize your own feelings as they take place and respond in a thoughtful, disciplined manner;

- *altruism*: a concern for the well-being of others;

- *personal motivation*: the drive to persist and achieve;

- *empathy*: the ability to understand and feel what others are feeling and communicate empathy appropriately;

- *the ability to love and be loved*: experiencing growth through intimacy and sharing.

These qualities can be nurtured by loving relationships and good choices. The very fact that you have chosen to examine the issues related to careers and your own growth shows your emotional intelligence is guiding your progress. The course you have selected will continue to nurture your development as a successful adult with a flourishing career, and a full, rewarding life.

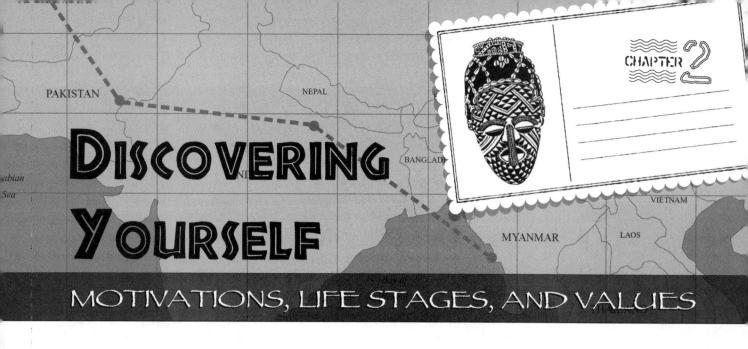

CHAPTER 2

DISCOVERING YOURSELF

MOTIVATIONS, LIFE STAGES, AND VALUES

Once I had abandoned the search for everyone else's truth, I quickly discovered that the job of defining my own truth was far more complex than I had anticipated.

INGRID BENGIS

Very likely, you are in the middle of the lifelong process of discovering who you are—not the person your parents want you to be, not the person your spouse and close friends think you should be, not the person your kids expect you to be, but the person you *are*. Self-discovery is a complicated process with no simple formula. It is the first and most important step in determining your career goals.

The assessment model presented here begins a process that in many ways will be self-propelling. Once you begin, you may find that you need little prompting to continue. In this chapter you learn more about your *motivations, life stages,* and *values*. Chapter 3 explores your *abilities and skills, personality,* and *interests*.

Those of you who are younger may struggle a bit with some areas of self-assessment that you have not yet encountered. Those of you with broad life experience may be a bit overwhelmed as you sort through the various aspects of your life. Change always involves some discomfort and anxiety. These are only the starting points from which you will begin your self-exploration. So be patient with yourself.

MOTIVATIONS: WHAT DRIVES YOU?

Motivations are the forces that move you to form goals and strive to achieve them. You may have heard high achievers referred to as having "a fire in the belly," an image that pictures someone who is consumed from within by a passion to reach a goal. Motivations are the "fire" or fuel that drives you forward.

Clearly, not all of us are motivated with the same amount of drive or by the same things. Some of us struggle just to get up in the morning, while others drive ourselves to the brink. Much of what motivates us originates in where we are psychologically and culturally.

Calvin and Hobbes

by Bill Watterson

Abraham Maslow, a noted psychologist, developed a model that describes how needs influence motivations. Maslow's "Hierarchy of Needs" has been used for the past 30 years to explain what moves people and gives their actions meaning. The model is shown in Figure 2.1.

Maslow suggested that human nature requires us to have our needs met in a pattern resembling a "climb" up a pyramid to a peak. To advance to the higher levels of need, you must first satisfy the needs at the base.

Think of it this way: You are one of the first inhabitants of a scarcely populated region of Earth.* As a primitive human you depend on a few basic skills and tools, passed on to you through your particular tribe. These

* My thanks to Felix Marshall for the inspiration for the cave man scenario.

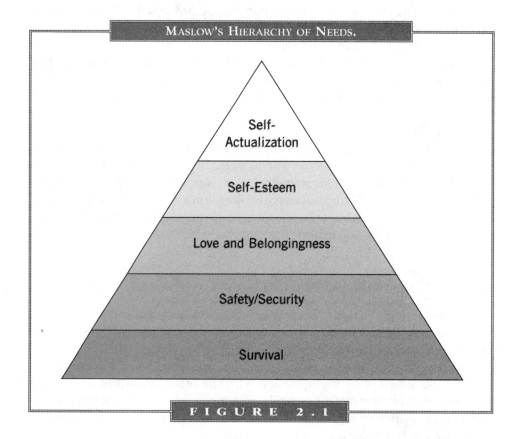

MASLOW'S HIERARCHY OF NEEDS.

Self-Actualization

Self-Esteem

Love and Belongingness

Safety/Security

Survival

FIGURE 2.1

skills and tools represent the accumulated knowledge of your group and as such are all that stands between you and . . . well, let's not dwell on that. Through a series of misadventures, you become separated from your tribe and are forced to survive on your own until you can get back to the safety of the group.

Every day of this separation is a challenge to find enough food to eat and to keep your body healthy while living in the harsh elements. You find a cave, cozy and dry, a real stroke of luck. You manage to find plants and a few edible bugs for nourishment. You have food, clothing, and shelter—you have met the needs of Maslow's most basic level, Survival.

You hear a noise outside the cave. Fortunately, you know how to make a fire, and the one at the mouth of your cave will keep unwelcome predators away. Your club is nearby and you feel quite secure. You have now reached the second level, Safety, or Security.

Still, you miss your home. You can't help recalling your spouse and your children. You would gladly return to the warmth of the home you knew with them. You may be warm and safe in your own cave, but you are alone, missing the benefits of Maslow's level three, Love and Belongingness.

As you grieve the loss of your loving home, you hear someone calling to you in the rudimentary language of your tribe. You listen and then respond. Soon you are reunited with your friends and family, who valued you enough to send out a search party. A happy reunion follows, and you are able to satisfy fully your need for love and belongingness.

Your return to the group is an occasion for great celebration. It seems that the tribe greatly missed your presence and your valued skills while you were gone. They are delighted to hear the exciting tales of your harrowing adventure. You are a significant participant in the group and have assumed an important role in your community. This level, Self-Esteem, represents your need to value your own importance and ability and your need for the tribe to value you as well. According to Maslow, esteem needs are basic to your growth as a healthy human being.

To advance to the highest level, Self-Actualization, requires being sensitive to our inner voice, which speaks within each of us. Self-actualization is the process of becoming everything that you are capable of and experiencing a sense of fulfillment and satisfaction with your choices in life. Only a small percentage of people reaches and sustains this level.

According to Maslow, to reach self-actualization, you must first proceed through the other levels. After all, it would be very difficult to experience contentment with your life choices if you had to focus primarily on seeking food to satisfy your hunger or shelter to keep you and your family safe.

It is common to be grappling with decisions and opportunities on different levels, especially when those decisions relate to your career. Many people simultaneously struggle with the challenges of preparing themselves for second careers and also supporting their families by remaining in jobs they've long since outgrown. They may be forced to cope with the frustrations of a job that is going nowhere for the short term; yet their efforts toward change elevate them to a higher level on Maslow's hierarchy, enhancing their self-esteem and expanding their vision of the future.

Exercise 2.1 helps you see where you are on Maslow's Hierarchy of Needs and how your place on it may influence the direction of your career path.

2.1 TAKE A CLOSER LOOK

Maslow's Pyramid

Take a look at the model of Maslow's Hierarchy of Needs and fill in the space with one- or two-word descriptions of ways in which you perceive your needs might be met at each level.

Self-Actualization

Self-Esteem

Love and Belongingness

Safety/Security

Survival

YOUR HIERARCHY OF NEEDS

Which levels have you completed?

_____

_____

Which have you completed partially?

_____

_____

Are you comfortable with where you find yourself? Are you at the highest point on the pyramid that you have ever been?

_____

_____

Are you looking forward to advancing to the next level? Why or why not?

_____

_____

Are you "stuck" in your present level? Why or why not?

_____

_____

Can you get "unstuck"? Do you want to?

_____

_____

Think about what is motivating you right now to examine your life and where you are going. At which level do your motivations place you?

_____

_____

Have you learned anything from the discussion of Maslow's hierarchy that relates to you and your motivations?

_____

_____

Discuss these questions with your group or with the class.

LIFE STAGES: WHERE DO YOU FIT?

For many years, prior to the advent of psychology as an acknowledged field of study, philosophers believed that there were only two life stages, childhood and adulthood. Even after theorists began to question this assumption, they still believed that adolescence was just a brief detour in the growth of humans and that growth essentially stopped when we physically reached adulthood. Now, on the basis of Erik Erikson's work and that of other psychologists, we realize that physical maturation is hardly the end of our growth as human beings. In fact, we continue to change and adapt throughout our lives.

There is still much to learn about each life stage, and psychological research is continually adding to our knowledge of adult growth. Figure 2.2 illustrates the most commonly recognized life stages and the experiences associated with them.

Much research still needs to be done concerning life stage development and how it translates to everyday living. We do know that each stage identified by Erikson presents different opportunities for growth through the events associated with that life stage. While some events may be linked to particular life stages, people can also experience events typically associated with one life stage during another part of their life. They may reencounter experiences they thought they had already dealt with conclusively. For example, you may assume the issue of finding a life partner is behind you when you marry. Then, suddenly, at 42 or 43, your loving spouse begins to seem like a stranger. You wonder what you might be missing in life by being tied down. Without knowing why, the issue is back in your life. You are reassessing your life, one of the growth experiences associated with that life stage. The resolution of your restless yearning depends on a range of issues related to you and your partner, your individual histories and temperaments, and how well you are able to work through conflicts in your relationship.

LIFE STAGE DEVELOPMENT.

Birth to Age 12 Childhood	Cognitive and social development; period of value development; modeling according to gender.
Age 13 to 18 Adolescence	Beginning of identity formation; period of intense questioning and testing of real versus ideal.
Age 18 to 22 Independent Adulthood	Continuation of identity formation; attempts to establish independent life and perhaps an intimate relationship.
Age 23 to 28 Adult Identity	Establishment of external place in society, i.e., decisions concerning career, relationships, personal experiences.
Age 29 to 32 Questioning	Attempts to integrate life choices; possible questioning of prior decisions with subsequent changes.
Age 33 to 35 Settling	Seeking stability; acceptance of adult decisions with goal of "rational" growth.
Age 36 to 45 Life Meaning	Reassessment; realization of mortality may initiate "midlife crisis."
Age 46 to 60 Resolution/Renewal	Based on midlife transition, may hold renewed vitality and challenge or loss of vigor and resignation.
Age 60 to 85 Retirement	Depending on health, possible "bonus" career to be realized on own terms; sense of satisfaction with life choices or despair over unsatisfying outcomes.

FIGURE 2.2

We are all faced with similar trade-offs throughout our lives. Seldom do our decisions yield clearcut outcomes, satisfaction guaranteed. The truly important issues are frequently ones that we visit more than once. In our increasingly open and flexible culture, we have many opportunities to revisit past choices and make responsible decisions.

Understanding the process of life stage development makes one fact dramatically clear: We all go through periods of growth and change. The inevitability of our growth makes finding a career that offers satisfaction and meaning a compelling goal. This author has known people who shrink from the prospect of four years of college because it seems like too long a time commitment. Pointing out that they will be four years older with or without the benefit of college education, so it might be worthwhile to invest their time and effort in something that will pay off, gives them a new perspective.

The right career can bring you a lifetime of fulfillment and growth. You have an outlet for using your unique talents, developing yourself through challenge and competition, learning to steady yourself through the trials of adult life, and reaping the rewards of doing a job to the best of your ability.

In Exercise 2.2, you will look at the life stages you have experienced, the events associated with them, and the opportunities that you may encounter in the future.

TAKE A CLOSER LOOK 2.2

Your Current Life Stage

Age _____   Life Stage _____

Review Figure 2.2. Find your life stage based on your age. Read the brief description corresponding to your age. Does the description reflect the way you see your current life stage?

_____

_____

If not, can you think of what circumstances in your life may have influenced your situation?

_____

_____

What do you hope to accomplish during this life stage?

_____

_____

Discuss your reactions with your group or the class.

VALUES: HOW WELL DO YOU KNOW YOURSELF?

Values are the things that we consider important or desirable. They represent needs that ideally become more clear and firm as we mature and learn more about who we are. As these values "crystallize" they shape our behavior and help us set goals. Values are shaped by our families, friends, churches, schools, textbooks, the media, and the whole range of our life experience. As we go through life, we encounter a variety of people and events, viewing them through the perspective of our values and their meaning to us.

While we may have only a small number of internalized values influencing us, they compete with each other to shape our actions through a complex structure of interrelationships. Let's say, for instance, that you value altruism, a concern for the well-being of others. You also value independence and autonomy. Your inclination toward altruistic careers might encourage you toward social work or counseling. Unfortunately, the salaries of social workers may not be sufficient to accommodate the competing value of independence. The decision is more complex if you have a need for prosperity. Only when values are prioritized can their competing influences be organized in a coherent pattern, a pattern that facilitates self-understanding and decision making.

Are the values that we are most in touch with today the ones that we are bound to follow for the rest of our lives? Much research indicates that while our attitudes and interests may change as a result of life experiences, our values remain relatively stable. We change and are influenced by life experiences, but our basis for understanding and evaluating our world is fairly consistent over time.

Think of your own life. While you probably do not prize the same things you did as a high school senior, your life is still a reflection of the core values to which you were exposed growing up. You've probably moved beyond the youthful idealism of your teenage years to a more mature view of the world and your place in it. Experiences gained through school, work, marriage, parenting, or any number of roles in the community can influence your perspective and give you a broader view of life without changing your values.

Let's look at an example to understand better the nature of values. You would like to own your own home, a result of your strong value for self-reliance. Owning your home is important and desirable. You begin to look for a house and soon find one that is suitable. You buy it and, now that you own your home, you no longer continue looking for a home. You now invest your energy in maintaining and enhancing your new home. Your basic value of owning a home as a way of being self-reliant has not changed but, as a result of your new experiences and growth, your actions have. You may indeed outgrow the house and look for another. Your value remains and you adjust it to meet the changing needs it reflects.

The same process may be influencing your present search for a new career. Perhaps your decision to look seriously at your career direction is a result of maturity and growth while still reflecting your deeper, unchanged values. Sometimes you may feel strongly about a value in the abstract, e.g., "equal job opportunities for all," but find yourself struggling with how those values are manifest in reality. You may feel that affirmative action initiatives are an excellent way to create opportunities for groups of people who have been closed out in the past—until just such a program results in a job rejection or demotion. In that case, it is a real test either to hold on to your original value or to question your belief.

Other situations may bring values into direct conflict. While you may look the part of the perfect corporate employee, your ability to relate with your "friends on the block" when you leave the office may make you feel as though you are living a double life. Do you keep your life divided, juggling your views to fit the situation you are in or do you find ways to harmonize your life? More threatening would be the situation in which one or the other side of your life demands your total commitment. While it is unlikely that would ever happen, your value for loyalty to friends and community may come in conflict with your value to succeed financially. Being able to resolve the tensions between those values will influence the direction of your life and career.

Our values ripple through every aspect of our lives to a greater or lesser extent. When we talk about jobs and the satisfaction we feel with our career choices, we can focus on a smaller, more manageable number of characteristics. We can begin to assess how our values affect our job/career priorities. Knowing clearly what *your* values are will enhance your ability to choose a gratifying career.

Exercise 2.3 gives you an opportunity to recognize your values as they relate to work and career and to prioritize their influence on your decision.

TAKE A CLOSER LOOK 2.3

Distinguishing Your Values

How much do you know about your values and the way they might influence your career and job choices?

Look at the list of values that follows. These values describe a wide variety of attributes associated with various work settings. Rate the degree of importance in choosing a career for yourself using the following scale.

1—Not important at all   3—Reasonably important
2—Somewhat important   4—Very important

_____ *Help society:* Do something to contribute to a better world

_____ *Help others:* Be involved in helping others in a direct way

_____ *Work with others:* Close working relationships with a group

_____ *Competition:* Pit my abilities against others with win/lose outcomes

_____ *Work under pressure:* Face situations with time constraints or where the quality of my work is judged critically

_____ *Power and authority:* Control work activities of others

_____ *Influence people:* Be in a position to change attitudes or opinions of others

_____ *Work alone:* Conduct work by myself, without contact with others

_____ *Knowledge:* Pursue knowledge, trust, and understanding

_____ *Personal growth:* Engage in work that offers me the opportunity to grow as a person

_____ *Creativity:* Engage in creative work, e.g., art, graphic design, photography, program planning, interior design, writing, composing, performing, and so on

_____ *Variety:* Have responsibilities that offer variety in content or setting

_____ *Stability and security:* Have a work situation that is predictable, with probability that I can keep my job

_____ *Recognition:* Be recognized for the quality of my work

_____ *Excitement:* Experience a high degree of excitement at work

_____ *Profit gain:* Have a strong possibility of earning large amounts of money

_____ *Location:* Work in a place near my home, with a short drive or bus ride

_____ *Fun:* Work in a setting where I am free to be playful, humorous, exuberant

_____ *Autonomy:* Have work responsibilities that allow me freedom to determine how and when the work is accomplished

_____ *Status:* Have a position that carries respect within the community

_____ *Advancement:* Have the opportunity to work hard and see rapid career advancement

_____ *Productive:* Produce tangibles, things I can see and touch

_____ *Aesthetic:* Create things that are beautiful and contribute to making the world more attractive

_____ *Achievement:* Experience a feeling of accomplishment for a job well done

_____ *Environment:* Work in a pleasant, clean, comfortable setting

_____ *Supervision:* Work as part of a team that is managed with fairness and appreciation

Now list the values you rated with a 4: very important.

_____

_____

Note the values you rated with a 3: reasonably important.

_____

_____

Do you see a pattern emerging? Can you see groupings that point to similar values in certain areas?

_____

_____

Take a look at the values you ranked with a 4. Ask yourself, "Is this important to me because *I* want it or because it will please others or win their respect and acceptance?"

_____

_____

Keep in mind that even if your values do not change, your priorities might as some needs are satisfied and others emerge. As you grow and change, continue to reassess and prioritize your values.

_____

_____

Discuss some of the new insights you may have discovered through this exercise with your group or the class.

KATIE'S STORY

Katie was facing her first career-planning class with a mixture of anticipation and skepticism. She'd been thinking and talking about what she might major in for so long it made her queasy to consider a whole term devoted to the subject. The fact that she was no closer to a decision than she had been when she was a high school freshman made her all the more apprehensive. After all the options and programs and possibilities she had considered, how could one class make a difference?

When she reached the classroom the first day, the instructor hadn't arrived yet. Katie took a seat near the front and looked over the textbook for the class. It looked like it would be fun to do the self-assessment exercises. She was surprised there wasn't more information about what careers were "hot." Within minutes the instructor for the class arrived and began to take attendance. "Do you want to be called 'Kathy' or 'Katherine'?" the instructor inquired when she got to Katie's name.

"'Katie' is fine," she managed. Furtively, she glanced around the room at her new classmates. The classroom was filled with students like herself, 18 or 19 years old, just getting started. An older man and a woman who looked like she might be in her late twenties were among the traditional students.

The instructor wrote her name on the board: Maggie Marshall. Katie sat up and listened intently as Maggie explained what would happen over the term and how to interpret the syllabus. Maggie was interesting and funny and shared a lot of information about her own career and how she had come to teach the career-planning class. Despite all of Katie's good feelings, she was unsure how the assignments would make any difference in her search for a career.

Katie wondered if anyone else was feeling similarly. After a break, the second half of the class included students' introductions, and Katie was relieved to hear several of the other students express their doubts about finding a career that they could be excited about. At least she was not alone. Maggie chatted amiably with each student after his or her introduction. At the end of class, Maggie explained that for their first assignment, each student was to "capture," or identify, a career dream and bring it to share with the class the following week. That actually sounded like it might be fun.

But Katie was surprised to find that she was struggling to pinpoint a career dream that she could tell the class. Every time she thought of a career that sounded interesting or fun, she came up with all the reasons why it just wouldn't work for her. Either the hours would be wrong or the pay too little or the work too hard. She felt like she was either too dumb or too young or just too inexperienced to consider anything that sounded the least bit interesting.

When it was Katie's turn to share her career dream at the next class, she knew she had to say something, so she flatly said she had always wanted to be a nurse. She was disappointed with herself, though, and after class she approached Maggie and explained her problem.

Maggie responded that sometimes when people are in situations in which they haven't had the chance to try out different types of roles or jobs, they may find it hard to choose. But just thinking about possibilities and considering them doesn't mean you have chosen them. It's just the first step in the process of finding a place in your life to satisfy your own hopes and needs. "Katie, are you sure that the things that you want to do are so far out of reach?" Maggie asked. "Before you decide that those things are impossible, try to get in touch with what you are feeling about yourself and your hopes for yourself. That's all the career dream represents . . . not a hard reality. It's just a way for you to set yourself free."

Katie left the class feeling better. She was ready to work on the assignments for next week, the work values assessment and a life stage development exercise. As she worked through the exercises, she reminded herself several times not to get stuck on making a final decision yet. She focused on being patient and letting her needs and interests surface slowly through the self-assessment process. She found out that her life stage involved establishing an independent life and continuing to form her identity. Her work values were focused on helping and influencing others and finding a way to be creative.

That seemed to strike a chord. She had always enjoyed art and had often been complimented on her work. But she didn't want to be an artist. That was too uncertain a path. As she considered the different possibilities in the exercises, she came upon the idea of teaching art, an idea she had never seriously considered before. Katie began to believe that there might be a career out there for her after all.

It was only the third class, so Katie had a great deal of work ahead of her. She still had to find out more about herself and the careers that might be available to her. But her conversations with Maggie kept her focused, and the exercises she completed had convinced her of two things: Finding a place for herself in her life might be a struggle, but she knew now that this was something only she could do. With her instructor's support, she was determined to make it happen.

Self-understanding can be an important part of choosing a career path and setting career goals. Exercise 2.4 may help you begin the process, using some of the tools we have already examined.

2.4 TAKE A CLOSER LOOK

Pulling It All Together

You have already begun to work to better understand yourself in the previous exercises. These questions will help you pull those impressions together.

What dreams did you start out with?

_____

_____

Where are you on Maslow's hierarchy?

_____

_____

What life stage are you in right now and what issues related to that stage are you currently considering?

_____

_____

_____

What do you want to accomplish in this life stage?

_____

_____

_____

What three work values did you respond to most strongly?

_____

_____

_____

How has identifying some of the factors that are important to you affected your understanding of yourself? Your career decision?

_____

_____

_____

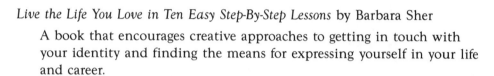

As a result of the first stage of your career adventure, you should have a good sense of the issues surrounding your motivations, the life stage you are in, the pressures associated with it, and information about your values concerning work and career. These areas of self-assessment all have a direct bearing on your career choice and will be considered again in later sections.

For now, it is important to realize that the unique combination of innate gifts and individual experiences with which you have been blessed are resources you will use to select a career and to find within yourself the courage and enthusiasm to make that choice a reality.

Other Sources and Suggested Reading

Live the Life You Love in Ten Easy Step-By-Step Lessons by Barbara Sher

A book that encourages creative approaches to getting in touch with your identity and finding the means for expressing yourself in your life and career.

Major in Success: Make College Easier, Fire Up Your Dreams, and Get a Very Cool Job by Patrick Combs

This book offers a good look at the whole process in a hip, fun format.

What Color Is Your Parachute? 2001 by Richard Nelson Bolles

This update of the classic manual for job hunters and career changers looks at the entire process of career decision making in a light, readable style.

Web Sites and Internet Resources

www.adm.uwaterloo.ca:80/infocecs/CRC/manual-home.html

The University of Waterloo, Canada, presents a comprehensive home page that includes a look at values, knowledge, and achievements.

www.bsu.edu/careers/values.html

Ball State University offers a values inventory on their Career Services Web page.

www.collegeboard.org

This site, sponsored by The College Board, is tailored for students beginning their career decision-making process. On the home page, click on site search on the menu bar. Click on Career Search, then click Questionnaire to access a full range of self-assessment tests.

CONTINUING YOUR SELF-DISCOVERY

SKILLS, PERSONALITY, AND INTERESTS

In the previous chapter, you began the process of self-assessment. This chapter gives you an opportunity to expand your knowledge of yourself by looking at three additional issues: *abilities and skills, personality,* and *interests.*

These three areas are valuable sources of information for developing your career decision. You will enrich your insight into your needs and how they can be met through your career.

ABILITIES/SKILLS: WERE YOU BORN WITH THEM?
CAN YOU LEARN THEM?

Abilities refer to those qualities that are part of you and the way that you relate to the world, intrinsic parts of who you are. An ability may be something as fundamental as understanding mathematics easily or it may be as intangible as facing a crisis calmly. Both of these are qualities that enable you to bring special talent to a particular situation.

The term *skills* is somewhat synonymous to abilities but has a more technical connotation. Generally, skills are those capabilities that can be acquired and developed through the exposure to and repetition of a task or learning process that may take place in a classroom or a lab, through training or study, or in a workplace. On the other hand, abilities are those talents or powers that are typically innate gifts and may be enhanced and developed to their maximum potential through study, training, or practice.

What are your unique talents and gifts? Your ability to identify and tap into both your inner capabilities and your skills will not only give you added confidence, but will also make you more marketable in the work world.

How can you identify and categorize career skills and abilities and match them up with career choices? The Department of Labor has a number of publications that explain how skills are related to career markets. The *Dictionary of Occupational Titles* and the *Guide for Occupational Exploration* (which we will look at in more detail in Chapter 4) describe specific categories that will help you evaluate your skills and abilities and explore how they may be relevant to further career development.

The skills and abilities listed in Figure 3.1 are grouped according to three categories: data, people, and things. As you survey the abilities and skills categorized, you may immediately see areas in which you consistently possess high-level skills. You may have become aware of these abilities through school, athletic events, hobbies, leisure activities, or other situations apart from paid employment. Your task now is to focus on what you have learned in the past and what your talents are now. You will identify settings for applying those talents in a later section.

SKILLS AND ABILITIES INVENTORY*

DATA

Synthesizing: Putting ideas and facts together in new ways to explain how things work; developing new ideas and theories.

Coordinating: Organizing things; planning projects; deciding in which order things must be done; checking to be sure the steps are done on time and correctly.

Analyzing: Studying information to find out what it means; deciding how to solve a problem.

Compiling: Collecting, arranging, or combining facts about data, people, or things and reporting the results.

Computing: Using arithmetic; reporting the results of computations and applying the data from those results.

Copying: Writing, listing, or entering numbers or letters exactly as seen.

Comparing: Deciding if data, people, or things are alike or different. Using rules to decide degree of difference.

PEOPLE

Mentoring: Helping people deal with problems; giving legal, scientific, clinical, spiritual, or other professional advice.

Negotiating: Talking over ideas, information, and opinions with others in order to reach positive solutions.

Instructing: Teaching people (or animals) by explaining, showing, or watching them practice; giving advice on a topic in which you have expertise.

Supervising: Directing workers by giving orders and explaining duties; making sure they do the work on time; acting as a team leader.

Entertaining: Amusing others; saying or doing things that people find interesting; working on stage, radio, or TV.

Persuading: Winning others over to purchase a product or service, or agree on a point of view.

Speaking/Signaling: Talking or making motions so people can understand and receiving information in return; giving verbal directions clearly and concisely so that listeners understand.

Serving: Helping people or animals; carrying out others' wants or wishes.

Taking Instruction/Helping: Doing as you are told; following orders without deciding whether they are right or wrong.

THINGS

Setting Up: Changing parts on machines; fixing mechanical objects if they break down; knowing how to operate several different machines.

Precision Working: Being responsible for making things that fit exact rules or standards; deciding which tools or materials to use to meet the specifications.

Operating/Controlling: Starting, stopping, and watching machines or equipment to be sure they are operating correctly; watching gauges, dials, and other devices, and changing valves or controls as needed.

Driving/Operating: Steering or guiding machines or tools; estimating distance, speed, and direction.

Manipulating: Moving, guiding, placing, or working things using your body or tools; selecting tools, objects, or materials.

Tending: Starting, stopping, and watching machines work; watching timers or gauges; making changes based on rules.

Feeding/Offbearing: Filling up or emptying machines that are run automatically or by other workers.

Handling: Moving or carrying things.

*Adapted from Marilyn Maze and Donald Mayall, *The Enhanced Guide for Occupational Exploration,* First Edition. Copyright © 1991 by Jist Works, Inc., Indianapolis. Reprinted with permission.

FIGURE 3.1

Exercise 3.1 is designed to assist you in determining what types of skills and abilities you possess and how those skills might be instrumental in choosing satisfying work.

TAKE A CLOSER LOOK 3.1

Acknowledge Your Abilities, Value Your Skills

Look at the categories and skills in Figure 3.1. Do you see any areas that you recognize in which you excel or possess a high level of capability?

_____

_____

How do you know you have these skills? Describe the setting in which you were able to demonstrate your ability.

_____

_____

Describe a specific incident associated with your demonstrated capability in which others recognized your skills.

_____

_____

What were the outcomes—tangible or intangible—of your having used that ability?

_____

_____

Describe your feelings while you were performing this skill and afterward.

_____

_____

Are you aware of any skills and abilities you possess that are not listed?

_____

_____

Do you recognize any categories of skills under which these "unlisted" skills would fit?

_____

_____

Discuss your reactions with your group or the class.

Calvin and Hobbes

by Bill Watterson

TRANSFERABLE SKILLS

Understanding your abilities and skills is vital to discovering who you are and what you have to offer, but this knowledge may not always determine your specific career path. Sometimes, like Calvin, we may find the things at which we are best have not yet found a market in the world of work. Just ask any mother or homemaker. Among your innate talents may lie the seed of your career.

All of your skills, whether rudimentary or highly developed, are transferable. *Transferable skills* are those that can be used in a variety of careers and work settings. If you have a particular ability that gives you a great deal of satisfaction, whether it's rocking your baby to sleep or sketching in your notebook while your teacher is lecturing, it may be the key to a career in which you can apply that ability.

Transferable skills are different from job-specific skills, or *work content skills.* Work content skills are skills directly related to a unique job description, such as operating a bulldozer, editing videotapes, or conducting lab tests.

Identifying your transferable skills can help you develop alternative career options. These skills are an especially valuable asset for career changers who have many talents but are seeking new ways and new settings in which to use them. Your transferable skills are often those you have used successfully during activities that you enjoyed. Using these skills gave you a strong sense of satisfaction.

Exercise 3.2 will help you identify your transferable skills.

 3.2   TAKE A CLOSER LOOK

Your Transferable Skills

Of all the skills we enjoy using, choosing ones that are transferable can help us envision ourselves in different work settings and can suggest career choices to explore further. You will identify your transferable skills by focusing on achievements or peak experiences that gave you a sense of satisfaction and fulfillment.

In the following space, list five achievements that you think were peak experiences, ones that allowed you to use your skills with good results. Note the details of your achievement, delineating the specifics of the event or task so that your notes resemble a job description. For example, rather than "Responded to a customer complaint," you might write "Greeted the customer, listened attentively to the complaint, asked questions to determine the exact nature of the problem, discussed possible remedies, contacted department, gathered information, resolved customer problem." After describing the event or events, list the skills that were necessary to achieve the results. For the above-mentioned episode, you might write down skills such as listening, remaining calm, negotiating, interpreting information, enlisting cooperation, and investigating and organizing resources. If necessary, review the list of skills on the preceding pages to help you identify those skills most critical to each of your specific achievements. The most important factor is that anything counts, whether you used a skill at work, school, home, or as part of a hobby. Your skills can be a valuable part of your career plan, so include everything that comes to mind!

ACHIEVEMENT EVENT #1

_____

_____

Facts Pertaining to Event

_____

_____

Skills Used to Achieve Results

_____

_____

ACHIEVEMENT EVENT #2

_____

_____

Facts Pertaining to Event

_____

_____

Skills Used to Achieve Results

_____

_____

ACHIEVEMENT EVENT #3

_____

_____

Facts Pertaining to Event

_____

_____

Skills Used to Achieve Results

_____

_____

ACHIEVEMENT EVENT #4

_____

_____

Facts Pertaining to Event

_____

_____

Skills Used to Achieve Results

_____

_____

ACHIEVEMENT EVENT #5

_____

_____

Facts Pertaining to Event

_____

_____

Skills Used to Achieve Results

_____

_____

Do you see a pattern of skills emerging? Discuss your reactions with your group or with the class.

ARE YOU READY FOR THE WORKPLACE OF THE FUTURE?

In April 1992, the Secretary of Labor's Commission on Achieving Necessary Skills (SCANS) released a report about the skills that will be necessary for the workplace of the future, "Workplace 2000." This report links workplace productivity to economic well-being and growth; productivity is directly related to the workers' skill level.

The SCANS report focuses attention on the new "high-performance workplace" and its emphasis on competency. The "high-performance workplace" has been implemented in companies throughout the country that have incorporated the best in leadership and technology innovations. These companies have redefined the competencies and skills necessary to thrive economically and have provided the engine that drove the unprecedented economic growth of the 1990s. The competencies and skills cited in Figure 3.2 formed the foundation necessary to revitalizing our economy. We refer to this foundation as "Workplace Know-How."

WORKPLACE KNOW-HOW.

The know-how identified by SCANS consists of five competencies and a three-part foundation of skills and personal qualities needed for solid job performance. These are:

WORKPLACE COMPETENCIES

Effective workers can productively use:

- *Resources*—They know how to allocate time, money, materials, space, and staff.
- *Interpersonal skills*—They can work on teams, teach others, serve customers, lead, negotiate, and work well with people from culturally diverse backgrounds.
- *Information*—They can acquire and evaluate data, organize and maintain files, interpret and communicate, and use computers to process information.
- *Systems*—They understand social, organizational, and technological systems; they can monitor and correct performance; and they can design or improve systems.

- *Technology*—They can select equipment and tools, apply technology to specific tasks, and maintain and troubleshoot equipment.

FOUNDATION SKILLS

Competent workers in the high-performance workplace need:

- *Basic skills*—reading, writing, arithmetic and mathematics, speaking and listening.
- *Thinking skills*—the ability to learn, to reason, to think creatively, to make decisions, and to solve problems.
- *Personal qualities*—individual responsibility, self-esteem and self-management, sociability, and integrity.

Source: *Learning a Living: A Blueprint for High Performance,* The Secretary's Commission on Achieving Necessary Skills Report for America 2000, Washington, D. C.: U. S. Department of Labor, April 1992.

FIGURE 3.2

Workers have found that they need the competencies and skills cited in the SCANS report to land a good job. Managers in organizations now require employees to work in teams, to assess critically their production systems, and to find the most efficient and cost-effective ways of accomplishing their work.

This author observed firsthand this managerial approach when visiting an automotive component plant. Every aspect of the production environment was constantly critiqued and explored for possible improvement. The managers' attention to continuous improvement was evident down to the detail of the traffic lanes that were used by forklifts in the plant area. In most American plants, these lanes are marked by parallel solid yellow lines. In this plant, the lines were marked by two lines of parallel yellow dots. The plant engineer explained that the use of dots to mark the lanes saves time and paint and accomplishes the same purpose.

Anyone seeking employment in this type of workplace will need more than a pulse to perform the work. Companies demand employees who are skilled, bright, motivated, and engaged in their work. Workplace know-how will become increasingly important in competing for jobs that offer the greatest opportunities for growth.

Research supports the necessity of skill development, not only as a means to securing rewarding employment but to steadily increasing productivity and wage growth. Richard Murnane and Frank Levy in their book *Teaching the New Basic Skills* provide convincing evidence that, in addition to basic proficiency in reading and math, skills in problem solving, communication, teamwork, and computer literacy contribute substantially to finding jobs that offer solid income and growth. More significantly, Department of Labor reports cite investments in education and computer training as critical elements in increasing productivity.

Exercise 3.3 will give you a glimpse of how you will fit into the workplace of the future.

3.3　TAKE A CLOSER LOOK

On-the-Job Know-How

Review the definitions of workplace know-how in Figure 3.2. Now recall your achievements, prior work experiences, and current educational situation, going through each competency and skill to see how you rate. Rank your level of competency and skill by circling the number below that you think best reflects your level, 1 representing little or no skill and 10 representing maximum achievable skill. Try to be as candid and honest as possible. This is part of finding out what you need to do to find your place in the world of work. It will help you know what you need to do to be competitive. Remember, *where* you acquired the skills is irrelevant here, just whether you have them.

Rate your workplace know-how on this chart. Review the criteria for each category before deciding on your competency level.

WORKPLACE COMPETENCIES

	NO SKILL									MAXIMUM SKILL
Resources	1	2	3	4	5	6	7	8	9	10
Interpersonal skills	1	2	3	4	5	6	7	8	9	10
Information	1	2	3	4	5	6	7	8	9	10
Systems	1	2	3	4	5	6	7	8	9	10
Technology	1	2	3	4	5	6	7	8	9	10

FOUNDATION SKILLS

Basic skills	1	2	3	4	5	6	7	8	9	10
Thinking skills	1	2	3	4	5	6	7	8	9	10
Personal qualities	1	2	3	4	5	6	7	8	9	10

How do you rate? Do you see areas in which you might improve your competency or skill level?

_____

How can you improve your skills in the areas where you see weaknesses?

_____

_____

Discuss your responses with your group or with the class.

WHAT MAKES YOUR PERSONALITY UNIQUE?

A particularly interesting area of self-assessment is personality or temperament. Your personality is composed of all your individual qualities. Your attitudes, behaviors, activities, and emotional reactions come together in your personality. Your personality reflects the way you view and respond to the world and the way you show the world who you are.

Ask any parent who has more than one child—they will repeat what psychologists know: *Everyone* is born with a distinct personality. Even identical twins, who share the same genetic makeup, take in and respond to their world differently. This uniqueness among individuals is a subject of endless fascination and study. Geneticists are beginning to trace some attitudes and behaviors to specific genes, a process that may reduce personality assessment to something resembling statistical analysis. For now, however, we rely on the work of psychologists to help us view how personality influences our lives.

Personality, however, is just one of many variables in career decision making. People with very different personalities may be drawn to the same career and people of a similar personality type may find themselves at opposite ends of the career spectrum. There are quiet, introspective salespeople and outgoing, gregarious accountants. Personality is only one dimension that influences career choice.

Have you ever been involved in a conversation in which someone says, "Oh, she's a typical teacher [banker, engineer, politician]"? Sometimes people make assumptions about someone's personality on the basis of their profession and vice versa. Some professions call to mind extreme, stereotypical traits. In the following section, remember that personality is only one factor to consider in your career choice. Keep all possibilities open. These exercises are meant to be guides to give you insight into yourself.

Jung's Psychological Types

An early pioneer in the area of personality development was C. G. Jung, a contemporary of Sigmund Freud. Jung developed a theory of psychological types in conjunction with an overall theory of personality development. Jung's typology led to the creation of a highly useful model for understanding personality.

Briefly, Jung's typology consists of four categories:

four attitudes   — Extroversion (E) or Introversion (I)
                          Judging (J) or Perceiving (P)*

and four functions — iNtuitive (N) or Sensing (S)
                          Feeling (F) or Thinking (T)

Each of the categories listed describes how people adapt and experience the world. By examining each one we can learn more about personality development and its influence.

*Jung initially referred to these as "rational" and "irrational."

Extroversion (E)/Introversion (I)

The category of extroversion/introversion in Jung's typology refers to the mode through which a person relates to the world.

If your preference is for *Introversion*, your orientation is primarily focused on the inner world. You might exhibit traits associated with quiet, reflective, or deliberate behavior.

If your preference is for *Extroversion*, your orientation is directed toward the outer world, usually displayed through outgoing, warm, candid behavior.

The attitudes described are best understood within the context of the psychological functions. Extroversion and introversion influence how each function operates in our personality.

iNtuitive (N)/Sensing (S)

This function relates to the way a person takes in information. If your dominant way of gathering information allows you to handle several different things at once, see the "big picture," and work easily with generalities, but you find it difficult to manage details, your typology would likely be labeled *iNtuitive*.

If you are more comfortable with specifics and prefer tangible results and literal interpretations, then you are probably a *Sensing* person.

Feeling (F)/Thinking (T)

Whether you are a Feeling or Thinking person relates to how you prefer to make decisions.

Feeling persons are sensitive to others' feelings and consider them important; they are rewarded by interacting with others and value getting along well with people.

Thinking persons are able to remain calm in a crisis, prefer level-headed objectivity to soft-hearted subjectivity, and are noted for their logical viewpoint.

Judging (J)/Perceiving (P)

The last category was originally termed "rational" and "irrational" by Jung. The current terms, judging and perceiving, are not meant to be interpreted literally. Jung's original "rational" component, now dubbed *Judging*, referred to a reflective, linear response that leads to a particular judgment with little tolerance for ambiguity.

The "irrational" component was related to the *Perceiving* function and referred to an ability to perceive intangibles and function well despite disorganization and ambiguity. These two attitudes correspond to the way we subjectively evaluate things.

Exercise 3.4 may help you focus on some of your personality traits.

Several highly respected personality tests have become quite popular in recent years as tools to help people discern their personality type and some of the characteristics associated with those types. It is important to remember, however, that such tests are not intended to be predictors of behavior

TAKE A CLOSER LOOK 3.4

Identifying Your Type

Let's examine each of Jung's eight categories separately to see which might describe you and your preferences. Place a check next to the phrases under each category that most accurately describe your style or preference. Mark down your "gut" reaction, trying not to read too much into each statement.

EXTROVERSION
- ❏ Prefer fast pace
- ❏ Enjoy variety

- ❏ Enjoy interacting with people
- ❏ High energy
- ❏ Open, self-disclosing
- ❏ Will talk with anyone about anything

_____ Total

_____ Category preference (E or I)

INTROVERSION
- ❏ Prefer planned activities
- ❏ Do one thing at a time until each task is completed
- ❏ Work in a setting with a low activity level
- ❏ Like to get away by yourself
- ❏ Enjoy working on things "in your head"
- ❏ Prefer to weigh all factors before deciding

_____ Total

INTUITIVE
- ❏ Prefer "big picture"
- ❏ Enjoy many things at once
- ❏ Seek new challenges
- ❏ Give weight to intangible factors
- ❏ Impatient with literal interpretations
- ❏ Eager to learn

_____ Total

_____ Category preference (N or S)

SENSING
- ❏ More comfortable with specifics
- ❏ Prefer working with details
- ❏ Uncomfortable with unfamiliar challenges
- ❏ Strict adherence to accuracy
- ❏ Resistant to "gut-level" responses
- ❏ Prefer literal interpretations

_____ Total

FEELING
- ❏ Sensitive
- ❏ Value others' feelings
- ❏ Enjoy interacting with people
- ❏ Work at relationships
- ❏ Subjective
- ❏ Capable of feeling deeply

_____ Total

_____ Category preference (F or T)

THINKING
- ❏ Orderly
- ❏ Enjoy working with numbers
- ❏ Not easily influenced by others' feelings
- ❏ Focused
- ❏ Calm under stress
- ❏ Objective

_____ Total

JUDGING

- ❏ Prefer step-by-step planning
- ❏ Thoughtful
- ❏ Motivated to reach closure
- ❏ Decisive
- ❏ Organized, linear
- ❏ Unrelenting in pursuit of goal

_____ Total

_____ Category preference (J or P)

PERCEIVING

- ❏ Comfortable with open-ended situations
- ❏ Tolerant
- ❏ Sensitive to intangibles
- ❏ Able to function despite disorganization
- ❏ Hesitant to exclude options
- ❏ Aware of full implications of issues

_____ Total

Note the letter from each category that shows your personality preference and indicate each preference below.

Your code

| _____ | _____ | _____ | _____ |
| E or I | N or S | F or T | J or P |

Based on your responses to the checklist, you will come up with one of the four-letter personality codes listed in Figure 3.3.

any more than a crystal ball would be. They are only tools in the overall process of growth and self-examination. Both the Myers-Briggs Type Indicator® (MBTI) and the Keirsey Temperament Sorter are based on Jung's psychological types. Both tests can enhance your insight into who you are and help in your self-assessment.

You may wish to take either the MBTI or the Keirsey Temperament Sorter if you are interested in a more thorough assessment instrument. The MBTI is available only from someone who is certified to administer that instrument. The Keirsey Temperament Sorter can be found in the book _Please Understand Me_ by David Keirsey and Marilyn Bates and through the Internet Web site. (See "Web Sites" at the end of the chapter.) Your instructor may be able to furnish more information regarding access and interpretation of these instruments.

FOUR-LETTER PERSONALITY CODES			
ISTJ	ISFJ	INFJ	INTJ
ISTP	ISFP	INFP	INTP
ESTP	ESFP	ENFP	ENTP
ESTJ	ESFJ	ENFJ	ENTJ

FIGURE 3.3

The MBTI applies a developed body of knowledge that correlates the four-letter code with career selection. The person administering the MBTI should be able to assist you in exploring further how the code can be interpreted as it relates to your career selection.

If you take the MBTI or the Keirsey instrument, share the results with your group or the class and your feelings about learning your personality type. Do the results match what you chose for yourself? Or were you surprised?

Fitting the Pieces Together

It may be possible to understand each of the categories and the various characteristics, but it is a bit more challenging to discern how the various aspects of your personality are integrated to form a particular personality type. Keirsey and Bates have devised extended profiles for each of the 16 four-letter types derived from Jung's theories. The profiles in *Please Understand Me* are summarized in Figure 3.4 and should offer a way of gaining insight into your unique view of the world.

Compare yourself with the personality types described in Exercise 3.5.

YOUR FOUR-LETTER PERSONALITY TYPE.

ENFJ ENFJs are the charismatic leaders who prize cooperation and value their interpersonal relationships over everything. Tolerant, empathetic, and highly intuitive, they are drawn to careers in counseling, teaching, ministry, the media, and performing.

INFJ An exceptional sense of intuition contributes to the complexity of INFJs. Their need to give of themselves makes them exceptional therapists and ministers. Caring, creative, and visionary, they also find satisfaction in writing and teaching.

ENFP Intense, emotional, and authentic are several words that describe ENFPs. Their enthusiastic approach to any task can be a powerful influence on others. They love being creative but become restless when bogged down with routine details. Careers in sales, politics, advertising, and writing are suitable outlets for their talents.

INFP INFPs are the dedicated idealists, capable of deep commitment to a cause or a person. Sensitive and understanding, they prefer harmony and can handle complicated situations but may bridle if forced into a stifling routine. Architecture, psychiatry, college teaching, or missionary work would appeal to INFPs.

ENTJ The ENTJs of the world are the leaders who take charge, provide structure, and drive a group forward. They are impatient with things that don't contribute to achieving the goal, whether they are structures that impede progress, illogical approaches, or people's feelings. Dedicated to their goals, ENTJs usually choose management and leadership positions in a variety of fields.

INTJ Confident and decisive, INTJs are the creative pragmatists who are continually looking for new and better ways to accomplish something. Highly intuitive, they can become lost in the challenge of developing an innovative approach to a problem. Scientific research and engineering are fields that offer an outlet for their abilities.

(continued)

FIGURE 3.4

ENTP   The sensitive and intuitive ENTPs are the problem solvers who can bring others along by using charm and enthusiasm. They enjoy improvising and innovating but only if the solutions work in the real world. This style can be awkward because ENTPs are not known for their attention to advance preparation. Nonconformists at times, they can be excellent teachers because they are always looking for new ways to get their point across.

INTP   Logical and literal with strong powers of concentration, INTPs are thinkers. They value intellectual pursuits but their curiosity can lead them in a dozen directions if they are not focused and directed. They prize logical thinking and can be abrupt if they see flaws in the logic of others. They are drawn quite naturally to scholarly and academic pursuits such as mathematics, philosophy, science, and teaching.

ESTJ   ESTJs are the responsible organizers. Rules, order, punctuality, and practicality are important to ESTJs, who believe those principles should be important to everyone else as well. Realistic, direct, and focused, they often work in management positions and are extremely dedicated to upholding duty and tradition.

ISTJ   Reliable, patient, and dependable are the words that best describe ISTJs. Despite the pressures they might experience, they have a quiet, conservative, practical demeanor. They are stable and able to perform consistently with details. ISTJs usually avoid risk taking. Careers suitable for this type include accountants, auditors, or tax examiners.

ESFJ   ESFJs are focused on the needs of other people and on maintaining harmonious relationships. They care about others' feelings and thoughts and are noted for their loyalty. Careers in administration, teaching, supervising, and coaching are excellent outlets for this type.

ISFJ   Stability and respect for tradition are hallmarks of ISFJs. Noted for being hardworking and reliable, they enjoy any opportunity to be of service to others. They are often found in nursing, library science, supervisory, or administrative work.

ESFP   ESFPs are the "stars" among us. Entertaining and warm, they have no difficulty creating excitement and performing, both on stage and off. Their sociability and enthusiasm often lead them to careers in public relations, sales, elementary school teaching, or nursing.

ESTP   Getting things done is the primary objective of ESTPs. Their smooth, charming style is irresistible and particularly useful when engaging others in tasks and projects. They care first and foremost about accomplishing a goal, however, and make no apologies for whatever must be done toward that end. They make outstanding administrators, promoters, business owners, and consultants.

ISTP   ISTPs are the practical craftspersons who relate well to any situation that calls for a hands-on effort. Not perfectionists, they are able to block out distractions and disorder so they can complete a project or achieve a goal. They enjoy practical and technical careers as diverse as rug making, heavy construction, professional sports, surgery, or weaving.

ISFP   The dreamers among us are probably ISFPs. Capable of intense feeling and highly tuned to physical sensation, they seek out opportunities for tangible experiences. The outdoors is a primary setting for their career interests as is the art studio, with its potter's wheel and brightly colored paints.

FIGURE 3.4

TAKE A CLOSER LOOK   3.5

A Glimpse in the Mirror

Now that you have learned a bit about your possible personality type and some of its character-istics, reflect briefly on how you see yourself.

From the previous exercise on personality type, what did you find your psychological type might be?

YOUR FOUR-LETTER PERSONALITY CODE

On these lines, note some key words from the text that are associated with your personality type.

_____   _____

_____   _____

_____   _____

Do these key words represent traits that you feel are true of you?

_____

_____

Look at the other descriptions, especially for those personality types that have letters in com-mon with your own. Do any of the key words describing other personality types remind you of yourself? Note those key words here.

_____   _____

_____   _____

_____   _____

Learning more about some of the characteristics associated with personality types has probably given you a better sense of some career areas that might appeal to you and bring you satisfaction.

_____

_____

Discuss the results of this exercise with your group or with the class.

A Cautionary Note

Please note several important issues when considering the categories or types just described:

- Everyone is gifted with each of the traits mentioned to a greater or less-er degree. The mix is unique to each person. For example, no one is always extroverted or consistently introverted. We adapt and incorporate behaviors that may lie on different ends of the continuum. The cate-gories simply allow us to identify better the areas in which we feel most comfortable, and they, in turn, influence our responses and actions.

- There is no right or wrong attitude or function, no good or bad trait or response. Each of us enjoys our own special "recipe" of attitudes and functions that combine to form how we meet the world and how the world meets us. There is no right or wrong way to be you. In fact, Jung's definition of true maturity involved the ability to learn who you are and accept the gifts and richness of your attributes, rather than try to figure out how you can change yourself to be something you are not.

- The codes described here are helpful tools in understanding a person's overall orientation but do not fully represent all the complexities that make up an individual's personality. No human being can be reduced to or explained by a set of letters. Nonetheless, we continue to use any means available to understand better what it means to be human.

- Finally, the career possibilities suggested here are necessarily a limited list of jobs. Don't be discouraged if a career option you may be considering isn't listed or conflicts with your personality type. The options suggested are designed to help you focus your career decision making; they are not life sentences to limit and control you. Trust your inner voice and follow its wisdom.

How Personalities Complement One Another

Part of Jung's definition of maturity included accepting yourself for the special person you are. Jung also suggested that it is important to our growth to accept other people and their different ways of being.

David Keirsey and Marilyn Bates, the developers of the Keirsey Temperament Sorter, have studied personality and its influence on relationships in depth. Keirsey and Bates's model breaks down personality types from the original four-letter codes to two-letter codes that are associated with particular temperaments. Figure 3.5 shows the two-letter temperament codes and the corresponding four-letter codes.

Each of the two-letter codes in this model is associated with specific temperament traits, as noted in Figure 3.6. These traits describe the behaviors and attitudes associated with the people with whom we might work, be friends, or choose as mates. In Figure 3.6, see if you can pick out yourself, either from your code or the description. Then pick out those of your friends and acquaintances.

TWO-LETTER TEMPERAMENT CODES.			
NT	**SP**	**SJ**	**NF**
INTP	ISTP	ISFJ	INFJ
ENTP	ESTP	ESFJ	ENFJ
INTJ	ISFP	ISTJ	INFP
ENTJ	ESFP	ESTJ	ENFP

FIGURE 3.5

KEIRSEY'S TEMPERAMENT TYPES AND TRAITS.

NTs:	About 12% of the population	Competent
	Want to understand ideas	Self-critical
	Never satisfied with results	Driven, seek knowledge
SPs:	About 38% of the population	Artists and performers
	Impulsive, enjoy a crisis	Highly changeable
	Add "electricity" in any setting	Dislike deadlines
SJs:	38% of the population	Prefer orderly setting
	Responsible and aware of duty	Rule/law-oriented
	Drawn to education, churches, hospitals as job settings	
NFs:	12% of the population	Seek meaning in life
	Very articulate and influential	Often drawn to writing
	Strive for self-actualization	Spiritual

FIGURE 3.6

Now that you have an idea of Keirsey's temperament codes, try Exercise 3.6 to see how you react to the personality differences you encounter.

TAKE A CLOSER LOOK 3.6

Love–Hate Between Types*

If you have taken the MBTI or the Keirsey Temperament Sorter, then you know your four- and two-letter codes. If not, try to determine which group you might be most comfortable in from the brief descriptions offered earlier.

Now divide up your class or group by two-letter types, with NFs and SPs in one group and SJs and NTs in the other. Once you are divided into groups, discuss the following question in your group. Have one member keep track of your responses.

What traits do you most dislike in the people in the other group?

_____

_____

_____

Have one of the people in your group read your responses aloud to the main group.

Now consider this question: What traits do you most like in the people in the other group?

_____

_____

_____

Again, share your impressions with the main group.

Surprised? Yes, for all the "strangeness" represented by the other personalities we encounter, we have to admit that they do have a lot to offer as well. Every group needs its creative, impulsive energy source along with dedicated, orderly producers. The beauty of the mix is in the balance it offers us. While there certainly are more NTs and SJs, the NFs and SPs make up in spirit and influence for what they lack in numbers. (It would almost seem to have been planned that way, but then I'm an NF and I see the "hidden" meaning in everything.)

Discuss your feelings about your type and the opposites as you view them now with your group or with the class.

* This exercise is adapted from the work done by Dr. Bruce Taylor, Janet Kalven, and Dr. Larry S. Rosen, based on Keirsey and Bates's *Please Understand Me.*

WHAT DO YOU ENJOY DOING?

Regardless of your age, you probably know what kinds of activities and subjects draw you in and cause you to be excited and passionate. Or perhaps, if you are a bit more subdued in your responses, you might refer to certain things that make you feel comfortable and at ease with yourself. These activities or areas are commonly known as your interests.

Interests can be powerful predictors of career suitability. You may find careers that match your values, fit your motivations, and correspond well with your life stage; but if your interests lie in other areas, then you may be dissatisfied with your choice. Typically, if you are strongly attracted to a certain career field, you may decide to pursue it despite a host of potential obstacles. Just take a trip to Hollywood and you will find hundreds, even thousands, of people whose interest in the entertainment industry outweighs other considerations. They will endure daily rejection, substandard living conditions, and years of uncertainty in hopes of being one of the chosen few who becomes a star.

John L. Holland has also explored the issue of interests and their relation to career choice. Holland's theories suggest that in our society most people fit into one of six personality types, largely determined by their interests. He further found that career choice was often a reflection of personality type. If you can identify your personality type by interests, then you can match your type with career choices that would complement your personality type.

People seek situations in which they can use their skills and express themselves in positive ways. Frequently, people of like personality are drawn to the same vocation. Tracing these "links" will open up a series of career possibilities that you can explore through using library resources. (We examine these resources in depth in the next chapter.)

If you have had a variety of life experiences, you may find the process of identifying your interests and preferences much simpler than someone who is younger or has not had different opportunities. Your knowledge about yourself and the world of work will be reflected in your interests and preferences. Young people with less exposure to a broad range of experiences may find this a bit challenging. Identifying your interests is an important step to self-understanding. The six personality types identified by Holland in Figure 3.7 may help you identify your interests.

HOLLAND'S PERSONALITY TYPES.

REALISTIC

People in this category usually prefer physical tasks, athletics, and outdoor activities; they enjoy working with their hands and using utensils and machines.

INVESTIGATIVE

People in this category are usually quiet, inquisitive, or analytical, and may be observant and enjoy academic and scientific pursuits.

ENTERPRISING

People in this category usually enjoy persuading or influencing others; they may seek leadership or management situations; they are comfortable organizing to achieve group goals; they prefer working with people.

ARTISTIC

People in this category usually prefer situations in which they can be creative and artistic; they may be flamboyant and imaginative, enjoying settings that are free of structure; some are visionary and independent.

CONVENTIONAL

People in this category usually prefer structure and order; they are comfortable with details of any variety—facts, numbers, any kind of data; and they find satisfaction in bringing situations to closure.

SOCIAL

People in this category usually gravitate to other people, regardless of the setting; they may have strong verbal and written communication skills and a special attraction to the helping professions.

FIGURE 3.7

If you are able to discern your personality type, usually identified by one dominant type and influenced to a lesser extent by one or two others, then you can start matching your interests with those of people working in particular professions. Use Exercise 3.7 to look at your interests.

TAKE A CLOSER LOOK 3.7

Assessing Your Interests

Take a look at the following interest areas and the related occupational titles. Based on your preferences, write out the possible occupational choices that are related to your interests.

INTEREST AREAS

ARTISTIC

Creative activities
Endeavors requiring imagination and innovation

RELATED OCCUPATIONS

Art, Music, Dance, Fine Arts, Theatre, Design, Commercial Art, Advertising, Writing, Sketching, Composing, Acting

INTEREST AREAS	RELATED OCCUPATIONS
SOCIAL	
Helping activities Activities that offer outlets for idealistic action Teaching, leading groups	Education, Counseling, Human Services, Work, Political Science, Health Care, Law Enforcement
CONVENTIONAL	
Methodical activities Activities requiring efficiency and systematic skills Following defined procedures and routines	Accounting, Business Management, Computer Systems, Clerical and Administrative Services
ENTERPRISING	
Managerial activities Endeavors requiring high energy and self-confidence Planning projects, selling, promoting and supervising	Management, Business and Hospital Administration, Purchasing, Human Resources, Public Administration, Retailing
REALISTIC	
Tangible activities Activities requiring operation and use of tools Working outdoors, tinkering with machines, sports	Architecture, Automotives, Engineering, Drafting and Design, Quality Control Engineering, Graphics Production
INVESTIGATIVE	
Problem-solving activities involving independent, intellectual tasks using natural curiosity and scientific methods to solve problems	Sciences, Medicine, Research, Laboratory Procedure and Analysis, Computer Programming and Systems Analysis

My interests are in: _____

Occupational areas: _____

A number of vocational interest tests similar to Exercise 3.7 are available today. Your responses are then used as a basis for developing possible career options. Holland's Self-Directed Search: A Guide to Educational and Vocational Planning (SDS), the Career Assessment Inventory (CAI), and the Strong Interest Inventory (SII) are among the most widely recognized instruments. Each of these tests is based on Holland's personality codes and offers a more comprehensive list of related career options. Holland's Self-Directed Search also includes measurement instruments for assessing leisure and educational interests. These tests are usually available through your college career counselor, who will assist you in interpreting the results.

Along with pencil-and-paper instruments, many colleges now have interactive computerized guidance systems available. These programs provide self-assessment and career-exploration exercises. DISCOVER and SIGI PLUS are two databases frequently used by career counselors to help students research their values, interests, and experiences. These programs automatically cross-reference your findings with possible occupational areas. We will look at these and other computer-based resources in more detail later.

Ask your instructor if it is possible to obtain one of these interest inventories, e.g., SII, CAI, or SDS. After you've had a chance to take the test(s), share with your group how you feel about the results. Do the results match what you might have chosen for yourself? Or were you surprised?

Keep in mind that your interests are subject to change. Just as your priorities may shift as you grow, which then affects the influence of your values, so too can your interests shift and adapt. The results of any instrument you take now are a "snapshot" at this point in your development.

LI'S STORY

Li was starting her first college term in a few weeks but felt totally lost. She had determined her class schedule on the basis of the answer to one critical question: "What degree will make it easiest for me to get a job when I graduate?" Li had looked over the college catalog, wondering what all the department codes and class numbers meant. She had thought about talking with an advisor but was afraid she would look foolish if she didn't know what she wanted to do.

As the first day of classes approached, Li realized that she was getting closer and closer to taking a path about which she felt increasingly uncomfortable. Her schedule was packed with math and science classes required for an engineering technology degree. She dreaded the classes and was having a hard time seeing herself working in that field. Something didn't fit.

Li finally admitted to herself that she needed help in finding out what would be a better fit for her. She made an appointment with a career counselor. The counselor, Brian, spent some time talking with Li about why she had decided on engineering technology in the first place. Li felt embarrassed telling him that she had chosen it because she was good with numbers and knew that she would be able to get a job in the field. Brian wasn't surprised and admitted that while many students made decisions with even less con-

sideration than that, it might be helpful if Li took some self-assessment instruments, such as the MBTI and the Career Assessment Inventory, before she made any big decisions. But the biggest part of her job would be to think more about what she enjoyed doing. She might eventually decide that engineering technology is indeed a good choice but if not, she would have a good idea of other options.

After completing the assessment instruments, Li wrote down all the activities and skills that interested her and matched her values. She had always enjoyed working with numbers but not the upper-level math that was required for engineering. She was an orderly person who felt good when everything fit together nicely. She was definitely interested in developing a marketable skill that would lead to job security. When she met with Brian to discuss the results of her tests, she was thinking about accounting as a possibility. The interest instrument and the personality indicator confirmed that accounting was one option that might be a good fit for Li.

There was a great deal that Li still had to find out, both about the field she was considering and about herself. She felt better knowing there was a process that would help her sort out what she wanted and how to achieve her goals.

3.8 TAKE A CLOSER LOOK

Pulling It All Together

Having read one student's story about coming to a new understanding of herself, you can probably see more clearly how looking at the different aspects of who you are can help you discover possible career directions. While the process can certainly include a more intuitive approach, it may help to set forth specifically the key factors that have been explored in this chapter, namely:

What skills did you identify as most important to you and your growth?

_____

_____

What transferable skills did you identify?

_____

_____

How did you rate in "Workplace Know-How"?

_____

_____

What were your four-letter and two-letter personality types?

_____

_____

What are some of the traits and characteristics associated with your personality type?

_____

_____

On the basis of your responses to the interest exercise, what was your interest area?

_____

_____

What are the occupational areas related to your interests?

_____

_____

Based on the information available to you in the college catalog, what majors relate to your interests and occupational areas?

_____

_____

If you were able to complete a personality or interest instrument, what occupational choices or college majors did you discover?

_____

_____

Did your process of self-assessment confirm the possibilities that you had considered or did it suggest careers that you had not considered before?

_____

_____

Careers to be explored:

_____

_____

_____

_____

Your career adventure is taking you farther along the path of insight into what a career might offer you. In this chapter, you examined your abilities, skills, personality, and interests. You explored those that are most rewarding to you and identified those that might be important in the workplace of the future. You developed a better understanding of your personality type and some of its characteristics. You also began to assess your interests and those activities and settings that appeal to you. Additionally, you probably have a clearer understanding of how those aspects of your personality relate to possible career choices.

If you are feeling frustrated and somewhat confused at this point, don't worry. Those feelings may be a sign that some of the assumptions you have held are in flux. You may be facing the reality of the work world for the first time—a significant step in itself. Over time, your feelings will resolve themselves as you adjust to what lies ahead. Keep a positive attitude and you may find things will fall into place very soon.

On the other hand, if you're feeling sure of yourself because you got just the results you had expected, be prepared. You never know what you may encounter as you continue your career adventure. That's what makes this process exciting. Keep an open mind.

Other Sources and Suggested Reading

College Success by Roberta Moore, Barbara Baker, and Arnold Packer
  A unique text that incorporates U. S. Department of Labor SCANS data into real-life workplace exercises.

Discover (A Computerized Guidance System) by American College Testing Program

This computerized career-planning program takes users through the spectrum of self-assessment and career-exploration issues in a user-friendly format.

Do What You Are: Discover the Perfect Career for You Through the Secrets of Personality Type by Paul D. Tieger and Barbara Barron-Tieger

This book examines personality types and possible career choices that complement each.

Making Vocational Choices: A Theory of Careers by John L. Holland

The Holland system of personality types and their relationship to career choice is explained in depth in this useful book.

Personality Types: Jung's Model of Typology by Daryl Sharp

A basic guide to Jung's theory of psychological types.

Please Understand Me by David Keirsey and Marilyn Bates

This book takes a closer look at personality types and their influence in the various aspects of life. The concepts are based on the personality theories of Carl Jung.

SIGI Plus (A Computerized Guidance System) by Educational Testing Service

This system offers many of the features necessary for self-assessment and career exploration as well as modules for local career market information.

Type Talk and Type Talk at Work by Otto Kroeger, with Janet M. Thuesen

Both of these books explore and expand on the Keirsey Temperament Sorter model and offer interesting insights on the impact of personality in contemporary work settings.

Web Sites and Internet Resources

www.collegeview.com

Click Career Center and then click Assessing Yourself for a number of assessment tests. Take your pick.

www.keirsey.com

This site offers the Keirsey Temperament Sorter from which to derive Jung's Four-Letter code.

www.mdani.demon.co.uk

An in-depth examination of Jungian psychology, including an online personality test.

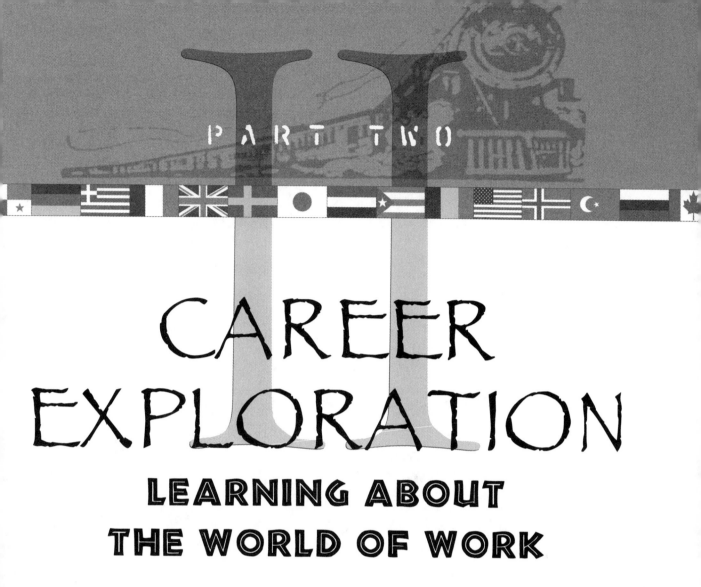

PART TWO

CAREER EXPLORATION

LEARNING ABOUT THE WORLD OF WORK

Being free to examine deeply who you are can be exciting and enlightening. Now it's time to explore aspects of the outside world. By this time you may have in mind a number of career possibilities that you identified through the self-assessment process. You are ready for your next step in your career adventure.

A key factor in your career decision will be your knowledge of the current career market. As you make your career decision, it is important to consider a broad range of information and

issues. Some issues relate to the basics of the position in which you have an interest—duties, salary, setting, and availability of openings. Other information crucial to this process relates to the general job market—the impact of technology on our way of doing work, trends in managing workers, and the influence of global competition.

As you gather information, the primary goal of this text is to help you focus on the place in the career spectrum where your unique talents can best be used and your individual needs can best be met.

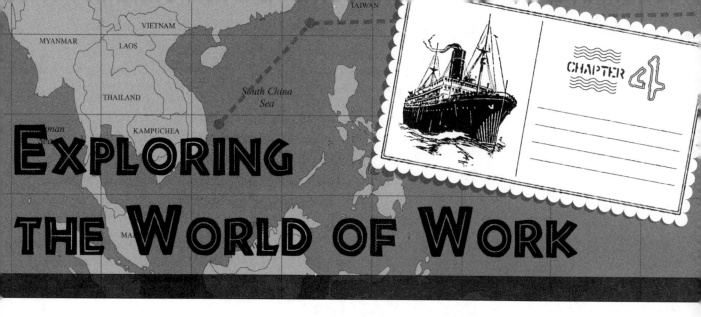

EXPLORING THE WORLD OF WORK

A t this point in the career adventure, you have the opportunity to explore the world of work. This part of your search is extremely important. As you plunge into the process of preparing for a career, you will benefit from understanding the career market. Without this knowledge, you might experience entering the job market as if you were jumping off a high dive without knowing how to swim. You might survive but you would definitely be in over your head.

This phase of the career decision-making process will yield much valuable information and perhaps a few surprises. The information-gathering process is an ongoing part of career planning throughout your life. You will continually use the skills that you develop as you investigate the job market, accept a position, change fields, and continue to grow in your career.

When you attend school, especially an institution of higher education, your expectations for success are naturally raised. You envision a higher-paying, high-level job that matches your academic skills—you imagine you can do anything! That's okay, as long as your expectations are grounded in reality. For example, a student comes to me glowing with excitement and announces that she's decided to be a sculptor. Her next step is to find out who is hiring sculptors and how much they are paying per hour. If she finds that there is very little demand for sculptors and the potential starting income may be low, she may still wish to pursue her goal. People who pursue their dream career, wherever it leads, deserve applause. However, they should also know that being committed to a career goal is fine, but knowing what lies ahead on your path is essential.

HOW CAN UNCLE SAM HELP?

In this chapter and those that follow, you will learn how to prepare for your chosen career. We will look at a variety of tools and resources designed to assist you in the process. In this section, we explore government publications, including the *Dictionary of Occupational Titles*, the *Guide for Occupational Exploration*, and the *Occupational Outlook Handbook*. These resources will provide you with a base of knowledge from which to broaden your search.

CHARLIE

"Don't forget, Charlie, I want to see your high
school diploma *tomorrow* or I'm gettin' me
another Frialator man!"

The *Dictionary of Occupational Titles (DOT)*

For over 60 years, the *Dictionary of Occupational Titles* has been the definitive document for cataloging jobs. Listing over 20,000 different jobs, it provides a standardized definition of positions and duties and it groups positions according to occupational clusters and skills. The occupations described in the *DOT* are organized by numerical codes that match a job's skills and functions. The *DOT* is updated regularly and represents a catalog of the evolution of the changing job culture since 1939. Figure 4.1 shows a sample page from the *DOT*.

A typical listing for a job in the *DOT* includes the position's nine-digit occupational code, the occupational title, the industry designation in which the job is categorized, any alternate titles, and a brief description of the tasks associated with the position. Positions can be found by checking the *DOT*'s alphabetical index, industry designation, or industry index.

Although the *DOT* was originally developed to assist employers in the task of standardizing workers' roles, it is also a tool in career decision making.

Because of the rate of change influencing the workplace, the Department of Labor has developed a database that identifies and describes the next generation of occupations in the workplace of the future. This database, the O*NET, is designed to replace the *Dictionary of Occupational Titles*, and presents information in the form of an interactive library source. Data on skills, training, requirements, worker characteristics, and labor mar-

101.167-010

GOE: 11.02.04 STRENGTH: L GED: R4 M2 L4 SVP: 5 DLU: 77

101   ARCHIVISTS

This group includes occupations concerned with collecting, evaluating, systemizing, preserving, and making available for reference public records and documents of historical significance.

101.167-010   ARCHIVIST (profess. & kin.)
Appraises and edits permanent records and historically valuable documents, participates in research activities based on archival materials, and directs safekeeping of archival documents and materials: Analyzes documents, such as government records, minutes of corporate board meetings, letters from famous persons, and charters of nonprofit foundations, by ascertaining date of writing, author, or original recipient of letter, to appraise value to posterity or to employing organization. Directs activities of workers engaged in cataloging and safekeeping of valuable materials and directs disposition of worthless materials. Prepares or directs preparation of document descriptions and reference aids for use of archives, such as accession lists, indexes, guides, bibliographies, abstracts, and microfilmed copies of documents. Directs filing and cross indexing of selected documents in alphabetical and chronological order. Advises government agencies, scholars, journalists, and others conducting research by supplying available materials and information according to familiarity with archives and with political, economic, military, and social history of period. Requests or recommends pertinent materials available in libraries, private colllections, or other archives. Selects and edits documents for publication and display, according to knowledge of subject, literary or journalistic expression, and techniques for presentation and display. May be designated according to subject matter specialty as Archivist, Economic History (profess. & kin.); Archivist, Military History (profess. & kin.); Archivist, Political History (profess. & kin.); or according to nature of employing institution as Archivist, Nonprofit Foundation (nonprofit organ.). In smaller organizations, may direct activities of libraries.
GOE: 11.03.03 STRENGTH: S GED: R5 M3 L5 SVP: 8 DLU: 77

102   MUSEUM CURATORS AND RELATED OCCUPATIONS

This group includes occupations concerned with administering museums, art galleries, arboreta, historical sites, and botanical and zoological gardens, and performing related services. Includes activities in collecting, authenticating, preserving, maintaining, exhibiting, researching, and furnishing information on collections of historical, artistic, scientific, or technological significance or of general public interest.

102.017-010   CURATOR (museums)
Directs and coordinates activities of workers engaged in operating exhibiting institution, such as museum, botanical garden, arboretum, art gallery, herbarium, or zoo: Directs activities concerned with instructional, acquisition, exhibitory, safekeeping, research, and public service objectives of institution. Assists in formulating and interpreting administrative policies of institution. Formulates plans for special research projects. Oversees curatorial, personnel, fiscal, technical, research, and clerical staff. Administers affairs of institution by corresponding and negotiating with administrators of other institutions to obtain exchange of loan collections or to exchange information or data, maintaining inventories, preparing budget, representing institution at scientific or association conferences, soliciting support for institution, and interviewing and hiring personnel. Obtains, develops, and organizes new collections to expand and improve educational and research facilities. Writes articles for publication in scientific journals. Consults with board of directors and professional personnel to plan and implement acquisitional, research, display and public service activities of institution. May participate in research activities. May be designated according to field of specialization as Curator, Art Gallery (museums); Curator, Herbarium (museums); Curator, Horticultural Museum (museums); Curator, Medical Museum (museums); Curator, Natural History Museum (museums); Curator, Zoological Museum (museums); Director, Industrial Museum (museums).
GOE: 11.07.04 STRENGTH: L GED: R6 M5 L6 SVP: 9 DLU: 77

102.117-010   SUPERVISOR, HISTORIC SITES (government ser.)
Directs and coordinates activities of personnel engaged in investigating, acquiring, marking, improving, and preserving historic sites and natural phenomena in conformity with state policy. Authorizes acquisition and improvement of sites, such as historic homes and battlefields, within allocated budget. Recommends appropriation of additional funds where necessary to purchase or restore landmarks. Negotiates with representatives of local governments, philanthropic organizations, and other interested groups to acquire properties. Provides information and encouragement to private individuals or civic groups attempting to acquire and maintain landmarks not considered feasible for state acquisition. Directs or participates in archeological research efforts in state parks. Directs design, preparation, and installation of museum exhibits and historical markers. Directs workers engaged in preparation of brochures, exhibits, maps, photographs, and similar materials to stimulate public interest in visiting sites. Serves as custodian of historic documents acquired during research efforts.
GOE: 11.05.03 STRENGTH: L GED: R5 M4 L5 SVP: 7 DLU: 77

102.117-014   DIRECTOR, MUSEUM-OR-ZOO (museums)
Administers affairs of museum, zoo, or similar establishment: Confers with institution's board of directors to formulate policies and plan overall operations.

Directs acquisition, education, research, public service, and development activities of institution, consulting with curatorial, administrative, and maintenance staff members to implement policies and initiate programs. Works with members of curatorial and administrative staffs to acquire additions to collections. Confers with administrative staff members to determine budget requirements, plan fund raising drives, prepare applications for grants from government agencies or private foundations, and solicit financial support for institution. Establishes and maintains contact with administrators of other institutions to exchange information concerning operations and plan, coordinate, or consolidate community service and education programs. Represents institution at professional and civic social events, conventions, and other gatherings to strengthen relationships with cultural and civic leaders, present lectures or participate in seminars, or explain institution's functions and seek financial support for projects. Reviews materials prepared by staff members, such as articles for journals, requests for grants, and reports on·institution programs, and approves materials or suggests changes. Instructs classes in institution's education program or as guest lecturer at university. Writes articles for technical journals or other publications.
GOE: 11.02.01 STRENGTH: S GED: R6 M4 L6 SVP: 8 DLU: 86

102.167-010   ART CONSERVATOR (museums)
Coordinates activities of subordinates engaged in examination. repair, and conservation of art objects: Examines art objects to determine condition, need for repair, method of preservation, and authenticity, using x rays, radiographs, and special lights. Directs curatorial and technical staffs on handling, mounting. care, and storage of art objects. Estimates cost of restoration work.
GOE: 01.06.02 STRENGTH: L GED: R5 M4 L4 SVP: 8 DLU: 77

102.167-014   HISTORIC-SITE ADMINISTRATOR (museums)
Manages operation of historic structure or site: Discusses house or site operation with governing body representatives to form or change policies. Oversees activities of building and grounds maintenance staff and other employees. Maintains roster of volunteer guides, and contacts volunteers to conduct tours of premises according to schedule. Conducts tours, explaining points of interest and answers visitors' questions. Studies documents, books, and other materials to obtain information concerning history of site or structure. Conducts classes in tour presentation methods for volunteer guides. Accepts group reservations for house tours and special social events. Arranges for refreshments, entertainment, and decorations for special events. Collects admission and special event fees, and maintains records of receipts, expenses, and numbers of persons served. Assists in planning publicity, and arranges for printing of brochures or placement of information in media. Inspects premises for evidence of deterioration and need for repair, and notifies governing body of such need.
GOE: 11.02.01 STRENGTH: L GED: R5 M4 L5 SVP: 5 DLU: 86

102.167-018   REGISTRAR, MUSEUM (museums)
Maintains records of accession, condition, and location of objects in museum collection, and oversees movement, packing, and shipping of objects to conform to insurance regulations: Observes unpacking of objects acquired by museum through gift, purchase, or loan to determine that damage or deterioration to objects has not occurred. Registers and assigns accession and catalog numbers to all objects in collection, according to established registration system. Composes concise description of objects, and records descriptions on file cards and in collection catalogs. Oversees handling, packing, movement, and inspection of all objects entering or leaving establishment, including traveling exhibits, and confers with other personnel to develop and initiate most practical methods of packing and shipping fragile or valuable objects. Maintains records of storage, exhibit, and loan locations of all objects in collection for use of establishment personnel, insurance representatives, and other persons utilizing facilities. Prepares acquisition reports for review of curatorial and administrative staff. Periodically reviews and evaluates registration and catalog system to maintain applicability, consistency, and operation. Recommends changes in recordkeeping procedures to achieve maximum accessibility to and efficient retrieval of collection objects. Arranges for insurance of objects on loan or special exhibition, or recommends insurance coverage on parts of or entire collection.
GOE: 07.01.02 STRENGTH: S GED: R5 M4 L5 SVP: 6 DLU: 86

102.261-010   CONSERVATION TECHNICIAN (museums)
Repairs and cleans art objects, such as pottery, statuary. etchings, or tapestries, to restore art objects' natural appearance: Studies descriptive information on object or conducts standard chemical and physical tests to determine such factors as age, composition, and original appearance, and plans methods or procedures for restoring object. Cleans object or broken pieces, using such methods as scraping and applying solvents to metal objects; washing statuary, using soap solutions; or cleaning and polishing furniture and silver objects. Repairs objects, using glue or solder, to assemble broken pieces, buffing assembled object where repaired, or repainting faded or incomplete designs with paint of same chemical composition and color in order to restore original appearance. Notifies supervisor when problem of restoration requires outside experts. Fabricates or repairs picture frames for paintings, using handtools and power tools and machines. Mounts pictures in frames.
GOE: 01.06.02 STRENGTH: M GED: R4 M4 L4 SVP: 6 DLU: 77

102.261-014   PAINTINGS RESTORER (profess. & kin.) alternate titles: paintings conservator
Restores damaged and faded paintings and preserves paintings, using techniques based on knowledge of art and art materials: Examines surfaces of paint

FIGURE 4.1

ket information are as close as your computer keyboard. The O*NET even offers a skill identification exercise that allows you to search for occupations based on your skills.

Both the O*NET and the DOT are accessible online. You can search the DOT online at **www.oalj.dol.gov/libdot.htm.** The O*NET is found at **online.onetcenter.org.**

Exercise 4.1 is designed to familiarize you with the DOT and the O*NET so that you can effectively take advantage of these extensive resources.

 TAKE A CLOSER LOOK

Finding Your Way Around the DOT

At first glance, the DOT can seem imposing. After your initial experience using it, you will feel at home. Most public and college libraries have the DOT in their reference section. The large DOT volume is often accompanied by smaller updates. These important items may contain information you need, especially if you are looking into a field that is undergoing change.

To begin, page through the volume and get a feel for how it is set up. As you can see, the jobs appear in occupational groups; thus, many of the job descriptions in a group may be very similar.

Read the following job titles. Using the alphabetical index at the back of the DOT, find and note the corresponding DOT code number.

Correction officer	_____
Costumer	_____
Head coach	_____
Teacher, art	_____
Nurse	_____
Director, motion picture	_____
Curator	_____
Psychologist, social	_____
Car repairer	_____
Electronic engineer	_____

You may find more than one subheading that designates the specific circumstances in which each job is performed. Using the nine-digit code number, look up a few of the descriptions. Note the differences between jobs with similar titles and the categories into which jobs are classified.

In the following spaces, list on the left the occupations that you identified in your self-assessment from Chapters 2 and 3, especially those from the interest instruments, as ones you would like to explore further. Then find the corresponding DOT code number in the alphabetical listing. Next, locate the definition in the main text and jot down a few of the key facts mentioned there. As you review the definition, note the job titles and descriptions for the positions on the page above and below the one you are looking up. Do those sound interesting as well?

CAREER TO EXPLORE _____   *DOT* CODE NUMBER _____
Key facts _____

_____

CAREER TO EXPLORE _____   *DOT* CODE NUMBER _____
Key facts _____

_____

CAREER TO EXPLORE _____   *DOT* CODE NUMBER _____
Key facts _____

_____

If you have access to the Internet, now try the O*NET (**online.onetcenter.org**). After you get to the home page, click on "Skills Search" and review the skill list offered there. Click the skills that you think would be a good fit for you in a work setting. After selecting the skill, click on "Find Occupations." What occupations match the skills you identified? List those that seem most interesting to you below. Click on an occupation in which you are interested. Review the broad definition or click on "Snapshot" for more details. Jot down pertinent details below. Click on "Related Occupations" and see what careers are similar to the one you have selected. Add those that appeal to you below.

OCCUPATIONS   "SNAPSHOT" DETAILS   RELATED OCCUPATIONS

_____   _____   _____

_____   _____   _____

_____   _____   _____

_____   _____   _____

Did the information you found in the *DOT* and the O*NET help you get a better idea of what occupational data is available? Were your expectations confirmed or were you surprised by some information? If you have had a number of different jobs, choose one and look it up in the *DOT* or the O*NET. Does the description match what you recall doing?

Discuss the results with your group or with the class.

The *Guide for Occupational Exploration (GOE)*

You have had a chance to do some preliminary research about occupations by using the *Dictionary of Occupational Titles.* Now you can begin to broaden your exploration.

The next step is to look beyond the particular definition of a position and see how the same or similar skills named in the description are used in related jobs. The best resource for compiling information about the broad view of any job is a manual known as the *Guide for Occupational Exploration (GOE)*, published by the U. S. Employment Service. Books such as the *Enhanced Guide for Occupational Exploration*, published by JIST Works, offer similar information along with data from the Department of Commerce, the Census Bureau, and other resources.

The GOE organizes information about job categories through a numerical system based on interest areas, work groups, and subgroups. The guide enables you to examine a variety of occupations that require the use of similar skills. Twelve major interest areas are profiled, delineating the requirements of occupations in each interest area. For instance, the area designated as "04-Protective" defines the interest as "An interest in using authority to protect people and property." The occupations in this category are divided into two work groups: safety and law enforcement, and security services. Job titles are listed under either of the two categories along with the names of related jobs. Finally, the work subgroups provide a six-digit code and title for jobs found in each work group.

One of the GOE's most valuable features is the question/answer format that describes the characteristics of a work group. Questions such as "What kind of work would you do?", "What skills and abilities do you need for this kind of work?", and "How do you know if you would like or could learn to do this kind of work?" are a few examples. Education and training are addressed, as well as issues that fall outside the subject of skills; for instance, the negative aspects of a given field.

To trace a particular job to the section of the GOE that coordinates it with similar occupations, use the alphabetical index in the back. You will find both the DOT number associated with that job and the six-digit GOE number. The GOE number correlates the position you are researching with the major categories of skills, interests, and related occupations to which it belongs.

Exercise 4.2 is designed to help you expand your exploration.

4.2 TAKE A CLOSER LOOK

A Family of Jobs

Start by surveying the classification table at the front of the GOE. This section, "Summary List of Interest Areas, Work Groups, and Subgroups," shows all the categories of occupations listed in the guide. Review the summary and note how the interest areas and different fields are grouped, how they are related, and how they differ.

Now turn to the alphabetical index at the back of the guide. Look up the job titles that you identified in your self-assessment exercises. Note the bold-faced six-digit code associated with that title, and jot the number down in the space below.

JOB TITLE _____   **SIX-DIGIT CODE** _____

Using the first two digits of the six-digit code, look up the interest area in Section II of the main text. Read the brief interest description. Using the next two digits of the six-digit code, find the work group related to the job you are researching. Look closely at the information on interests, skills, and settings associated with this work group. Write down this information below.

KIND OF WORK

_____

_____

Skills and abilities needed

_____

_____

_____

How do you know you would like or could learn this kind of work?

_____

_____

_____

Preparation necessary

_____

_____

_____

Other information

_____

_____

_____

Finally, find the job you are researching. Note the subgroup of jobs in which it is found and the titles of jobs and _DOT_ or SOC code numbers that are in the same subgroup. Now go back to the _DOT_ or O*NET and check the description of the new positions, noting key facts.

Related Job Title/_DOT_ Number/O*NET SOC Code

_____

Related Job Title/_DOT_ Number/O*NET SOC Code

_____

Related Job Title/_DOT_ Number/O*NET SOC Code

_____

Does the information provided in the _GOE_ give you a better idea of how jobs are related by interest area?

_____

Are you aware of any related jobs or careers that you may not have considered before?

_____

Do the skill requirements of the positions you have researched indicate that you will need to acquire new skills or further training in order to perform the job duties?

_____

The exercise you have just completed has helped you to look beyond what might have seemed like your only choice. It is important to keep a positive, open focus on what you are trying to achieve. Your goal is to find a full, rewarding career, not to fall into a trap from which you must later free yourself. Try to stay positive and flexible. It will help broaden your notion of what will work for you.

Discuss your new view of your career field with the group or class.

The *Occupational Outlook Handbook (OOH)*

As your career search expands, information about the opportunities for growth and availability of jobs becomes more important. As a career counselor, this author has had many students approach me with questions such as "In which field will I be sure to get a job when I graduate?" or "Which job pays the most?" Salary and job availability are only two factors for you to consider in your career choice.

Wouldn't it be wonderful to own a crystal ball that could assure happiness and contentment? Students in the real world have to rely on more ordinary resources to help them assess the career market. The most readily available and comprehensive resource on job prospects is the *Occupational Outlook Handbook (OOH)*, a publication of the Department of Labor. The *OOH* is a manual distributed every two years and is most commonly available in the reference section of your college or public library or on the Internet at **http://stats.bls.gov.** It profiles over 330 occupations and millions of jobs found within those occupations. A sample page from the *OOH* is shown in Figure 4.2. Figure 4.3 is the home page for the Bureau of Labor Statistics at which you can access the *OOH* online. The information in the *OOH* ranges from the type of work found in particular jobs, the working conditions, employment statistics, training, qualifications and advancement to earnings, outlook for future employment, and sources for additional information. Cross-references to *DOT* codes are available as well as references to state offices that offer relevant local information. The current issue of the *OOH* offers projections on employment up to the year 2008. As you review the *OOH*, you may be tempted to view the data presented as the final authority on job availability. Although the information presented is helpful within the context of national trends, the specifics about the job outlook in your geographic area may differ or even run contrary to those cited in the *OOH*. *The Occupational Outlook Quarterly*, a DOL publication that updates occupational data, also offers in-depth examinations of stats on various careers during the interim between new editions of the *OOH*. These documents are only a start in your investigation. You will acquire a broad perspective on a career field and learn detailed facts about the field; then you will be informed when you talk with others about careers.

Information on job outlook is a highlight of the *OOH*. Figures 4.4 and 4.5 list high-paying jobs that, according to the *OOH*, are expected to experience the most growth by the year 2008.

Both figures reveal a number of important things. Figure 4.4 shows that the technology sector of the labor market will produce the greatest increase

Professional and Technical Occupations 139

Science Technicians

(O*NET 22599F, 24502A, 24502B, 24502C, 24502D, 24505A, 24505B, 24505C, 24505D, 24505E, 24508A, 24508B, 24511B, 24511E, 24599A, 24599B, 24599C, and 25323)

Significant Points

- Science technicians in production jobs often work in 8-hour shifts around the clock.

- Job opportunities are expected to be very good for qualified graduates of science technician training programs or applied science technology programs who are well trained on equipment used in laboratories and production facilities.

Nature of the Work

Science technicians use the principles and theories of science and mathematics to solve problems in research and development and to help invent and improve products and processes. However, their jobs are more practically oriented than those of scientists. Technicians set up, operate, and maintain laboratory instruments, monitor experiments, make observations, calculate and record results, and often develop conclusions. They must keep detailed logs of all their work-related activities. Those who work in production monitor manufacturing processes and may be involved in ensuring quality by testing products for proper proportions of ingredients, purity, or for strength and durability.

As laboratory instrumentation and procedures have become more complex in recent years, the role of science technicians in research and development has expanded. In addition to performing routine tasks, many technicians also develop and adapt laboratory procedures to achieve the best results, interpret data, and devise solutions to problems, under the direction of scientists. Moreover, technicians must master the laboratory equipment, so they can adjust settings when necessary, and recognize when equipment is malfunctioning.

The increasing use of robotics to perform many routine tasks has freed technicians to operate more sophisticated laboratory equipment. Science technicians make extensive use of computers, computer-interfaced equipment, robotics, and high-technology industrial applications, such as biological engineering.

Most science technicians specialize, learning skills and working in the same disciplines as scientists. Occupational titles, therefore, tend to follow the same structure as scientists. *Agricultural technicians* work with agricultural scientists in food, fiber, and animal research, production, and processing. Some conduct tests and experiments to improve the yield and quality of crops or to increase the resistance of plants and animals to disease, insects, or other hazards. Other agricultural technicians do animal breeding and nutrition work.

Biological technicians work with biologists studying living organisms. Many assist scientists who conduct medical research—helping to find a cure for cancer or AIDS, for example. Those who work in pharmaceutical companies help develop and manufacture medicinal and pharmaceutical preparations. Those working in the field of microbiology generally work as lab assistants, studying living organisms and infectious agents. Biological technicians also analyze organic substances, such as blood, food, and drugs, and some examine evidence in criminal investigations. Biological technicians working in biotechnology labs use the knowledge and techniques gained from basic research by scientists, including gene splicing and recombinant DNA, and apply these techniques in product development.

Chemical technicians work with chemists and chemical engineers, developing and using chemicals and related products and equipment. Most do research and development, testing, or other laboratory work. For example, they might test packaging for design, integrity of materials, and environmental acceptability; assemble and operate new equipment to develop new products; monitor product quality; or develop new production techniques. Some chemical technicians collect and analyze samples of air and water to monitor pollution levels. Those who focus on basic research might produce compounds through complex organic synthesis. Chemical technicians within chemical plants are also referred to as *process technicians.* They may operate equipment, monitor plant processes and analyze plant materials.

Environmental technicians perform laboratory and field tests to monitor environmental resources and determine the contaminants and sources of pollution. They may collect samples for testing or be involved in abating, controlling, or remediating sources of environmental pollutants. Some are responsible for waste management operations, control and management of hazardous materials inventory, or general activities involving regulatory compliance. There is a growing emphasis on pollution prevention activities.

Nuclear technicians operate nuclear test and research equipment, monitor radiation, and assist nuclear engineers and physicists in research. Some also operate remote control equipment to manipulate radioactive materials or materials to be exposed to radioactivity.

Petroleum technicians measure and record physical and geologic conditions in oil or gas wells, using instruments lowered into wells or by analysis of the mud from wells. In oil and gas exploration, these technicians collect and examine geological data or test geological samples to determine petroleum and mineral content. Some petroleum technicians, called *scouts,* collect information about oil and gas well drilling operations, geological and geophysical prospecting, and land or lease contracts.

Other science technicians collect weather information or assist oceanographers.

Working Conditions

Science technicians work under a wide variety of conditions. Most work indoors, usually in laboratories, and have regular hours. Some occasionally work irregular hours to monitor experiments that can't be completed during regular working hours. Production technicians often work in 8-hour shifts around the clock.

Science technicians put theory into practice.

FIGURE 4.2

BUREAU OF LABOR STATISTICS HOME PAGE.

U.S Department of Labor

Bureau of Labor Statistics

| BLS Home | New from BLS | Contacts at BLS | Search BLS |

Text Version

- Data
- Economy at a Glance
- News Releases
- Regional Information
- Publications
- Occupational Outlook Handbook
- Surveys & Programs
- K–12 Page
- Mission, Management and Jobs
- Subscribe to BLS News
- Freedom of Information Act (FOIA)
- Privacy and Security Statement
- FEDSTATS
- Other Statistical Sites
- Feedback about Content
- Feedback about Site (Technical)
- DOL Customer Survey
- Jobs in BLS – Washington, DC
- Jobs in BLS – Regions

ECONOMY AT A GLANCE
U.S. Economy · Industries · Regions, States, and Metropolitan Areas

CAREER GUIDES
Occupational Outlook Handbook · Career Guide to Industries

INFLATION AND SPENDING
Consumer Prices · Inflation Calculator · Producer Prices · International Prices · Employment Costs · Consumer Spending

WORKING AND LOOKING FOR WORK
Employment · Unemployment Rate · Employment Projections · More...

HOW MUCH PEOPLE EARN
Average Hourly Earnings · Wages by Area and Occupation · Employment Costs · Employee Benefits · Collective Bargaining

WORKER SAFETY AND HEALTH
Injuries and Illnesses · Fatalities

PRODUCTIVITY
Business and Manufacturing · Industry · Multifactor Productivity

INTERNATIONAL STATISTICS
International Comparisons · International Prices

ONLINE MAGAZINES
Monthly Labor Review · Compensation and Working Conditions · Occupational Outlook Quarterly · MLR: The Editor's Desk

ECONOMIC ANALYSIS AND INFORMATION OFFICES
Atlanta · Boston · Chicago · Dallas · Kansas City · New York · Philadelphia · San Francisco

TOOLS
Data Access · Inflation Calculator · Wage Query

CAREERS IN BLS
Jobs in BLS - Washington, DC · Jobs in BLS - Regions · Fellowships

Latest Numbers

CPI:
+0.6% in Jan 2001

Unemployment Rate:
4.2% in Feb 2001

Payroll Employment:
+135,000 in Feb 2001

Average Hourly Earnings:
+$0.07 in Feb 2001

PPI:
+1.1% in Jan 2001

ECI:
+0.8% in 4th Qtr of 2000

Productivity:
+2.2% in 4th Qtr of 2000

U.S. Import Price Index:
+0.1% in Feb 2001

Bureau of Labor Statistics
labstat.helpdesk@bls.gov
Last Updated: March 15, 2001
URL: http://stats.bls.gov/blshome.htm

FIGURE 4.3

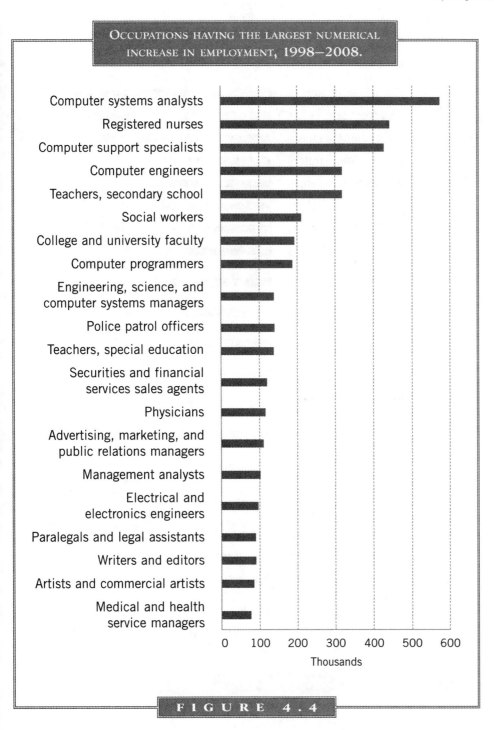

OCCUPATIONS HAVING THE LARGEST NUMERICAL INCREASE IN EMPLOYMENT, 1998–2008.

FIGURE 4.4

in jobs. Figure 4.5 shows that the fastest growth will take place in computer technology. The charts confirm that recent trends in the labor market will continue with real growth in service positions, particularly in computers and health care, with continuing decreases in manufacturing.

Exercise 4.3 will further familiarize you with the OOH and other resources and with how to determine the outlook for the career you are exploring. Make additional copies of the following exercise as needed to accommodate all the job titles you are researching.

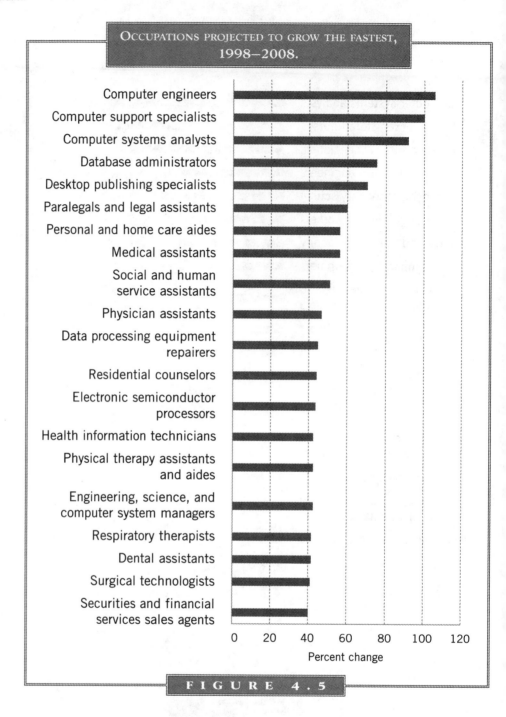

OCCUPATIONS PROJECTED TO GROW THE FASTEST, 1998–2008.

FIGURE 4.5

4.3 TAKE A CLOSER LOOK

Putting Predictions in Perspective

Choose one of the job titles you identified in the *Dictionary of Occupational Titles* or *Guide for Occupational Exploration* exercises, and use the alphabetical index in the back of the *Occupational Outlook Handbook* or on the Web site to find the section that addresses projections for your field. Answer the questions on the basis of the information you gather.

How specific is the information related to your field? Does it mention the actual job title or a broad category of jobs?

_____

_____

How does the information about the job compare to that found in the _DOT?_

_____

_____

Does the information cover national projections or regional?

_____

_____

Are the projections specific (statistical, percentage of increase) or general (expected to grow, expected to decline)?

_____

_____

Is this information helpful? If so, in what way?

_____

_____

What else should you consider when researching a particular job's outlook for future growth?

_____

_____

Where can you get additional information?

_____

_____

As you gather data about career possibilities, try to suspend your inclination to throw out any possibility that might present a challenge. Be sure that you have exhausted every possibility before you dismiss any options. Have faith in yourself and you will achieve your goal.

Discuss with your class or group the information you have uncovered.

WHAT IS COMPUTER-ASSISTED CAREER GUIDANCE?

Just as you were able to acquire information about careers and trends from the Internet, there are a number of computerized systems that are valuable resources in making career decisions. Both as a tool in self-assessment and as an information database for job markets and educational institutions, computers offer another way to approach career issues. While a session with a computer may never take the place of face-to-face counseling with a professional, many students can still benefit from using computers.

The computerized guidance systems that are currently available offer a variety of programs and modules from which to choose. The most popular programs are profiled briefly here.

Discover II and SIGI PLUS

These computerized career information systems match students' self-assessment responses against occupations and then offer a complete database of information about occupations. Although there are minor differences between the two programs, both programs were developed with a strong foundation in career development theory and offer colorful and user-friendly programs. Updates provide multimedia enhancements with videos of professionals at work and background music. Most valuable is the depth and amount of information about careers and the world of work that is available at the touch of a button. Students can learn more about specific jobs, salaries, duties, outlook, and what professionals like and dislike about their jobs. Files related to financial aid, colleges, technical schools, and military programs are also available. An added benefit lies in each system's ability to store student information and responses, allowing the student to return to the program for long-term use.

Career Information System (CIS) and Guidance Information System (GIS 3.0)

Both the Career Information System (CIS), published by CIS out of the University of Oregon, and the Guidance Information System (GIS 3.0), published and managed by Riverside Publishing/Houghton Mifflin, offer data similar to those available on Discover and SIGI PLUS. In addition, both CIS and GIS offer modules that provide users with information about state and local job markets gleaned from the state government's labor data. Self-assessment modules as well as information about occupations, military programs, educational institutions, and financial aid are available in both databases.

As with any tool that you use to make a career decision, computers can make the process more manageable. But, just as you have found with interest tests and personality exercises, they do not provide a magic answer that will lead you directly to the career of your dreams. As a resource, they allow you access to a wealth of information and may assist you in gaining insight, but they will never completely replace the hard work necessary to make a career choice.

Discuss with your instructor or counselor whether any of the programs mentioned previously are available on your campus. If so, schedule an appointment to use the system. Discuss your experience with the computer-assisted career guidance system with your group or with the class.

USING INFORMATION TECHNOLOGY IN YOUR CAREER SEARCH

Just as you used the library to research background information about companies, it is now possible to use the Internet to research organizations, job leads, and other career-related information. If you have a computer, modem,

Internet software, and an Internet service provider (like America Online), then a typical search will yield literally hundreds of thousands of references. It is an incomparable source of information, but can offer too much of a good thing. With just the touch of a button, you can be buried under Web sources that may hold valuable information or may be a maze of useless data and advertising. A few simple steps will make the time you spend on the Internet more productive.

1. *Use two or three search terms, clarifying with markers.*
   - Use *and* or a *plus sign (+)* to narrow your search (accountants AND treasury + Internal Revenue Service);
   - Use *or* or a *slash (/)* to broaden your search (college or university, college/university);
   - Use *not* or a *minus (–) sign* to indicate a word that should not appear (cowboys *not* NFL, cowboys–NFL);
   - Use *near* when the words should be close to each other (cost *NEAR* accounting);
   - To limit to an exact phrase, put it in quotation marks; Career Information System without quotation marks gives over 130 returns on Yahoo.com. "Career Information System" gives 10.

2. *Use guidelines provided at the search engine sites to facilitate your search.* Each search engine has tips on the best way to gather data. Take a few minutes to familiarize yourself with the recommended short cuts.

3. *Use sources that you can rely on.* Yahoo and LookSmart search engines offer directories, or online guides, at their home page that are evaluated by human experts. These vertical portals, or "vertals," save time by linking you when possible directly to the most useful sites.

4. *Evaluate Internet resources before relying on the data found there.* Keep the following in mind when reviewing information found on the Internet.
   - Who is the author? Is the author the originator of the data? What are his credentials, background, education, experience?
   - What organization supports the site? What is the relationship between the author and the site sponsor? Does the site sponsor monitor the information or is the author biased in favor of the sponsor?
   - Is the information current?
   - What is the purpose of the data? To inform? To persuade? To explain?
   - For which audience is the information intended?
   - How does the information offered here compare to other sites as well as non-Internet sources?

Figures 4.6 and 4.7 offer examples of Web sites that you might wish to visit as you search the Internet. Figure 4.6 is a Web site sponsored by the National Association of Colleges and Employers (NACE). JobWeb (copyright NACE) organizes information about jobs, employers, career planning, and job hunting in a colorful, interesting format that is user friendly and appeal-

THE JOBWEB HOME PAGE.

ONLINE CAREER FAIR

Click HERE for preferred employers of college graduates

jobweb

CONTACT US | SEARCH

EMPLOYER INFO | JOB SEARCH TOOLS | RESOURCES | BEYOND COLLEGE | PRESS | STORE

Friday, 03/16/2001

Starting Salary Offers

Find Your Next Job: JobWeb's Online Career Fair

Search for College Career Fair

Site Map

What do you think of JobWeb?

NACE Member Information

Personalize JobWeb!

Media Kit

TODAY'S TIP

A salutation or greeting is important in an e-mail message. Say "Good morning," or use some other greeting.

JOBWEB HIGHLIGHTS

Experience Pays Off

EMPLOYMENT STATUS	EXPERIENCE	RESPONDENTS AVERAGE SALARIES
First positions after graduation	Grad with intern/co-op experience	$19,400
	Grad without intern/co-op experience	$18,700
Current position	Grad with intern/co-op experience	$21,800
	Grad without intern/co-op experience	$21,000

Source: Winter 2000 *Journal of Career Planning & Employment*

Students: Employer of Choices

Which would you rather work for?

Dot com: 5.64%

Federal government: 21.18%

Fortune 500: 27.00%

Own company: 26.27%

Small company: 19.91%

Total Votes: 1100

NACEWEB

Interviewers' Favorite Questions

"Tell me about yourself," an interviewer intones, adjusting her glasses and gazing steadily into your eyes. What should you tell a recruiter or hiring manager?

Soft Economy Means Grads Must Work Harder to Find Good Jobs

Experts say students won't be forced to defer their dreams of finding a good job, despite reports of corporate layoffs and hiring freezes.

Do You Have a Job Yet?

Corporate layoffs, plummeting stock market values, an overall softening of the economy—does it have you worried? Talk to us in JobWeb's Job Talk.

New Graduates See Gains in Starting Salary Offers

In spite of talk of softening in the economy, a new salary offer report shows that graduates in many fields are getting higher starting salary offers than they did last year.

ask the experts

This week's question:
• I am applying for jobs as a writer/editor. How do I send the clips? Melanie Huff, career services coordinator at the Columbia University Graduate School of Journalism, offers some expert advice.

Come to JobWeb each Monday for new articles and information.

Home | Employer Info | Job Search Tools | Resources
Beyond College | Press | Store | Contact Us | Search | Site Map

Copyright© National Association of Colleges and Employers
62 Highland Avenue, Bethlehem, PA 18017-9085
Phone: 610/868-1421 or 800/544-5272 • Fax: 610/868-0208
Webmaster

FIGURE 4.6

The Riley Guide

Employment Opportunities
and Job Resources on the Internet

www.rileyguide.com
www.dbm.com/jobguide/

Compiled by Margaret F. Dikel

Do you see the URL (www.dbm.com/jobguide/) for this site in the Address or Location bar?
Can't bookmark this site because you're caught in a frame from another site?
Use this link **to break free!**

How can I help you?

New This Week: **I've found some Great Books for you!**

NEW What's New NEW **March 16, 2001**

Prepare for a Job Search || Resumes & Cover Letters

Targeting & Researching Employers, etc.

Executing Your Job Search Campaign || Job Listings!

Networking, Interviewing, & Negotiating || Salary Guides & Guidance

Information For Recruiters || A-Z Index || About the Guide

 This marker at the top and bottom of each page
will always bring you back here.

Wish you could review the Riley Guide in a language other than English?

Try the Babelfish Translator Service. **Enter the URL of the page you want, select a language (English to French,**
Italian, Spanish, Portuguese, or German), and go. It's not perfect, but I hope it will help.

The Riley Guide is here to guide you through the many online sites and services that are useful for your job
search. We do not post jobs nor resumes, we don't review resumes, and we cannot forward them to others on
your behalf. We will happily consider linking to your website **if it provides job leads or other helpful information**
for job seekers.

 "This is the best by far. If I could only go to one   *"Margaret Riley Dikel is the preeminent expert on*
gateway job site on the Web, this would be it."   *Internet job hunting. And the Riley Guide is an*
-- Richard Bolles, JobHuntersBible.com   *invaluable tool for savvy job hunters."*
    --Tony Lee, Editor in Chief, Careerjournal.com, from
    The Wall Street Journal Interactive Edition.

If you find any problems or know of additional resources not included, please send email to webmaster@rileyguide.com .
Comments and suggestions to improve the guide are always welcome. I regret that I cannot answer all of your inquiries,
but I will try to incorporate the answers into the guide.

Copyright 1998 - 2001, Margaret F. Dikel. Permission to reproduce and/or distribute printed copies of these pages is
hereby granted for non-profit purposes only. No changes may be made to these copies without the express permission
of the author. All other requests for copying and distribution including electronic distribution must be directed to the
author. Permission is granted for you to link to this page or The Riley Guide at any time, but the location address (URL)
must not be hidden through the use of frames. Please read our disclaimers.

 The Riley Guide, **www.dbm.com/jobguide/ or www.rileyguide.com**
Supported by Drake Beam Morin
webmaster@rileyguide.com

Reprinted with permission, Margaret Riley Dikel, *The Riley Guide* (www.rileyguide.com).

FIGURE 4.7

ing. This site is one of dozens that offer information you need about organizations, jobs, and careers and can be accessed at **www.jobweb.com/**.

Figure 4.7 is the home page for The Riley Guide, a highly regarded site sponsored by Drake Beam and Morin, an outplacement firm that offers a wide range of information on both the process and particulars of career planning and job seeking. This site (www.dbm.com/jobguide) is recommended for the information and the links it features. It even provides a basic tutorial for web searching. As you learn new ways to explore careers, you will also have the chance to take the pulse of the job market by seeing what jobs are currently available.

Most colleges now offer Internet access to their students. Using the Internet to conduct your career exploration provides you with valuable information and allows you to become more of a part of the continuing technology transition. Take advantage of it.

WHICH WAY TO YOUR COLLEGE CAREER CENTER?

One of the most valuable sources for current career information is your college career center. On some campuses it may be called career services or perhaps career counseling. Whatever its name, it is the best place to find many of the resources mentioned in this chapter as well as to obtain one-on-one career counseling. As a bonus, many career centers have corporate libraries that store up-to-date information about local and regional companies, their products, and the local economy.

If your school is a member of NACE, you will find copies of their annual publication on job seeking. This free magazine for college students is published in several editions devoted to specific career areas, including health care, business, and science; also included are profiles about specific companies.

WHAT'S THE BIG PICTURE?

In the last section, we saw an example of how information on job growth can be complex and misleading. To have a solid understanding of a career field, take the time to look at more than just the information related to a specific position. It is important to be informed on the job and in the

Calvin and Hobbes   by Bill Watterson

career as a whole as well as the labor market in which it exists. Be aware both of the national and local trends and economic and cultural trends that affect our society.

Futurists such as John Naisbitt and Watts Wacker contend that the rate of change in our society will be continuous rather than sporadic. As major institutions struggle to meet the challenge that change presents, individuals will have to stretch their emotional, psychological, and physical resources to meet the new demands.

Now more than ever, your understanding of how trends in our society and culture will affect your career is essential to your success and satisfaction in that field. Knowing what to expect places your decision in a context that will enable you to choose wisely and prepare yourself for what lies ahead.

TRENDS IN THE WORKPLACE.

- *The work force will reflect the increasing diversity of our society.*   The larger proportion of minority group members and women and the increase in average age of our population will be a factor in the changing composition of the work force. As baby boomers reach retirement age, the impact will be realized in those careers that have the highest concentration of aging workers: education, public administration, management, transportation, and health services.

- *Workers will attempt to reintegrate home and work life.*   Companies and workers will find new ways to make work and home life compatible, reversing a 100-year trend. On-site child care, job sharing, and working from home are examples of innovations that are already benefiting some corporations through increased worker loyalty and greater profitability. Look for more innovations as corporations attempt to create 'a great place to work' through additional services like counseling on health, legal, and financial matters as well as more personal and community service time.

- *A greater number of jobs will be created in many small businesses rather than from the large business sector.*   New business start-ups will continue to offer the greatest opportunity for employment. Large business will continue to trim employees and contract for work in an effort to remain competitive and show profits. New business relationships will assure economic survival by adding capabilities through new strategic alliances without adding cost or growth to the organization. The so-called old economy corporations, made from bricks and mortar, will survive and thrive depending on how well they can integrate new dot-com features into their culture. Competition will come from unexpected places as travel agents found when they realized that their greatest threat wasn't from the travel agency across the street but from the personal computer (pc) that their former clients could now use to book their own tours.

- *Competition from foreign countries will contribute to the continued growth of a global economy.* Opportunities for growth in foreign markets will push the U. S. economy to open further while we struggle to keep up with scientific and technical competition from abroad. Corporate alliances across disciplines and national borders will rival political alliances, creating new power bases, new leadership roles. Globalization and technology are inextricably linked and will continue to change the way we interact. E-commerce, online education, and telecommuting—even intercontinental telecommuting—will become increasingly common. The advantages customarily associated with U. S. citizenship and residency will diminish as information technologies reshape the way work and resources are distributed.

(continued)

FIGURE 4.8

CONTINUED.

■ *Increasingly, the nature of work will demand a knowledge-based work force.*   Jobs requiring little skill and training are disappearing. Technology and the global economy have increased the need for further training after high school and made it a prerequisite to employment even in entry-level positions. Manufacturing will continue to shift jobs to foreign competitors until computer technology takes over the production setting. When this takes place, some manufacturing jobs could be reclaimed if our work force is prepared with the required higher-level skills. Corporations with particular shortages of skills in information technology areas will offer programs that entice workers at younger ages into fields through subsidized training, guaranteed positions, and bonuses for long-term service. College graduates from some disciplines, specifically health, engineering, education, and information technology, will be in high demand while others will find themselves facing diminished opportunities and underemployment.

■ *Further change will take place in the relationship between employees and employers.*   Human resources planning will play a major role in reestablishing the way workers interact with their employers. The traditional career path of upward mobility through one organization to retirement is already a thing of the past. "Outsourcing," or contracting for portfolio or freelance and temporary employees who work on an as-needed basis, has become a way for corporations to reduce overhead and save money. In all organizations, "human capital," the organization's investment in its employees and their ability to innovate and respond quickly to market forces, will determine which organizations will survive into the next century. Employees will take responsibility for their careers, recognizing that performance and skill development are what count. Employers who are willing to respond by sharing profits and encouraging employee participation in the organization's success will create the synergy necessary to keep pace with the marketplace.

F I G U R E   4 . 8

Researchers have identified a number of trends that will have a lasting impact on the world of work. Figure 4.8 consists of a compilation of a few noteworthy themes that are currently being played out in our work force.

As you can see, our world will be undergoing dramatic change as we transition from the old industrial economy into the new information age. You will be part of that change. Being informed on these and other issues will provide you with an invaluable base from which to make decisions.

As you embark on your quest for a new career, you may find that the rapid rate of change is continually shifting the shape or the career you have chosen. You may need further training. If so, four factors have a strong influence on the success that college students achieve upon graduating. Your success will be determined in large part by:

■ *what you study*—Some fields of study will continue to enjoy growth and job availability.

■ *how hard you work at school*—Applying yourself to your studies will result in better job prospects after graduation.

■ *what actual skills you develop*—Your ability to demonstrate your value to an employer as soon after graduation as possible will make you a preferred candidate for employment.

■ *the level of hands-on experience you've had*—Any opportunities to become involved in hands-on work experience—even unpaid experience—helps build your credibility for later employment. This includes co-op positions, internships, and volunteer and part-time jobs.

All these are variables that you control. Even more important, knowing what you want, knowing what to expect, making your choice, and working hard have a greater impact than any external forces.

Next is an example of how one student used the resources discussed in this chapter to make his decision.

MITCH'S STORY

As a student, Mitch was struggling to find a place for himself in the spectrum of college majors. Mitch's father had worked his entire life as a carpenter in the construction trades. Mitch had always been around skilled tradesmen and had wielded a hammer since he was five years old. He loved the work environment and the sense of satisfaction he received from working with his hands but was uncomfortable with the instability of the construction business. He had seen his father suffer through periods of instability and wanted a more secure career. His family supported his decision to continue his education as a way to broaden his experience and allow him more autonomy in his career.

Unfortunately, he wasn't sure what career could give him the same satisfaction as carpentry and provide the opportunity for growth that a college education represented. Mitch looked up the position of carpenter in the *Guide for Occupational Exploration* under the "Mechanical" section. Under that main heading he found areas that sounded interesting to him, such as engineering, craft technology, quality control, and equipment operation. As he scanned the various categories under "Mechanical," he found several that offered opportunities for growth combined with the hands-on skills with which he was familiar. Architecture and civil engineering from design areas were possibilities that would require a bachelor's degree or more, while programs in drafting and surveying were available at the two-year-col-

lege level. Disciplines such as quality control engineering and equipment operation were secondary choices that also interested Mitch.

Mitch's research on the Internet led him to the Bureau of Labor Statistics home page. He clicked on the *Occupational Outlook Handbook* and the information there indicated that the job outlook for architects would be good through the year 2008, with at least average growth. The prospects in drafting were expected to be a bit slower than average. The *OOH* emphasized that both careers were highly dependent on economic changes and would be among the first affected in a recession. Mitch was prepared for this because of his knowledge about the construction field. Mitch believed that he could compete for employment in the predicted economic environment. His family's support and his prior success in meeting his employer's requirements were good indicators of his future success. Long-term trends further contributed to his belief that service occupations (architecture or drafting), which integrated computerized design into their approaches would fill a market niche for many years to come.

His initial research behind him, Mitch now set out to find how accurate his understanding was regarding the occupations he found interesting. His next step was to begin talking with people who actually worked in these fields. Mitch knew that the road ahead might offer obstacles, but he was beginning to feel that he would be realistically prepared for whatever happened.

4.4 TAKE A CLOSER LOOK

Pulling It All Together

Now that you've taken a look at specific careers, you have a base from which to make choices about your career. Use this as a way to consolidate your information.

What careers did you find from the *DOT/GOE* and Internet search that seem to offer you what you are seeking?

_____

_____

_____

What does the *OOH* say about the field/job in which you are interested? The O*NET?

_____

_____

_____

What national trends recognized from the popular press are relevant or significant in terms of your career choice?

_____

_____

_____

Discuss the results of your exploration up to now with the class or with your group.

At this point in your career adventure, you have acquired a great deal of knowledge about the different types of careers that appeal to you and could meet your needs. You are familiar with resources in the library—the *Dictionary of Occupational Titles* and the *Occupational Outlook Handbook*—that offer specific information about the duties, settings, skills, salaries, and outlook for a particular occupation. You are also familiar with the *Guide for Occupational Exploration*, which has provided you with a perspective on related jobs and skill areas. Computers with access to the Internet may be available to you as a source to further your career search, and your college career center has valuable resources from which you can learn more about the national and local economy. Finally, you have begun to broaden your exploration to include learning about overall economic and social trends and their effect on the job market. With all of this new knowledge, you are creating a sound basis for making an informed career decision.

A LOOK BACK

Other Sources and Suggested Reading

The resources discussed in this chapter are the best place to develop a perspective on your chosen career field. In addition, your college or public library has numerous publications available from which you can obtain even more information.

The resources cited are a few of those we have found most useful for students exploring their career choices.

100 Best Careers for the 21st Century by Shelly Field

This is a good resource for future career trends.

American Salaries and Wages Survey, 5th Edition published by Gale Research

This book presents the salaries of thousands of occupations on both a national and local level.

The American Almanac of Jobs and Salaries by John W. Wright

Statistics are accompanied by career trends for a broad range of disciplines.

Best Bet Internet: Reference and Research When You Don't Have Time to Mess Around by Shirley Duglin Kennedy

This book offers dozens of tips for making the time you spend on the internet productive.

A Big Splash in a Small Pond: Finding A Great Job In A Small Company by R. Linda Resnick with Kerry H. Pechter, and William C. Dunkelberg

The opportunities available through small business and entrepreneurial ventures are too numerous to ignore. This book encourages you to take seriously this exciting area of the labor market.

Clicks and Mortar: Passion Driven Growth in an Internet Driven World by David S. Pottruck and Terry Pearce

As information technology continues to influence careers, companies will be reexamining issues of leadership and decision making. This book profiles one organization's transition as it confronts the challenges of change.

Department of Labor Publications

The Department of Labor offers career information books through the United States Employment Service. These books focus on specific careers such as criminal justice, environmental protection, or health and medicine. These are useful for the extended examination of the occupations and are available wherever U. S. government publications are found.

Encyclopedia of Careers and Vocational Guidance, 11th Edition published by Ferguson Publishing Company

This is a comprehensive guide to careers and vocational information.

Liberal Arts Advantage: How to Turn Your Degree into a Great Job by Gregory Giangrande

For anyone convinced that a liberal arts degree is the only one for them, this book will give you a preview of how to connect in the job market.

Peterson's Internships 2001 published by Peterson's, a division of Thomson Learning

Although you may not be ready for an internship or job hunt at this point, this volume will give you a feel for the types of jobs available. The areas range from business to creative arts, from the environment to international and public affairs.

Working for Your Uncle produced by the editors of the Federal Jobs Digest

This book assists those individuals who wish to work for the federal government. It is an informative guide to the labyrinthine world of federal employment with specific information on the hiring process.

Web Sites and Internet Resources

Some of the most valuable information on the Internet is provided by the U. S. Department of Labor (DOL).

www.acinet.org

The Department of Labor presents this site, America's Career InfoNet. It offers a full range of career exploration data.

www.ajb.dni.us

This DOL site, America's Job Bank, is a national job posting site.

www.alx.org

This site, America's Learning Exchange, also from the DOL, addresses training and education options.

www.jobweb.org

The National Association of Colleges and Employers (NACE) provides everything you need for career exploration at this site.

www.salary.com

Want to know the salary for an occupation in a particular city? Try this site for information on salaries and wages.

http://stats.bls.gov

This Department of Labor site offers all the latest statistics on jobs and the labor market available from the library sources including the *Occupational Outlook Handbook*.

NETWORKING

ESTABLISHING CONTACTS & SUPPORT

It wasn't long ago that the definition of "network" was limited to a type of hardware we associate with electronic components. For the past 20 years, however, we have expanded the meaning of the word to include a system of relationships that can have a dramatic effect on you and your career. Indeed, networking is a necessary part of establishing and maintaining a rewarding, meaningful career.

A network is a group of social and work acquaintances who know who you are and what you do or hope to do. It can include people from the most informal of settings, such as the woman who sits next to you at the ballpark, or formal business associates, such as the president of the company where you once worked. Both of these people are members of a club and may not even know it. It's the "Friends of You" (FOY) Club. Obviously, we are using the word "friends" in this case to refer to anyone who might be in a position to assist you in your career.

Whether the members of the FOY Club are familiar to you on a close or more distant basis is of little importance. What is important is:

- *Your network is unique to you.* No one else has the exact same combination of relatives, acquaintances, and associates. Your FOY Club is a distinctive asset that is unique and valuable.

- *Your network can be expanded to meet your career needs.* It would be easy to limit your club membership only to those people whom you have met up to now. There are dozens of others—friends of "friends of you," if you will, who could play a role in your career growth. All you have to do is meet them . . . a task that can seem intimidating but is in fact easy. We will discuss how to do this in a later section.

- *Your network will help you understand the local career market much better than any resource you can examine in a library.* Talking to people who are actually working in the field in which you are interested will provide you with a balanced insight into the job as well as an understanding of job availability, good places to work, and future trends in the field.

- *Your network will help you to begin establishing yourself in your chosen career field.* If you don't already know anyone who is working in a particular career that you are exploring, now is the time to meet these individuals. The people you meet now may be there later, when you are ready to enter the field, waiting to give you a welcome boost.

- *Your network can be a means of visualizing yourself in your new profession.* As you meet with people at their places of work and talk with them, you will begin to imagine yourself actually performing the job just as you will learn the language of a new career. This initial phase of visualization in a profession will be a sustaining vision as you move toward your goal.

The process of invigorating your network so you can put it to work begins by organizing the members of your current network, the FOY Club.

IDENTIFYING YOUR EXISTING NETWORK

In my work with hundreds of students over the years, it has been gratifying to help them discover just how extensive their personal networks are. It is not uncommon for students to find that a family member or neighbor or previous classmate is working in a field in which they are interested. Exercise 5.1 helps you identify the range of your network by listing any friends and acquaintances who could tell you more about their careers.

 5.1 TAKE A CLOSER LOOK

Your "FOY Club"

Think about your FOY Club, your circle of friends and acquaintances. Then look at the categories of people and jot down any names that come to mind. You may be surprised to learn how many people you can think of while doing this exercise. Be sure to include everyone who comes to mind, including people you might not have seen in years.

Family members

_____

_____

Classmates/roommates

_____

_____

Coworkers

_____

_____

Former coworkers

_____

_____

Social club members

_____

_____

Neighbors

_____

_____

Sports team members/competitors

_____

_____

Social friends

_____

_____

Fellow volunteers

_____

_____

Former girl-/boyfriends

_____

_____

People from place of worship

_____

_____

Parents' friends and associates

_____

_____

People with the same hobby

_____

_____

Incidental acquaintances (e.g., bus stop companions)

_____

_____

Were you surprised by the number of people you could name? Granted, you may already know that many of the people on your list are working in jobs that hold no interest to you. More significant, did you find anyone in your circle of contacts who is working in the field you are investigating? If not, don't be concerned. You are about to enlarge the circle.

EXPANDING YOUR NETWORK

The best first step is to contact people with whom you are comfortable and familiar. After you have gathered leads and information from them, take the leap—reach out beyond the familiarity of your existing network to the larger career community.

To expand your network, start by identifying resources that you believe will yield names relevant to your field of interest. Keep a record of names, telephone numbers, and business addresses of people who work in your career area. Even if you don't know anyone in the career you're interested in, you may know *someone who knows someone* in that career.

If you find that your present circle of contacts is limited, don't despair. There are other avenues by which to continue your exploration. One of the most effective methods of expanding your network is to become acquainted with the members of the professional organization associated with your area of interest. These groups usually meet monthly to discuss topics relevant to the profession and to network among themselves. Students are often able to arrange membership at a reduced fee. These meetings can provide a gold mine of information about the professions and available jobs. If you have zeroed in on a particular field that has a local professional organization, get in touch with the person in charge of new members and inquire about attending meetings or obtaining referrals. Most organizations are happy to work with someone who may later join the group.

Along with formal professional organizations, informal networking groups are a valuable resource for referrals and information. These groups are often more accessible than professional associations. You might find listings in your local newspaper under group meetings. If not, keep your ear to the ground when contacting new people and find out what you can about how *they* network. This is another route toward finding a group that will offer encouragement and support.

If you are undertaking a midlife career transition, then your professional network may already be quite extensive. Everyone with whom you have worked in prior positions is a member of your FOY Club. Even if they work in careers that don't interest you, they are another source of contacts and information. More significantly, if you were a valued member of your former associates' work group, you can ask them for advice, information, and recommendations. You need only to enlist them into your group.

Many colleges have lists of alumni who are available to assist students in their career investigations. These people are graduates who have settled in the geographic area near their alma mater. Check with the career services or alumni offices at your school to see if they offer this service to students. Alumni are an excellent resource for job market information and are usually glad to help, so feel free to approach them for a brief phone or in-person interview, even if you feel a little uncomfortable. Once you've done it, you'll find it gets easier and easier.

If by chance your school does not offer this service, it's time to head back to the library in search of directories for local companies and organizations. Resources such as the *Harris Industrial Directory* or the *Career Guide 2000* by Dun & Bradstreet offer an array of information about organizations on a state-by-state basis. Just scan them initially. Then focus in on your state and city. You will find information on the type of business these companies do, their addresses, phone numbers, perhaps a brief historical synopsis or even the names of the organization's executives. The primary value of checking these directories is to locate specific organizations that might employ people in your field of interest. You might also find names of possible network partners in the directories of professional organizations, chamber of commerce publications, or in local newspaper articles highlighting companies.

Of course, for many careers, you need go only as far as the yellow pages to find the names of many people who are working in a particular discipline. Medicine, law, accounting, publishing, and data processing are just a few of the areas in which professionals are listed under their area of expertise.

Internet contacts can assist you with information about professions and jobs through contact with listserv groups, "bulletin boards," and online chat. While these contacts can yield a great deal of information, it is only as good as its source. It may be difficult to determine the validity of the contact you've made and, more significantly, something that holds true about a career in California may mean little if you live 3,000 miles away. Also, getting data from the Internet is an easy way to do research, but it may do nothing to help you meet people who could be helpful down the road. Of course, trying to meet network contacts through the Internet has its own pitfalls, such as being taken advantage of by unscrupulous individuals. Using the Web is no substitute to meeting people face-to-face.

The key factor in expanding your network is making contact with *the actual persons who are performing the work that interests you*, not the human resources office, the secretary, the receptionist, the operator, or "Steve47" from your online server. Once you actually talk with the person who can help you, you are much more likely to arrange a meeting with her.

Use Exercise 5.2 to compile a list of new network partners.

TAKE A CLOSER LOOK 5.2

Develop Contacts

Using any resource available to you (newspaper articles, directories, yellow pages), including your circle of friends and family, make a list of five companies or organizations in your area that might employ people in your field of interest.

COMPANIES/ORGANIZATIONS/PHONE NUMBERS

1. _____
2. _____
3. _____
4. _____
5. _____

Write the name of the organization and the phone number at the top of a blank sheet of notebook paper. Under it, place anything else that you think is important to remember about this company (e.g., type of product, number of employees) that you may have picked up from your research. Figure 5.1 illustrates a typical company sheet and the type of information that might be pertinent. If you don't have a great deal of information to put down, that's all right. That will be the goal of your telephone conversation—to gather more information.

After determining the area within the organization in which the jobs you are interested in might be found (e.g., engineering, marketing, accounting, public relations), call the main phone number and ask for the name of the manager of that department. Most operators will provide you that information; some may also give the extension or ask you if you want to be connected. For now, just get the name.

Some operators will explain that the company does not give out the information over the phone. If this happens, explain that you are a college student working on a project and your assignment requires you to contact a person in accounting, or marketing, or whatever. Then your request may get forwarded to human resources. Since you are not seeking a position at this time, just information, you may be able to get some names or tips from the human resources person. If not, simply offer your thanks and move on to the next company.

Once you have the name of the person in the department you are interested in, add it to the other information on your notebook sheet. You are now ready to expand your list of contacts through information networking.

Discuss with your group or class how your actual inquiries were received.

INFORMATION NETWORKING

Information networking, the process of meeting face-to-face with a professional in the field you are researching, is one of the most valuable methods for gathering data about a career field. This type of career research was popularized during the 1970s by Richard Nelson Bolles in his book *What Color Is Your Parachute?* and has become an integral part of any career or job search.

When contemplating information networking, the first question most people ask is "Whom will I interview?" As mentioned earlier, the easiest place to start is with your existing network, those contacts and acquaintances already in the FOY Club. They are your networking partners right now. With very little effort, you can enlist their help in your career exploration.

ARRANGING YOUR NETWORK MEETING

You have now reached the part of networking that typically causes the most anxiety: arranging network meetings. For many of you these may be your first business phone conversations. For others, this process may bring back memories of other business conversations that were less than pleasurable. Perhaps it's just the idea of calling someone with a request that makes you hesitate.

If you experience anxiety or hesitation, try to relax and take one step at a time. Remember, you are a college student completing an assignment. The community is a resource that supports your institution through taxes, donations, endowments, and a variety of other means. This is one of those other means. Students from your school return to the community after graduation

Acme Engineering, Inc.
3376 Industrial Parkway
Chicago, Illinois 60601

(312) 498-6255

Major product/service: Industrial engineering consulting

Areas of specialization:

Number of employees: 23

President:

Executive officers:

Engineering department manager/head:

Staff engineers:

Annual sales/receipts:

Additional information/comments:

Date of interview: _____   Time: _____

Contact: _____

FIGURE 5.1

and contribute to the organizations they join. It is in the best interests of the people with whom you will be talking to support you in your search. Feel free to ask for their insight and help—they undoubtedly have been helped by others before them . . . and you will do the same later, when you are a wizened veteran of your chosen career. Besides, people love to talk about themselves, and you're going to give them the chance to do just that.

To start, try the following role-play exercise with someone in your class to get a feel for how it works.

5.3 TAKE A CLOSER LOOK

Practice Your Telephone Style

Once you obtain the name and number of the person with whom you would like to arrange an interview, you want to be concise, because her time is valuable. Get right to the point by using the telephone dialogue that follows. Practice the dialogue with a partner or make up one of your own to use with a new contact. Constructing your own dialogue will help you to sharpen and tailor your responses so that you will feel comfortable when you make your calls.

"ARRANGING THE MEETING" DIALOGUE

Operator: "Good morning, Acme Engineering."

You: "Good morning. May I please speak to Ms. Charlotte Ramsey?"

Operator: "One moment, please."

Ms. Ramsey: "Engineering, Charlotte Ramsey."

You: "Hello, Ms. Ramsey. My name is John Black and I am a student at Omega University here in Summitville. I am conducting research into engineering careers. I'm not looking for a job, just some information. I am wondering if you would have 15 or 20 minutes to chat with me at your convenience about your job and about engineering in general?"

Ms. Ramsey: "I'm quite busy. I'm not really sure I can help you."

You: "I'm sure that any information you can share will be very valuable to me, and I promise I won't take more time than you can spare. Perhaps I could come out and chat with you next week some time? Say Tuesday perhaps?"

Ms. Ramsey: "Well, all right. Next Tuesday at 10:30 A.M. would be good. I can talk to you for a short time then."

You: "Thank you, Ms. Ramsey. I look forward to meeting you."

How did the dialogue feel? Maybe a little stiff the first time, but you'll become more comfortable with it as you practice and use it. Vary the responses in your group to see how you might react under different circumstances. Role-play situations in which your contact is rude, rushed, distracted, resistant, evasive, or disorganized.

Discuss your practice experiences with your group or with the class.

Now you are ready to make calls. Choose a time when you are sure to have a quiet space where you will be undisturbed. As a courtesy to the person you are contacting, avoid making calls on Monday, a particularly busy day for most people. When you are making the actual calls, suggest a date for the interview that is completely open for you so that your network partner does not have to rearrange her schedule to accommodate your needs. Once you have a date and time set, *write it down* on your data sheet for that company. Promptness is essential.

A word on voice mail: You may find that your call will be answered by a machine or an electronic messaging system (voice mail). If you are uncomfortable with the idea of leaving your name and number on the tape, you may wish to keep trying until you reach the person. You may become quite frustrated since some people use voice mail as a way of screening calls. If this happens, leave a brief message stating your name, why you're calling, and when you will try to reach the person again. If you are still unsuccessful in contacting the person directly, you may then want to leave a number where you can be reached. Don't wait for them to call you, though. In the long run, it may be more productive for you to try reaching someone else who is more accessible.

PREPARING FOR YOUR NETWORK MEETING

You have successfully arranged a meeting! It is time to do your homework and prepare yourself for the interview. The most important fact to remember is that this meeting is *not* a job interview. Meeting with contacts to inquire about their field is part of your ongoing career exploration, not a campaign to obtain a job. Think of your contact as a potential guide through unfamiliar territory—someone who will point out the pitfalls of your exploration as well as where to go for the best view. Focusing on this will free you and your network partner from the pressures associated with job seeking. In addition, your preparation for the interview includes two other areas—your appearance, and the questions you will ask.

The simplest aspect of any network meeting is making sure that you dress appropriately. Typical campus attire would not be appropriate for this meeting. If you can, find out how people at the company dress. Respect your interviewer and take the time to conform to the dress code of his environment. Appropriate dress usually consists of a tie, jacket, and dress trousers for men, and a blouse, jacket, and skirt, a suit, or a simple dress for women. Also, make sure that your hair is combed neatly, nails trimmed, and shoes polished.

Ensure that you are on time for your meeting by "dry-running" your route to the organization the day before (remember to factor in "rush hour" traffic). On the day of the meeting, arrive at least five minutes early as a way of demonstrating your dependability and to give yourself time to relax in the lobby before the appointment.

The rest of your preparation should focus on making a list of questions you wish to ask your new contact. You may have only 15 to 20 minutes so it is best to ask clear, concise questions. Some examples follow.

- What are the specific duties associated with your position?
- How did you obtain your present job?
- How would I prepare myself to enter this field?
- Where do you see this field going within the next 5 to 10 years?
- What do you like most about your job?
- What do you like least about your job?
- Who else would you recommend I speak with who knows about this field?

Any interview with a professional in the career field you are exploring should include questions about that person's specific duties. After you have interviewed several contacts, you will see how people with the same job titles may perform very different jobs. Asking how the person got into her position will give you an idea of how career paths evolve.

The other questions you might ask focus on the type of preparation needed to enter the field and what might happen in the field in the future. If your allotted interview time is quite short, you might be limited to just these questions. You may find, however, that the person is willing to expand the interview beyond the time limit. Most people are quite generous with their time when they are discussing something they enjoy.

Be flexible enough that you can improvise, too, as the conversation progresses. Take advantage of any opportunity to pursue an area that interests you even if it deviates from your prepared set of questions. You can always get back to those.

Also, be prepared to discuss *your* interest in the career. Review in your mind how you came to choose this path—this will encourage a meaningful exchange. If you are in the middle of a career change and are comfortable sharing your experiences with your network partner, you will have an excellent opportunity to connect on a professional level. Your background and maturity can be a plus, but be careful not to talk negatively about a former employer or company.

The final question, "Who else would you recommend I speak with who knows about this field?" will provide you with another contact for your network, hence another avenue to explore and expand in your career network.

If you drew a picture of your network after meeting with a few contacts, you might find that it looks like a road map. In some respects it is a road map that intersects with you. As you interview more and more people, you may hear the same names repeated as "the people to know" in your field. If you have already met them, then pat yourself on the back. You have made valuable contacts and, if you were well prepared, you probably made a good impression. If you haven't made contact with one of these key people, you may want to do so. Such a meeting could prove valuable later on.

FOLLOWING UP

After your network meeting, follow up with a thank-you letter or note, which brings your first encounter with that person to favorable closure. "Closure" doesn't necessarily mean that you will have no further contact with that person, however. Remember, they are members of the FOY Club now.

If, as a result of your network meetings, you decide to make a commitment to enter that career, you may want to include that in your thank-you note. Figure 5.2 is an example of a short note expressing your gratitude. If it is appropriate, mention that you hope to be able to call on this person in the future for advice and insight. As your study of the field continues, you may wish to write to those contacts you have made through the networking process to update them on your search and progress. These individuals may be key players in the realization of your professional goals.

85 Green Street
Chicago, Illinois 60601
March 23, 2001

Ms. Charlotte Ramsey
Acme Engineering, Inc.
3376 Industrial Parkway
Chicago, Illinois 60601

Dear Ms. Ramsey:

Thank you for the opportunity to meet with you last Tuesday to
share your insights on industrial engineering. Our discussion was
most helpful and has confirmed my interest in pursuing industrial
engineering as my profession.

I will be continuing my studies toward my degree at the College of
DuPage in the fall. Your informed perspective has been of great
value to me. With your permission, I would like to let you know of
my progress.

Again, I deeply appreciate your time and consideration.

Sincerely,

Lori Vance

FIGURE 5.2

FINDING MENTORS AND SPONSORS

Having a contact helps you to understand how a local career market has
developed and what might be possible, but your contact may provide even
greater benefits. Occasionally, you may encounter an individual who is willing to do more than just give information. A person who plays the role of
mentor or sponsor can have a significant impact on your career. But finding
someone to provide that support can be tricky.

The roles of mentor and sponsor have become a more visible reality during the last 20 years. Mentors and sponsors have been around for years in an informal context, usually assisting young men through the transitions of their careers. When women began to enter the world of work, they found that they were frequently excluded from the relationships and informal settings such as the locker room at the country club, where mentoring commonly occurs. Therefore, women began actively to seek out individuals of either gender who could support them in their professional lives.

Some of the contacts were mentors, people who were experienced in their field, veterans of career wars, who could offer insight, encouragement, and a steadying influence on young people trying to succeed. Others became sponsors, individuals who were willing to promote actively a newcomer for opportunities within their organizations.

These alliances are certainly advantageous, but they are not without risk. Some young workers have been exploited by unscrupulous individuals. And some professionals have been victimized by young people pushing for a career boost. People on both sides of the relationship have experienced betrayal, scandal, and ethical blunders. That said, however, the advantages of having a mentor far outweigh the disadvantages.

The best opportunities to develop relationships of this type usually occur in actual work settings, where you can get to know someone well. In turn, that person will have the chance to see you at work and to establish a feeling of mutual respect and trust. Students who have had a cooperative work experience often encounter a coworker who will take the time to encourage them. The person who extends a helping hand might then become a source of continuing support.

Occasionally, prior to work experience, a person from your network may suggest that you keep in touch with them as you continue your academic work. If you are comfortable with the suggestion, you may find that this person may become a mentor or even a sponsor. If you are unsure, discuss the situation in detail with your college advisor, your parents, or your spouse. Make sure that all contacts with your potential mentor/sponsor take place in a professional setting and involve issues related to your career and training. If you become uncomfortable with any aspect of the relationship, you are not obligated to continue. Simply thank the person and end the association.

You may be wondering how mentors and sponsors benefit from their relationship with you. Many professionals enjoy the experience of nurturing fresh talent. In addition, the more successful they are in developing a corps of gifted new workers within the organization or within the field, the more their reputation in the company and the field is enhanced. If they are successful in establishing you as a hot new addition to the company, they have just added another loyal member to their own Friends of You Club. Keep that in mind. Networking never ends.

JOB SHADOWING

A different type of informational interview is known as *job shadowing*. This process involves an extended interview in which you accompany the professional whom you are visiting as he carries out the duties of a typical day's work. While this setup is not as commonly utilized as a network meeting, it is becoming recognized as a valuable career education tool. The most visible sign of this trend is "Taking Our Daughters/Sons to Work Day," when working men and women arrange for their children to observe them at their work settings. This effort is intended to raise the consciousness of our young people about career possibilities and has led to the general acknowledgment that all young people need to know more about the career marketplace.

You can learn a great deal by actually "walking through" a day with someone—you get a front-row seat to their world of work. If it is possible for you to arrange this type of extended informational meeting, do so. It will be well worth your time.

While visiting any business organization, try to absorb as much as possible about the jobs employees perform. Observe the types of communication they are involved in, how they handle themselves in various situations, what is expected of them, how others respond to them, the tone and style of the organization, and the pace at which they conduct their duties. Paying attention to such details may tell you more about the job and the organization than the information you learned verbally.

You may discover as a result of networking or job shadowing that a career you thought you'd enjoy isn't right for you after all. It may not seem like it at the time, but that realization is a blessing. It is better to learn this now than to spend years preparing for a career that turns out to be a bad fit.

If you find after an interview that you are not as interested in a career, it may be the result of one of two things.

1. You may be learning the true nature of the work for the first time, and you may realize that it isn't right for you. If this is the case, regroup and take another look at the self-assessment and library research you did. See if there is anything in those two steps that led you down this cul-de-sac, and take steps to get back on track. You may have interpreted some of the results a bit rigidly, and now would be a good time to open yourself up to something else that interests you.

   Testing and probing are part of making a choice. Changing your mind (or your major) is something most college students do, sometimes more than once. It is a normal and necessary part of finding a career that's right for you.

2. You may have talked to the "wrong" people. I require my students to talk to at least three people (college instructors excluded). Connecting with as many people as possible provides you with the broad view that you will need to consider all the aspects of a career. If you meet people who have nothing positive to say about their jobs, keep looking. Just because the job is not a good fit for them doesn't mean you won't love it.

Exercise 5.4 is designed to help you recap what you have learned so far from your networking experience.

ELIZABETH'S STORY

Elizabeth was beginning her freshman year in college and was unsure of her major. She found in her self-assessment that she is interested in careers in which she can use her strong skills in math and science, and that she enjoys tasks that involve some problem solving. As a result, Elizabeth thought she might like to pursue a career in engineering.

Engineering is a vast field, and Elizabeth felt that she needed to focus more. After looking at the O*NET, *GOE,* and the *OOH* online, she decided that she needed more information about what different engineers do on their jobs. She decided to conduct information interviews with engineers specializing in a variety of areas of engineering.

Her existing network yielded two contacts who specialized in different types of engineering. One was a friend of her father's who was an architect, the other a former neighbor who was an environmental engineer. Both were available for networking meetings, and Elizabeth visited both at their places of employment.

The architect was a woman who worked at a firm that specialized in medical/health care facility design. This meeting showed Elizabeth how one person interacts with professionals from a variety of disciplines on a long-term project. The woman described the type of work and training she had been involved in that led to her current job. She also candidly described some of the obstacles she had had to overcome to achieve a position of responsibility.

In her second interview, Elizabeth met with the environmental engineer at a site that was being investigated for hazardous waste cleanup. Elizabeth was in no danger, but she did get to wear a hard hat and went with the engineer to meet the site manager. She enjoyed the atmosphere and found the work to be a great deal more complex than she had originally anticipated.

Elizabeth decided that it would be valuable to expand her network to an area related to manufacturing. She contacted a local automotive company and spoke with a supervisor in the design department. He referred her to an engineer in the department who was responsible for the redesign and improvement of a passenger-side airbag system. Elizabeth was surprised that a young woman who had graduated from college just three years before was responsible for redesigning this system.

Elizabeth's meeting included a short tour of the plant's production area, where she was introduced to other engineers in her network partner's department. Elizabeth was most impressed with the respect that her new contact enjoyed among her colleagues and with how much she loved her work. The woman shared with her that she had found her academic work extremely difficult, but she was glad she had stuck with it because she enjoyed her professional work much more. At the end of the meeting, the engineer suggested that they keep in touch as Elizabeth progressed through school.

Elizabeth learned a lot from these meetings. She was in the process of deciding about the field in which she might spend most of her working life, so the meetings were instrumental in helping her form her perspective. She was now more sure that engineering would offer her the challenges she was seeking. As she began the preliminary academic work to prepare for that career, she resolved to look further into the possibilities offered at her school in the mechanical and industrial engineering fields.

Pulling It All Together

List all the contacts you have made who have provided you with helpful information about the career you are exploring. Then note the information that you found to be most helpful. Also, note anything that you found of special interest during your meetings.

CONTACT/ORGANIZATION _____

Helpful information

_____

_____

Observations

_____

_____

CONTACT/ORGANIZATION _____

Helpful information

_____

_____

Observations

_____

_____

CONTACT/ORGANIZATION _____

Helpful information

_____

_____

Observations

_____

_____

Were you able to develop other contacts for future reference from referrals during your meetings? If so, list them here.

_____

_____

NAME/ORGANIZATION/PHONE NUMBERS

_____

_____

As a result of your meetings, have you begun to determine a possible career? If so, write it here.

_____

_____

If you are still undecided, have you narrowed your search to one or two possibilities? What are they?

_____

_____

Did you find from your meetings that the career you had an interest in is not a good fit for you?

_____

_____

If you answered yes to the previous question, are there related areas that interest you that you uncovered from networking, or will you need to look in another area?

_____

_____

Have any of your new contacts offered to act as a resource to you as you continue your career preparation?

_____

_____

Discuss the results of your networking experience with your group or the class.

If you have followed the suggestions for doing this part of your career exploration, you will have developed a much better understanding of the career in which you have an interest. You have probed the boundaries of your existing network to identify people you might already know who would be a willing resource for you. You have learned more about the career area that interests you and the type of work involved in that occupation. You have begun to expand your network into areas that are directly related to your future career, or you have found from your meetings that the area you thought you'd enjoy actually might not be the right fit. You may even have initiated a professional association that could benefit you and your new network partner for many years.

Networking is a component of career development that is here to stay. If you have tried the approaches described here, you have already benefited from this process. Be prepared in the future for a call from someone like yourself who will be asking you to take some time to provide information and encouragement. Make sure you respond generously, just as your new friends have responded to you.

A LOOK BACK

Other Sources and Suggested Reading

A Foot in the Door: Networking Your Way into the Hidden Job Market by Katharine Hansen

> While this book is better suited for those who are ready to seek employment, it provides useful insight into the networking process.

Information Interviewing: How To Tap Your Hidden Job Market by Martha Stoodley

> This is a good resource for anyone going through career transition. A guidebook for experienced careerists about ways to create career visibility, it offers insight to people just entering the job market into how networks can benefit all participants.

Power Schmoozing: The New Etiquette for Social and Business Success by Terri Mandell

> Knowing what to say after you get through the door is an incomparable tool. This book makes it easier to feel comfortable in situations you may be experiencing for the first time.

What Color Is Your Parachute? by Richard Nelson Bolles

> Since its initial publication in 1970, this manual for career decision making has become an all-around resource for anyone contemplating a career move. While the methods Bolles proposes are not for everyone, the philosophy of investigating careers in order to make an informed decision is presented in an interesting, "user-friendly" style.

Web Sites and Internet Resources

www.careermag.com

> This is a full-service career site with articles, job openings, and information on employers.

www.careers.yahoo.com

> This Yahoo directory is an outstanding source of career information. Click on 'Advice' then click on 'Networking Effectively' for articles and information from the *Wall Street Journal* on networking.

www.mentornet.net

> Although this site is focused on serving women in engineering and science, it is a good example of how networking on the internet can be accomplished. If you happen to meet the criteria for participation, you may wish to apply for a mentor to assist you in your career development.

DECISION MAKING AND GOAL SETTING

CHAPTER 6

I magine yourself at the oceanside looking through the viewfinder of your camera at a sailboat gliding atop the waves. Your first glimpse is cloudy and blurred, but as you start learning how to adjust the focus, you are able to see the boat more clearly. That process of focusing a camera is similar to what happens in this phase of your career adventure, decision making and goal setting.

Now you are focusing in on just what your career choices are and determining the best way to achieve your career goals. Up until now, you have spent time gathering and interpreting information, some of it about you, some of it about the outside world. You have completed the necessary steps to make some choices about your career direction.

"But," you say, "I've made dozens of decisions just to get to this point in my career search. Don't all those decisions count?" Of course they do. You have made many important choices. These decisions were part of your self-discovery and your exploration of the career market. They set your direction up to this point by excluding options that didn't meet your needs and by including possibilities that kept you on your present course. Making these preliminary decisions has given you direction, stability, and momentum.

You are now ready to leave this phase of exploration and move to a new level of decision making, a level beyond information gathering. Decision making will help you to organize your thoughts and feelings as they evolve about what you have learned in your experience and research and to develop meaningful career goals. The key word is *evolve*. This process is an evolution, a refining. You will now strive to establish goals that are achievable and that will set you on a definite path and still allow you to be your own person.

In reality, you never stop exploring. You have selected a direction but you want to keep all avenues open as you learn more about your path. As physicist Richard Feynman said in Clark McKowen's *Thinking About Thinking*, "I can live with doubt and uncertainty and not knowing. I think it's much more interesting to live not knowing than to have answers which might be wrong."

You may change your mind many times before you find the career that fits you. That is part of the excitement and wonder of choosing. No one knows for sure if their decisions will lead to sure-fire success or even a sense of satisfaction. We do know that you can always change your mind. You are not required to live with unsatisfying choices.

DECISION-MAKING STYLES

People approach career decisions in much the same way that they approach other decisions in their lives. Some people prefer to analyze data and think things through while others "go with their gut," relying on how they feel about the issues.

Some of you may know people who never contemplate any purchase, even something as simple as shampoo, without consulting a consumer buying guide. Referring to outside resources and analyzing all the data about choices is one way of doing research on decision outcomes. Other people chart and graph every scintilla of information until all they know about a subject is down on paper. Only then can they make a choice. Another option is to take a sheet of paper, draw a line down the middle, and write "pro" above one column and "con" above the other. These are all valid techniques for making decisions using the *cognitive approach*. People who are comfortable with this approach rely on reason and logic to determine their choices.

Other people prefer to make decisions based on feelings. Sure, they think about issues, but when all is said and done, "facts" may take on a secondary role. It may be that the facts are what produce the feelings. Others would claim that sensitivity to all the issues, implied and unspoken, actually enhances judgment since it factors in more than what's on paper. This approach, which is *intuitive*, is just as useful as the cognitive approach.

Which approach—the cognitive or the intuitive—works best for you? The only way to know which style is best for you is to take a look at your track record on decisions you have made in the past. Did your decisions yield the results that you had hoped? Were you satisfied with the outcomes? If your answer is yes, then you may have a style of decision making that works for you, whether it is cognitive or intuitive. Current research shows that people who use both intuitive abilities in combination with cognitive analysis make effective, wise career decisions. If you found that the results of your decisions have been disappointing, you may want to try some of the alternative techniques presented in this section.

You already have an idea about your decision-making style from taking the personality exercise in Chapter 3. As you may recall, the third letter in Jung's four-letter code represents how you prefer to make decisions. "T" people prefer logical, structured approaches and "F" people are the gut-level types. Both the cognitive and intuitive models are presented here. Try to determine if one fits you better than the other and how you might use both to make decisions.

DECISION-MAKING TECHNIQUES

So far in your career adventure, you have taken the following steps:

- *Self-Assessment*—You started by looking at yourself—your motivations, life stage, values, interests, personality, and skills. From this base you began your career exploration, looking first at broad categories of occupations that interested you.

- *Career Exploration*—You expanded your knowledge through research into jobs and careers that fell under the occupations to which you were initially drawn. You may have begun to do some actual decision making by discarding certain types of jobs and zeroing in on others that sounded right.

- *Networking*—You talked with people who were actually doing the work that interested you. This was your "reality check" to determine if your understanding of the job matched the real-world experience of others.

WHAT ARE YOUR PRIORITIES? WHAT ARE YOUR OPTIONS?

Now it's time to narrow your focus and set your goal. Think about what issues will carry the most weight in your decision to follow a particular career path. Setting priorities is critical to making your choice. Consider what is most important to you in a job in order to evaluate whether one career path is better for you than another. What do you believe about yourself and your career needs? By now you should have an idea of your priorities. You should also know from your research how the career options you are considering stack up. If the differences between your needs and the careers you are considering are dramatic, now is the time to find out. One way of evaluating alternatives is to set up a checklist that compares your career priorities with the career options you are considering. This point-by-point comparison helps you to see how a certain career choice might meet your needs.

TAKE A CLOSER LOOK 6.1

Career Option Checklist

This checklist gives you a chance to compare your career priorities with your career options. The categories on the left represent some possible career priorities, needs, and preferences you may have identified through self-assessment and career exploration. The blanks at the end of the list are for priorities you may have identified as important that aren't mentioned in this list. As you review these priorities, in the center column, rate the importance of each issue in terms of your career needs: Use a number 10 to indicate items of highest priority and descending numbers to indicate items of lesser importance. The number 1 would thus indicate an item that is unimportant to you.

After you have rated each priority, use the column on the right to jot down any relevant information you obtained through career exploration about the career option you are considering. For example, if you've identified a salary range of $30,000–$35,000 in your preferred geographical region, fill in that information. If you find you aren't sure how your career option stacks up against the priorities you have set, you may need to return to the resources or contacts you used in prior chapters for that information. If you are currently considering more than one career option, follow the same process, checking how your choices match your priorities and compare with each other.

CAREER OPTION _____

CAREER PRIORITIES	RATE (1–10)	RELEVANT INFORMATION
Salary range	_____	_____
Availability of jobs	_____	_____
Opportunity for advancement	_____	_____
Interesting work	_____	_____
Good benefits	_____	_____
Pleasant work atmosphere	_____	_____
Location of job	_____	_____
Job stability	_____	_____
Value to community	_____	_____
Variety of tasks/duties involved	_____	_____
Setting (indoor/outdoor, office, hospital, and so on)	_____	_____
Family friendly/flexibility	_____	_____
_____	_____	_____
_____	_____	_____

After completing this process for your career option, does the information you have assembled confirm your gut feelings about this career being a good choice for you?

_____

_____

If not, what else could you do to ensure that the option or options you are considering are appropriate?

_____

_____

Discuss the checklist exercise with your group or with the class.

WHAT ARE YOUR GOALS?

By this point, you have devoted a great deal of effort and time to your career exploration. You deserve to feel satisfied and excited about where you are going. Part of the excitement comes from knowing that you are already on your way simply because you have made a choice (or perhaps choices). You may face obstacles ahead, but your enthusiasm for your goals will sustain you through the rough spots. You are now ready to set forth your goals.

One way to maintain your enthusiasm is to make a commitment to a stated (long-term) goal and then develop a plan that will allow you to move toward that goal on a step-by-step basis (using short-term goals). Begin by establishing your *destination:* your long-term goal. Then look at the steps that lie between you and that end point.

Exercise 6.2 offers you a way to start moving toward your goal.

TAKE A CLOSER LOOK 6.2

Your Long-Term Goal

State your career goal in a clear, specific way. To get started, fill in the Goal Commitment Statement.

MY CAREER GOAL

I, _____ , will seek to enter the field of

_____ , with the intent of becoming

a(n) _____ . I will undertake and complete

the training necessary to become a respected participant in this field and do whatever is neces-

sary to maintain my commitment to my chosen discipline. I will review my progress toward my

goal every six months and be prepared for unforeseen contingencies.

Signed _____   Date _____

WHAT'S NEXT?

What will it take for you to achieve your stated goal? Find out what stands between you and reaching what you have set out for yourself, and determine what you may need to do to keep your momentum going. I refer to this as fact finding.

Exercise 6.3 helps you think about what you need to do to achieve your goal.

TAKE A CLOSER LOOK 6.3

Fact Finding

The process of achieving your goal is already under way. To be successful, you will need to anticipate what resources are necessary to meet the challenges ahead. Using the information that you have developed from your self-assessment and career exploration, make a short list of the resources you will need to make your goal a reality. You may not be able to anticipate every obstacle you might encounter, but you will be much better prepared to overcome them if you marshal your resources now.

FURTHER INFORMATION NEEDED (LIBRARY WORK, NETWORKING):

Do you need to talk to anyone or do more research about your career goal? Do you know where training is available?

_____

_____

FURTHER TRAINING NEEDED (COLLEGE, TECHNICAL, EXPERIENTIAL):

Do you need to contact specific institutions that specialize in the field you want to enter? Will you need to relocate?

_____

_____

ECONOMIC NEEDS (LIVING EXPENSES, TUITION, CARE OF DEPENDENTS):

Will you need financial support to enter the career field? Are you eligible for financial aid? Will you have to take a paid job while preparing to enter the field?

_____

_____

PERSONAL SUPPORT SYSTEM (FAMILY, FRIENDS):

Are your parents or family aware of your career goals? Do they understand the reasons for your career choices? Do your friends support your goals?

_____

_____

CONTACTS NEEDED (COLLEGE ADVISORS, FACULTY MEMBERS, PLACEMENT PERSONNEL):

Whom do you need to talk with to find out how to be accepted in a program? Who can help you with financial aid? What about living arrangements? Do you know anyone who might help you get started in the career field through entry-level work?

_____

_____

SKILLS NEEDED (TELEPHONE, VERBAL, WRITTEN):

What skills do you need to acquire to accomplish your goals? Do you need to grow beyond the comfortable behaviors that have worked up to now? Will you need to adapt your behavior to fit in better in your new career?

_____

_____

OTHER POSSIBLE RESOURCES (PLACES TO FIND EMPLOYMENT):

Are there organizations in which you can find employment or volunteer work in areas related to your career field?

_____

_____

Some of the resources you have listed may already be a part of your life. If not, obtaining the support you need to accomplish your goal will become part of your overall strategy, especially if you are considering a change that will take you into a different social and economic circle.

To complete your plan, make note of all the things you can think of that will move you toward accomplishing your goal. The list might include such things as arranging finances, changing housing location, talking with family and friends about your goal, or scheduling interviews with college administrators. The list may even include changes you would like to make in your own habits and behaviors that will make it easier to reach your goal. Come up with as many as you can think of and be as specific as possible. List them in the space below.

STEPS TO THE GOAL

1. _____

2. _____

3. _____

4. _____

5. _____

6. _____

THE ONE-YEAR PLAN OF ACTION

You have set your long-term goal and identified the resources necessary to reach it. You are aware of the steps you must take to realize your goal. The final component in this process is developing your plan of action to accomplish your goals. This plan of action consists of accomplishing a series of short-term goals that will take you closer to accomplishing your long-term goal.

Determining short-term goals is a critical step toward your eventual goal of a rewarding career. We all know people who announce boldly that they've decided what to do with their lives. We might run into them six months later and find that they are no closer to their goal. They may still believe that they can reach their goal. They just don't know how to break the process down into manageable steps and accomplish them one by one. Deciding is only the first step. Making many small steps toward the goal is what actually gets you there. These short-term goals are the key to success. Map out those steps into a one-year plan of action—a road map to follow toward your goal. Your short-term goals then become the benchmarks by which you will measure your progress, build your momentum, and keep your focus. Include points during the year's plan when you step back, assess your progress, and fine-tune your direction.

TAKE A CLOSER LOOK

Setting Short-Term Goals

Read the following statements. Complete the sentences with the information in the previous exercise. Some examples of statements you might use are offered. For instance:

"These are the things I can do within the next week to take me closer to my goal": Discuss my plans with my family and identify any changes we might have to make to help me reach my goal. Make an appointment to meet with a financial aid advisor to discuss grants and aid.

_____

_____

"These are the things I can do within the next month to take me closer to my goal": Register for classes in my major. Arrange for child care during class schedule.

_____

_____

"These are the things I can do within the next six months to take me closer to my goal": Meet with career counselor to discuss opportunities for part-time employment in field. Explore co-ops and internships.

_____

_____

"These are the things I can do within the next year that will take me closer to my goal": Join study group or campus club related to major. If none exists, start one.

_____

_____

Discuss the results of the goal-setting exercise with your group or with the class.

CONSOLIDATING YOUR RESOURCES

Exercise 6.4 required you to think in a concrete way about the resources you will need to accomplish your goal. The list included a variety of items, both economic and personal. The people who will be involved in your journey are probably supportive and encouraging and will make an effort to help you on your way. In some cases, however, you may find that you are not getting the help you need—people don't understand or aren't concerned whether you succeed or not. In such cases, stay focused on yourself and your goal. Concentrate on using your skills to work effectively within the system and continue to reach out in a personal way to those people who can and will help you. Surviving and even flourishing in pursuit of your goal will require you to use all your energy and resources.

You may stumble upon some unanticipated obstacles in your path—people who are important to you may actively discourage you and express doubt about your choices. If your parents or spouse are uncomfortable with the career goal you have chosen, they may unwittingly make it much more difficult for you. If you announce that you are switching your major from pre-med to archaeology and that next semester you will be going on a dig in Zambia, don't be surprised if your plan is met with less than enthusiastic support from your tuition-paying parents. They may be wondering just what is going on up at that college and if you are in touch with reality. In fact, your decision may be quite reasonable, and you can present the data you have gathered through self-assessment and career exploration. Your parents usually just need to know on what you are basing your decision.

If you find that even with convincing arguments, your family is still skeptical, try to remain positive. You can make it happen. Sometimes in life we have to go out on the skinny limb. We can't live in ways that meet every-one else's needs and expectations. If this happens to you, make sure you have your own "cheering section" to keep you focused on your goals. You can usu-ally find recruits for this role among your professors and fellow students. Most important, be your own cheerleader—pat yourself on the back when things go well and give yourself a break when they seem to fall apart.

Career decision making is the heart of your career adventure. It requires courage, strength, and resolve. Now is the time to start developing the psy-chological "muscle" that will get you through the rough spots in life. Enjoy your chance to choose. You are exactly where you want to be.

DEALING WITH UNCERTAINTY: AFFIRMATIONS

In the book *Bang the Drum Slowly* by Mark Harris, the baseball players play a card game called Tegwar to amuse themselves when on the road. Usually two players set up the game in the lobby of the hotel and start playing. As the game continues, passersby stop to watch and ask questions about the game. Just when the observers think they understand the rules, the ball play-ers introduce a new rule that turns the game around. Sometimes the onlookers join the game, pretending to follow every hand only to end up more confused than before. The rules of the game keep changing. That's because they are playing "Tegwar: The Exciting Game Without Any Rules."

Sometimes when you are experiencing the ups and downs that go with any career you may feel like you are actually playing Tegwar and, in a sense, you are. You will have to make decisions without enough information or based on assumptions that you can't confirm. Checklists and goal setting help, but they can't eliminate all uncertainty and risk. Anxiety comes with uncer-tainty. If you are struggling with choosing, try to remain as flexible as possible. That is your best insurance against the unpredictability of the future.

Keep in mind that you are well prepared and maintain a positive out-look. One way to maintain that positive outlook is through *affirmations*. Affirmations are statements you can use to give yourself a boost when you experience doubt and uncertainty. When you feel discouraged, try repeating some of these statements as a way to steady yourself during the rough spots.

"I make good decisions and I am happy with the results."
"If I don't like the outcome, I am smart enough to know how to change things."
"I always achieve my goals."
"I'm gifted and energetic and I believe in myself."
"I'm lucky to be here and the people I meet feel lucky to know me."

Say these affirmations over and over as many times a day as you need. You will be surprised at how the use of affirmative statements refocuses your energy in a positive way.

Exercise 6.5 will help you develop your own affirmations.

Positive Self-Talk

Everyone has had negative experiences that cause self-doubt. But our faith in our ability to accomplish our goals can be reinforced through affirmations. Repeating affirming statements is simply an acknowledgment of what you may already believe but may have come to doubt because of a bad experience.

Think about a situation that might make you feel uncomfortable, hesitant, or even fearful. Maybe it's entering a classroom full of new faces or completing a final test. Whatever it might be, imagine yourself experiencing that same difficult situation in a way that you never have before—as your ideal self—confident, self-assured, at ease.

How do you look in this fantasy? Describe yourself as you might look and feel.

_____

_____

Pick a few words that describe how you are in your fantasy. Then develop an affirmation using those words to describe yourself in a positive, encouraging way.

_____

_____

Use the following space to come up with more affirmations to encourage and support yourself.

_____

_____

Repeat the affirmations, eyes closed, putting your trust in the words you have chosen. How do you feel now?

_____

_____

Discuss your responses to your affirmations with your group or with the class.

One final word. Students sometimes ask me if the day will come when they won't have doubts about themselves and the choices they make. They are disappointed when they find that even the most competent and respected professionals have moments when they question themselves and wonder if they can pull it off. If you are truly growing and challenging yourself, there may be times when self-doubt will cause you to hesitate. Your challenge is to keep trying, keep getting better. You might have fears but they needn't paralyze you. Facing your fears and doing your best is part of meeting the challenge to grow. You are working to achieve *long-term* goals. It's worth the risk.

CHARLIE'S STORY

Charlie was confused about what he wanted. He was trying to make a career decision, but his parents were pressuring him to major in engineering, a field they believed would offer him a steady job after graduation. Charlie was interested in engineering and found that some aspects of the field matched his needs. But he wasn't sure if it was really what *he* wanted. Math was a struggle for Charlie, and he felt that his parents' support could not compensate for his lack of ability. For his part, Charlie loved to travel and thought that working in a hotel would be interesting and exciting.

Charlie gamely went through the networking process, talking with several engineers, and he had favorable responses from the people he contacted. One of the engineers he interviewed suggested that Charlie call him when he graduated to see if there was anything he could do for Charlie. Despite those encouraging results, Charlie was still worried. The only way to complete the decision-making process would be for him to find out if he could in fact perform academically in math courses. This might help him decide whether he would like engineering as a career.

The first math course Charlie took, college algebra, confirmed his worst fears. He ended the term with a C–, even though he had labored valiantly over the material. He had less time to devote to his other classes, and he ended the quarter with more doubts than before.

Charlie knew he could probably still pursue engineering if he wanted to and with extra effort could graduate in that field. He realized that he had to look at all the options available to him in some kind of systematic way if he was ever going to come to a decision. After identifying his priorities, Charlie found that salary and security weren't as important to him as doing interesting work in a friendly atmosphere. He liked to work with data, but he was more interested in interacting with people.

Charlie laid out the two options he was considering on a checklist. The engineering career would offer a number of settings in which he could work as well as various fields. The other option that interested Charlie was to work in the hotel and hospitality industry. After doing some research, Charlie learned that a job in hotel management and other related positions in similar settings offered salaries that were lower than those of engineers.

In comparing the options, Charlie found that despite some of the advantages of a career in engineering, he clearly preferred a business career that would get him into hotel management. In hotel management, he would find the interaction with people, the opportunity to work in a cosmopolitan setting, and a diversity of tasks—all priorities he had worked to discover in his career decision-making process.

Charlie recognized that gaining his parents' support was important to achieving his career goal. His plan of action was to compile information to assist his parents in seeing a balanced view of his choice. At Christmas, Charlie went home and discussed his situation with his parents. His father noted that Charlie needed a "solid" career. Charlie was convinced that he could have a fulfilling, solid career in business, with a specialty in hotel management. He also told his parents that he felt confident in pursuing his own goals and that he would be willing to accept the consequences of his decision. He was sure he could be successful in the field he preferred.

Given Charlie's feelings about the decision he was facing and the thoughtful answers he had for their questions, his parents acknowledged that it was indeed Charlie's decision. While they were still somewhat skeptical about his choice, they encouraged him to keep an open mind and offered their full support.

For his part, Charlie knew that to ensure his success he would have to inform his parents about his progress and future plans. Charlie valued their support and was prepared to do whatever was necessary to maintain it. But he also felt strongly that if his parents chose not to stand behind him, he would still remain on his chosen path—the right path for Charlie—and would be able to move toward his goal on his own if necessary.

6.6 TAKE A CLOSER LOOK

Pulling It All Together

Read the following statements and answer them as honestly and realistically as you can.

The most important issues for me in any job/career are:

_____

_____

The options on my career option checklist were:

_____

_____

The most favorable options on my checklist were:

_____

_____

My career goal is:

_____

_____

My realistic and achievable plan of action and short-term goals are:

_____

_____

Discuss any reactions you have to this chapter with your group or the class.

This chapter has given you the tools you need to have a better, more focused view of where you are going. By now, you are able to set priorities and criteria for evaluating choices and can complete a career option checklist that helps you compare your options.

You have also been able to set long- and short-term goals. You have stated your goals with conviction and have developed a coherent plan of action that you can begin using right now to start on your new path. You have anticipated what lies ahead and you are affirming your belief in your ability to achieve your goals.

A LOOK BACK

Does this mean you are finished with your career decision making? While you may have made a choice that will lay the foundation for your career for some time to come, you will probably come back to some of these tools in the future. As you grow you will continue to be presented with choices regarding your career.

Have faith in your ability to make the right decision. Stay flexible and keep a positive focus. These attitudes will be crucial in helping you reach your goals.

Other Sources and Suggested Reading

The Confident Decision Maker: How to Make the Right Business and Personal Decisions Every Time by Roger Dawson

This author begins by identifying the qualities that make people good decision makers. From there the process is broken down and presented in a way that motivates the reader to try the techniques immediately. The book is an excellent guide for all types of decision making. Note the chapter on Intuitive Decision Making. This is also available on audiocassette.

Following Your Path by Alexandra Collins Dickerman

This is a workbook that takes you on a journey of self-discovery to your intuitive side. The use of myths, symbols, and images highlights a fascinating examination of the power of your own intuition.

How to Make Instant Decisions and Remain Happy & Sane by Zelma Barinov

A book that limits the jargon and offers fresh techniques for coming to closure more quickly; easy to read with good use of the author's personal insight.

Smart Choices: A Practical Guide to Making Better Decisions by John S. Hammond, Ralph L. Keeney, and Howard Raiffa

This is an excellent resource for a systematic, step-by-step decision-making model.

Web Sites and Internet Resources

www.byu.edu/ccc/Career_Planning/assistance/decision.htm

A great decision-making site from Brigham Young University. The "Suggestions for Building Decision-Making Confidence" is worth the trip.

www.coloradocollege.edu/CareerCenter/Services/DecisionModel.html

This site is a brief, seven-step model on career decision making.

www.ub-careers.buffalo.edu

The SUNY-Buffalo offers this site on career decision making with links to a range of other internet resources. Click on the arrow at "Menu of Frequently Requested Topics"; click on "Career Decisions" and "Go."

PART THREE

THE JOB CAMPAIGN

ORGANIZING YOUR SEARCH

You are now prepared to take the next step in your career adventure: organizing your job campaign. This phase of your career development will provide the tools for actually entering the job market—your resume, cover letter, interview preparation, and job marketing skills.

Any formula for success includes being ready for opportunities when they arise. You have prepared for your decision by doing research on yourself and on careers. You will continue to move toward your chosen career by gaining the technical and academic training you need to be a competent professional. It is time to focus on

gaining the skills that will allow you to showcase your abilities when you are job hunting. This is an opportunity that might not happen for several years or it could happen next week. You will be ready for the challenge of competing in an increasingly crowded and complex job market.

Your next task is to organize your research about yourself and careers into a portfolio that markets you successfully. You are entitled to succeed. The way you use your information and training will make the difference in whether you stand out as a shining star or get lost in the crowd.

DESIGNING YOUR RESUME AND COVER LETTERS

W hat is the vision you created of the professional you would like to become? Entering the career market is your route to realize that vision. You can accomplish that only if you can effectively communicate to others what you see in yourself. The resume is the primary vehicle for introducing yourself to employers who can assist you in reaching your goal.

CONVEYING WHO YOU ARE

A resume is a business document created to help employers and candidates talk about possible employment. It is expected to reflect systematic organization characteristic of most business documents. The trick is, however, to conform to those expectations and still present yourself as an individual. Your resume should highlight the unique blend of skills and experiences that makes you the ideal candidate for a position, while still respecting the conventions and expectations of the work world. You control what information is included in your resume. A well-crafted resume emphasizes only those aspects of your background that make you a serious competitor for a job.

Make no mistake. This is a competition, and there will be situations in which you compete against other well-qualified candidates. Designing a resume that presents your abilities best will give you the necessary edge to be successful.

Various styles of resumes serve the needs of job seekers in different ways. Your challenge is to find a resume style with which you feel comfortable. Ideally, it will allow you to describe your background in ways that suit the various opportunities available to you and also to convey your abilities competitively and honestly. Once you decide which resume style works best for you, then you develop the content based on your background, taking into account the needs of the specific employer.

THERE'S NO SUCH THING AS A "SURE-FIRE" RESUME

In any library or bookstore you will find a great number of resume manuals that advertise a set way to write resumes that "win" jobs—if you simply follow the formulas in the book. There are as many ways of writing resumes as there are resume writers and, so far, the "sure-fire," guaranteed-to-get-you-a-job resume has yet to be developed.

Only one resume will work best for you—the one you develop using information about your special combination of skills, abilities, training, education, experiences, and qualifications. Be conscious of the standard formats when developing your resume, but know that any one style prescribed by a book can never take into account all of your needs for a particular situation.

The reason that resume writing defies simplistic formulas is that resume *reading* is highly subjective. If you show your resume to 10 different people, some may think it is perfect, some will suggest minor changes, and others may suggest substantial revisions. Depending on the circumstances, any or all of them may be correct. People in charge of hiring are just like your well-meaning advisors. They apply their personal preferences and idiosyncrasies when evaluating resumes. Trying to predict how a particular employer will respond is nearly impossible.

The only logical way to create your resume is to be able to identify and describe those aspects of your background that relate to the potential position and then select a style of resume that showcases you and your abilities to your best advantage. Next we will look at different styles of resumes and what each style offers job seekers.

RESUME STYLES

Almost all resume formats and variations can be categorized under one of three resume styles: chronological, functional, or achievement/accomplishment.

Chronological Resume

The resume style with which most people are familiar is the *chronological resume*. This resume focuses primarily on work experience and presents your background in *reverse* chronological order. This means that you list your most recent position first and your earliest job last.

Most employers prefer this resume style since the focus is on your work history, the factor they consider most relevant. The chronological style is excellent if you are seeking employment in a field in which you have an established and successful track record. The emphasis on work experience presents your background in a way that helps the employer visualize you in that position. The format shows a natural progression, from the bottom of the page to the top, of increasing responsibility and growth, culminating with your stated objective at the top, which should relate to the job for which you are applying. It is an ideal style for you if you have had a long career in one discipline and want to continue to work in that field. The chronological resume in Figure 7.1 illustrates how this style enhances the candidate's appropriateness for the job.

THE CHRONOLOGICAL RESUME.

Julie Reese

315 Cedar Street
Parnell, Iowa 52325

(319) 658-9341
jreese@netlink.net

Profile: Accounting professional with broad range of experiences; strong background in computer accounting applications

Professional Experience:

Basic Printing, Inc., Parnell, Iowa
Accounting Assistant, 1999 to present

Responsible for assisting controller in performance of accounting functions, including posting journal entries, general ledger, forecasting, and accounts payable/accounts receivable; some tax experience.
* Specialized Skills: Microsoft Excel/Word, Windows

Hawkins' Lithography, Parnell, Iowa
Accounting Clerk, 1994 to 1999
Responsible for posting to general ledger and journal entries.

Education:

University of Iowa, Iowa City, Iowa
Graduated 2001, Bachelor of Science
Major: Accounting
GPA: 3.6

Special Achievements: 1999 Recipient, Parnell Jaycee's "Outstanding Young Woman" Scholarship; Dean's List

Extracurricular Activities:

Member, Accounting Club, 1996–2001
University of Iowa Alumni Association

FIGURE 7.1

Emphasizing your work experience may work well if you have a strong background in the field in which you are applying, but this technique is less effective if you don't have much prior experience. For this reason, the principal drawback of chronological resumes is the focus on work experience. If your employment has been primarily in the food service industry, for example, there may be little that you can state to help an employer see you as a serious professional in another area. You may have an excellent academic record, plenty of organizing experience from volunteer projects, and maybe even co-op experience. If you use a chronological resume that highlights your work at the fast-food franchise, you may project an image of yourself standing behind a counter, while the more relevant data is buried at the bottom of your resume.

Work experience unrelated to the job you currently seek is not totally irrelevant. Steady employment of any type speaks well of you as an applicant and, more important, identifies skills (e.g., customer service, managerial responsibility, performing under pressure) that could benefit future employers. You must learn to identify and describe those skills using the appropriate format. It is critical that your first presentation to a potential employer establish an image that matches the employer's needs and assumptions about the job the employer wishes to fill. The goal of your resume is to make the connection between yourself and the employer's vision of the skills needed to fill the job, as different as they might be from what you have done in the past. A chronological resume style might not always be the best style through which to accomplish this task.

Functional Resume

The *functional resume* highlights the skills and abilities of the job seeker rather than the settings in which the person obtained those skills. This makes it an ideal resume for the midlife career changer or someone with limited work experience in the field. Figure 7.2 shows a sample functional resume.

The functional resume may seem to be the perfect resume format since it focuses on the skills relevant to the position you seek. While it is typically an excellent format for anyone trying to enter a career in which they have little experience, it is not the best style for the job seeker who has a strong work background. The functional style simply doesn't offer the proper forum to show the depth of skill and career maturity that comes from extended or relevant work experience. In addition, a list of your skills isn't a helpful sales tool if you have nothing in your background to establish how you obtained those skills. Related academic study is helpful, but most employers are skeptical that it can completely take the place of hands-on experience for developing a high level of proficiency in any field.

Achievement/Accomplishment Resume

The *achievement* or *accomplishment resume* uses many of the same elements of the previous styles with one important difference. It uses actual events from prior experiences and training as the method for conveying informa-

David Muñoz

654 WALNUT DRIVE   (303) 365-5729
AURORA, COLORADO 80012   dmunoz@earthlink.net

Summary   Seasoned self-starter able to create opportunities and make the
                         sale seeks a position in sales and marketing

Skills and Abilities   ■ Recognized abilities in all areas of market forecasting
                         ■ Knowledgeable in marketing aspects of product development
                         ■ Practiced in developing sales leads and creating interest
                         ■ Well-developed organizational skills
                         ■ Able to make the sale; strong closer

Education   University of Colorado, Boulder, Colorado
                         Graduated 2001, Bachelor of Science
                         Major: Business Administration/Marketing
                         GPA: 3.4

Awards and   Dean's List, 1999, 2000
Achievements   Member, National Honor Society

Work Experience   Steve's Place, Aurora, Colorado
                         Salesperson for clothing retailer, 2000 to present

                         Hale's Quick Stop Photos, Boulder, Colorado
                         Customer service and sales for photo development outlet,
                         1998 to 2000

Extracurricular   Volunteer, United Way, Special Funds Committee
Activities   Member, National Marketing Association, Aurora Chapter

FIGURE 7.2

tion about you. This type of resume provides the employer with the basics of your training and work life and also substantiates your skill through outlining your past accomplishments. Figure 7.3 illustrates one style of the accomplishment resume.

As noted in Figure 7.3, the achievements associated with the work Ray is performing support the image that he is attempting to convey—that of a motivated self-starter capable of making the sale.

Every employer is interested in two aspects of your background:

1. *What can you do?*   This is the skill question. Effectively answering this lets the employer know what you are capable of contributing from the very start.

2. *What have you done?*   This is the "prove it" question. You may have the skill, but that in itself may not be enough. Citing your achievements enhances your credibility. It is the most powerful and understated way of backing up what you claim to be able to do.

The functional and chronological formats are good vehicles for describing your skills and history but do little to establish the dynamic image conveyed by the achievement resume. The latter type of resume is especially beneficial to people with extensive experiential background who are facing particular career obstacles, such as job displacement through downsizing. Start building an achievement resume even if you don't expect to be laid off. Everyone, even individuals with standard sales or counter work experience, has accomplishments that can be quantified. In a later exercise we will generate ideas for listing accomplishments and achievements.

WHICH STYLE IS RIGHT FOR YOU?

The style of resume you choose is largely determined by the type of position for which you are applying. If the position is in a field in which you have a significant amount of experience, you may wish to use the chronological style. It will meet the employer's expectations and highlight your strengths in the field.

If you are trying to enter a new career field or looking for your first job out of college, you may want to consider the functional style. This style shines a bright light where it belongs, on your ability to do the job, not on the places where you developed your ability.

If you can identify events in your life that you feel are noteworthy and will make you an appealing candidate for a position, then the achievement resume is probably the resume style for you.

As we proceed through the various phases of developing a resume, you will see how you can integrate elements of each format based on specific situations to give your resume a customized look. You can custom design your resume simply by shuffling the various components of the resume to suit the specific needs of the job you seek. Keep an updated copy of your resume on a word processing diskette to make revising your resume fast and easy.

When deciding which style of resume to use, ask yourself, "What are my strongest qualifications for the job?" Your answer, whether it relates to aca-

THE ACHIEVEMENT/ACCOMPLISHMENT RESUME.

RAY GRANT

733 Elm Street   (919) 822-1562
Kinston, North Carolina 28502   raygrant43@aol.com

SUMMARY OF QUALIFICATIONS

Skilled sales/customer service professional able to anticipate and respond to customer needs; technical sales orientation

EXPERIENCE

The Hershey Chocolate Company, Hershey, Pennsylvania
Sales Representative, July 2000 to present

Responsible for service and expansion of major wholesale accounts in the Kinston area; coordinate corporate promotions and advertising campaign through wholesalers; negotiate ad rates and charges; monitor use of displays, product samples, pricing, distribution, and warehouse inventory.

ACCOMPLISHMENTS

- Increased sales volume with two major grocery wholesalers by over 30 percent

- Received Outstanding Quarterly Sales Representative Award three times in one year

- Developed team approach to marketing product with local store managers

EDUCATION

East Carolina University, Greensboro, North Carolina
Graduated 2000, Bachelor of Arts
Major: Liberal Arts/Communications
GPA: 3.0

SPECIAL ACTIVITIES

Volunteer, Small Business Development
Center, Kinston Office
Assisted small business owners in various development activities, including creating employee handbooks and developing and presenting training.

FIGURE 7.3

demic skill, technical training, or work experience, will help you determine which style will present you in the best light.

Once you have decided on a resume style, begin to focus on developing the content for your resume.

DEVELOPING CONTENT FOR YOUR RESUME

What information should you include in (or exclude from) your resume? Remember, you want to create a picture with words, which lets the employer imagine you in the job for which you're applying. Think about the following two questions:

- What skills are needed to do the job for which I am applying?
- What experiences and training have I had that match those skills?

One other aspect to consider when writing your resume is that human resource professionals at large companies may scan resumes and store them in computer files in an effort to control paper flow. When resumes are later retrieved, they are often called up according to certain key words; for example, if a company conducts a search based on the criteria of "B. S., engineering, mechanical, automotive," they first will be referred to the resumes of people who meet all criteria, next, to those that meet most but not all, and so on.

Key words that describe the parameters of the job to be filled may determine whose resume is read and whose remains in database limbo. Thus, depending upon the type of job you seek and the companies to which you apply, you may need to prepare yourself for a job search on two levels—one for people and one for electronic resources. Until now, the goal has always been to get someone to read your resume in order to get a shot at an interview. Now, with some firms your resume won't even be read unless it is developed with a clear understanding of the position you want. That requires some thoughtful work on the content of your resume.

If you are just beginning a new career, you probably will not have had any positions that relate directly to the job you're seeking. That's nothing to be discouraged about. All jobs can be broken down into specific tasks, regardless of their setting. Focus on the tasks that most closely parallel the tasks and skills necessary for the job you seek. For example, perhaps you have an extensive background in retailing and customer service but would like to work in human services. By focusing on certain aspects of customer service you can establish your qualifications in that field. Skills such as sensitivity to customer concerns, listening skills, and the ability to work under pressure contribute to your portfolio as a human services professional. Combine these skills with your academic background and you can begin to see that you have a strong foundation for a winning resume.

The same process is equally effective for other disciplines. If your work experience has been in one area and you want to get started in another profession, focus on the skills that relate to your new job, regardless of their importance in your current role. It's what you are going to do with them that counts, not where you got them. If you already have paid experience in a field, you are halfway there. Use Exercise 7.1 as a way to find the parallels that will help you achieve your goal.

Finding Parallel Skills

In this exercise, you distill your prior experiences and skills into a summary that matches the job you are seeking. By now you have done the homework necessary to know which skills are important in the job to which you aspire. See if you can match your experiences (including jobs, internships, volunteer work, workshops, courses and laboratories, etc.) and the skills acquired through them to the skills needed in your future career.

SKILLS REQUIRED IN THE JOB YOU WANT	RELATED SKILLS YOU'VE DEVELOPED IN PRIOR JOBS AND OTHER EXPERIENCES

Keep in mind that even the most routine and basic jobs offer the opportunity to use and master skills that can become the building blocks for other positions. Try to find the parallel skills that intersect with job titles and categories. These skills will help you determine what to include in your resume. As you develop the components of your resume, reinforce your qualifications by including experiences and examples that reflect your skills as they relate to the position you want.

Discuss the results of this exercise with your group or the class.

COMPONENTS OF A RESUME

The six basic components of a resume are the *identifiers*, the *summary* or *profile*, *skills*, *employment history* or *work experience*, *education* or *training*, and *related information*. We examine next each of these separate areas.

Component 1: The Identifiers

The identifiers on your resume are those parts that tell the employer your name and how you can be reached. While these are the most straightforward parts of the resume, it is quite common for people to forget to include their phone numbers or overlook a typographical error in their names. Be sure to proofread your resume to ensure there are no errors. Neglecting even a small item in resume writing tells the employer a lot about your attention to detail and your ability to present yourself professionally.

A good rule to remember when seeking employment is that written responses are most often rejections but phone calls are usually invitations to an interview. That's why your correct phone number is critical. When you include the phone numbers where you can be reached, be sure that anyone answering the telephone at those places knows who you are and that a potential employer might be calling. Even the most open-minded employer will be irritated by rude responses and loud background music. If you have an answering machine, be sure your outgoing message is clear and free of any "cute" devices, such as background music or funny sounds.

If appropriate, also include your e-mail address and fax number.

Component 2: The Summary/Profile

The summary or profile component of a resume is a statement about you, your background and strengths as they relate to the position you seek. It usually goes at the beginning of the resume, immediately following the identifiers. This component evolved from the old "objective," a part of the resume that stated the job seeker's goal. The use of a summary or profile statement accomplishes the same thing by focusing attention on your ability to do the job.

This component can be a valuable part of your resume, but you must use it carefully. If your summary statement is vague or too general, you will not be providing useful information. I have personally seen hundreds of resumes that began with an all-purpose statement: "A strong performer able to use my skills and abilities in any setting." People who begin their resume with this type of statement would do better to exclude it altogether or to change it to a specific statement.

A well-crafted summary or profile statement ideally should do three things:

1. Communicate that you are a thoughtful, mature individual with a clear idea of who you are and what you are able to do.
2. Briefly summarize your primary skills as they parallel the position, draw the employer's interest in you as a potential employee, and encourage her to continue reading the rest of the resume.
3. Assert your goals and commitment to growth.

Developing a summary or profile that accomplishes all of these things is not an easy task. Ideally, your profile, and your entire resume, should be tailored for the specific job for which you are applying. That isn't always possible, however, especially if you are providing a resume to be distributed by a third party, such as the college services office. In most cases, however, to be a competitive candidate for a position, your resume must correlate closely to the specific needs of the position, beginning with the summary. Once you have the summary or profile, the rest of your resume will fall into place.

Some profiles can be disarmingly simple. One of my students who was a union carpenter felt strongly that a two-word phrase, "Skilled carpenter," would accurately reflect who she was. The type of profession you are entering will often determine how you frame your statement.

Occasionally, students feel that a summary statement is limiting. They prefer to leave out specifics, hoping to increase their marketability in a broad range of positions. If you feel this way, you can try putting together a resume without a summary or profile, making sure that you don't fall into the trap of trying to be all things to all people. Stay focused and you may find that the resume can be just as effective.

Exercise 7.2 gives you ideas about developing a strong career summary statement.

TAKE A CLOSER LOOK 7.2

A Practice Summary Statement

Your work on your summary or profile statement will continue throughout your career as you grow, develop your skills, and seek new goals. To get started, try the fill-in-the-blanks format below.

"A(n) _____(a)_____ background in _____(b)_____ with ability in _____(c)_____ and _____(d)_____ ."

Doesn't look like much at this point. That's okay. It's your job to provide the specifics depending on your career goal, interests, and specialized experiences that fit the situation. Here's an example of a summary that might work using this format.

"A broad background in human resources development with ability to develop and implement programs."

Or:

"Specialized experience in elementary/preschool education with emphasis on special needs populations."

Each blank has a purpose. Blank (a) gives you the chance to present a positive description of your experience. Blank (b) offers the category of experience that your background falls under: accounting, education, business, engineering, management, health care, and so on. Blanks (c) and (d) allow you to focus your skills on specifics that spotlight your greatest strengths.

Now develop your own summary or profile using the parts of the format that you think work best for you. Review the following list of words to help you fill in the blanks.

BLANK (A)

strong	broad	proven	extensive
effective	advanced	outstanding	demonstrated

BLANK (B)

administration	accounting	sales	education
human services	research	management	programming
marketing	customer service	graphics	engineering
business	library services	food service	retailing

BLANKS (C) AND (D)

(These terms should be related directly to the job or field in which you are applying.)

implementing programs	initiating programs	developing programs	administering programs
organizing	problem solving	troubleshooting	team building
taxes/cost accounting	design/layout	coding/debugging	developing leads/closing
programming/systems analysis	counseling/referral	acute/critical care	Java/Web design

If the suggested model seems like too much, don't worry. Just take what you need to get started. For example:

"Recognized performer, able to provide full range of accounting support services."
"Chronic and long-term care specialist, familiar with needs of geriatric clients."
"Public relations expertise with specialized skills in copywriting and marketing development."

Any of these models or your own statement are fine as long as they set the right tone for the employer by briefly expressing your unique combinations of strengths and interests.

Discuss the results of this exercise with your group or the class.

Component 3: Skills

Sometimes students with little paid experience in their field find that resume writing is just one long, discouraging exercise. They've spent years preparing for their first job, but when they begin to summarize everything they've learned using conventional resume formats their background looks insignificant, hardly representative of their hard work and preparation. If this is true for you, then you will have better results emphasizing your skills over your paid experience. A combination format that focuses on skills will allow you to flesh out your resume using experiences from a variety of sources: part-time jobs, co-op and intern experiences, volunteer work, lab work, classroom learning.

The growing reliance of human resource professionals on electronic support increases the significance of the skills section of your resume. When a person doing hiring determines the parameters for a job and then searches the database of resumes for key words, the computer will scan those resumes and extract those that meet the parameters, with those meeting the greatest number of parameters pulled first, those meeting fewer parameters pulled second, and so on. You can see how a thorough survey of your skills in a resume becomes critical.

The skills component of your resume is simply a series of statements that expand on the profile statement by describing in detail the abilities and qualifications that are suited to the position you seek. This section builds credibility for the statement with which you began the resume. Here are a few examples.

"Knowledgeable in all aspects of tax compliance accounting"

"Strong written and verbal communication skills"

"Skilled in Web design and the use of JavaScript"

"Experienced in use of scientific methods and observation"

"Able to read blueprints"

"Capable in full range of administrative and clerical skills"

As you develop a broader, deeper knowledge of your chosen field, you can expand this part of your resume to reflect your increasing level of skill, citing specific "buzz" words that not only identify you as a pro but also better flag your resume for electronic search. These skills deserve to be highlighted in a special section. You have worked to acquire them. Showcase them in a way that markets you effectively. Exercise 7.3 will help you develop skills statements.

TAKE A CLOSER LOOK 7.3

Highlighting Your Skills

When developing your skill statements, keep in mind the exercises in Chapter 3 devoted to skills and abilities. Remember to focus on those parts of your skill portfolio that are relevant to the position you seek. Use the phrases below to start developing a few statements that communicate concisely your greatest strengths.

"Knowledgeable in all areas devoted to _____."

"Strong background in _____."

"Able to _____."

"Exceptional _____ skills."

"Experienced in _____."

"Knowledgeable in use of the following (software, machines, and so on) _____."

Continue to develop statements that highlight your relevant skills. Focus on skills that are as specific as possible to the job for which you are applying. The more detail you can include, the better—you can include as many as five or six statements in this special section, more if you have strong credentials in a particular area.

Discuss the results of this exercise with your group or with the class.

Component 4: Work Experience

Your employment history or work experience is a significant part of your resume. Most employers will not consider someone a viable candidate without some knowledge of that person's employment background. At some point during college, you should begin to look for opportunities to acquire hands-on experience in your field. Part-time jobs, volunteer work, and co-op/internship positions are all fruitful areas for you to begin your career and add to your resume. When you detail your experience, mention where you worked, your job title, and how long you worked in that position. Remember: If you are competing for the chance to interview alongside people who have qualifications as strong as yours, strive to showcase your experience in a format that best highlights your capabilities.

Your prior employment can be divided into two aspects:

■ *Your routine duties.*   These were the responsibilities you were expected to fulfill on a daily basis. The particulars might be cut-and-dried and may sound at times like your job description.

■ *Your accomplishments.*   These are the high points of your work or academic life that serve as the basis of the achievement resume. They usually reflect your unique combination of skills and abilities.

When describing routine duties, use phrases and action words that convey a dynamic image. Words such as "designed," "managed," "organized," "supervised," "wrote," and "created" work better at establishing an active image than do words like "was responsible for" or "acted as." Figure 7.4 lists

ACTION VERBS.					
activate	conceive	file	market	promote	revise
address	conceptualize	forecast	monitor	prove	schedule
administer	conduct	formulate	move	provide	select
allocate	contact	gather	negotiate	publicize	sell
approve	convert	generate	observe	purchase	service
arbitrate	coordinate	guide	obtain	question	set up
assembled	create	handle	operate	realize	shape
assess	cultivate	head	order	receive	ship
assist	decode	hire	organize	recommend	solve
attain	define	identify	originate	reconcile	speak
balance	design	illustrate	oversee	recruit	structure
bring about	dispense	implement	participate	refer	succeed
buy	display	improve	perform	refine	supervise
calculate	distribute	increase	persuade	regulate	supply
coach	edit	initiate	place	reorganize	test
collect	entertain	install	plan	repair	train
command	estimate	interview	prepare	report	update
communicate	evaluate	investigate	present	represent	upgrade
compile	examine	lead	process	research	validate
complete	explain	lecture	produce	resolve	verify
compute	facilitate	manage	program	review	write

FIGURE 7.4

some of the action verbs you might use in describing prior jobs. Keep in mind that you should use present tense for your current position and past tense (-ed) for prior jobs.

You have to get the employer's attention quickly and keep it, so use short, concise paragraphs, without pronouns and modifiers that may bog down your description. Succinct phrases do not need to be complete sentences. Limit your paragraph on routine duties to no more than six lines. Accomplishments should include one brief statement highlighting the specific results you achieved.

In most cases, the experience component should include only jobs you have held within the last 10 years. Emphasize jobs and skills that are relevant to the job you're seeking. Focus on skills so that if the employer is using an electronic database to store resumes, mentioning relevant skills will ensure that your resume is "grabbed" when the computer does a key word search. If a job is not related to the field you're entering, omit or condense it. State only the basics, using one line to describe your duties. "Various customer-service-related duties" serves the purpose.

Look at the following example. The paragraph on routine duties is a concise overview of the person's responsibilities. The accomplishment statements tell the reader that the person was involved, responsible, and willing to go beyond what was expected to help the organization.

EXPERIENCE:

KREMER'S SUPPLY, INC., Vestron, Washington

Mail Clerk, 12/99 to present

Responsibilities include sorting and delivering mail to all personnel in company of over 150 employees; organizing and distributing packages and priority mail; arranging for overnight shipment of priority packages; delivering messages for executive personnel.

ACCOMPLISHMENTS:
- Reorganized mail sorting system resulting in approximate savings of $800 annually
- Supervised mail room duties when mail room manager was absent

The figure of $800 savings noted in the first accomplishment was developed by estimating the average amount of time saved on a weekly basis and multiplying it by the hourly rate of the employee. When extrapolated, the annual savings might be $800. Estimates and approximations are legitimate methods for calculating quantifiable results of an accomplishment.

Exercise 7.4 will help you think about your experience profile and the accomplishments you have had in your jobs.

TAKE A CLOSER LOOK 7.4

Showcasing Your Work Experience

To describe your work experience, focus first on your routine duties and then on the accomplishments that resulted from applying your skills. Remember to emphasize the skills that relate to the job for which you are applying.

EXPERIENCE:

Company name, city, state

_____

Title/dates of employment

_____

Duties:

_____

_____

Accomplishments:

_____

_____

If you are having trouble coming up with accomplishments, answer these questions:

Have you ever supervised anyone?

Have you ever worked as part of a team on a specific project?

Did you ever see a problem and suggest a solution that was adopted? Did it save time or money?

Did you ever improve an existing system or situation? Did the improvement save or increase funds?

Did you sell anything? Did you meet your goals? Did you exceed your goals?

Did you receive awards for your work, as an individual or part of a team?

Did the workload increase while you were on a job? Did you handle the increase successfully?

Develop a concise description of your experience at all the recent and relevant positions you have had.

JOB A

_____

_____

JOB B

_____

_____

JOB C

_____

_____

Review the information you have compiled about your experiences and see if it reflects your current job goal and the skills that might be needed. If you see something that may detract from your relevant skills or aren't sure if the information applies, leave it out. Be brief and focused.

Discuss the results of this exercise with your group or with the class.

Component 5: Education/Training

When presenting your education, the key factor again is whether the training you have had is relevant to the stated objective. Anything—college, seminars, workshops, work, or military training—that is related to the objective is important to include in this component of your resume. The format to present this information is quite flexible, and this example is only one of many possibilities.

EDUCATION

Columbia University, New York, New York
Graduated 2001, Bachelor of Science
Major: Business Administration
GPA: 3.5, magna cum laude

The basics of this component are the name of the institution from which you received your training, the location, the year you graduated (or attended), the degree conferred, and major area of study. Include your grade point average only if you have achieved a GPA of 3.0 or above; a lower GPA does not "show" well on a resume.

If you have been fortunate enough to attend workshops or seminars related to your field, either on your own or through your job, include these under a subheading in this section of the resume. You can choose to group these experiences either chronologically, providing dates, or under subject headings. A title such as "Additional Training" or "Seminar Training" suffices to indicate the education subcategory.

Some of you may have prior educational experiences or classes from one or two years of college that you wish to include. Perhaps the time you spent involved in previous study fills a gap in your resume. Emphasize only the information you feel will help you. Note the institution, location, dates, if not too long ago, and the type of study in which you engaged. A statement such as "Various business courses" offers enough pertinent information for the prospective employer.

If training you received is not relevant to the goal of your job search, you risk hurting your chances for getting the job by including it. It is understandable that you would want to acknowledge your efforts; however, sometimes unrelated information can detract from the vision you are trying to create. For example, Paul was seeking a job in risk management and felt that his prior training in truck-driving school could be helpful. It was only after some discussion and several rejection letters that I was able to convince Paul that his history as a truck driver might be confusing and distracting to the conservative insurance executives who were considering him for a position. He removed the statement about his prior unrelated training from his resume; within a month he was offered a position with a large property management company.

"...Hmmm... Under your favorite three activities: 'Hanging around Riverside Mall, hanging around Quail Run Mall and hanging around Chestnut Hill Mall.'"

Component 6: Related Information

The final component of your resume is a section on related information. This section can include any information that doesn't fall under another component and further supports your appropriateness for the job. Included in this area would be:

- awards or scholarships you may have received
- extracurricular activities
- licenses and certifications related to your career field
- memberships or offices held in professional organizations
- published works
- community involvement

As in all the previous components, keep the focus on the skills or abilities that directly relate to the employer's need and to your objective. You might well be proud of your hobbies and outside activities, but employers' reactions might be considerably less enthusiastic, as you can see from the response of the employer in the cartoon.

Now complete Exercise 7.5, listing some of the things that you might include in this component of your resume.

7.5 TAKE A CLOSER LOOK

The Whole You

The related information component of the resume gives you the opportunity to broaden your image for an employer; however, choose carefully when providing these details. Fill in the categories that might be helpful in presenting yourself.

PROFESSIONL MEMBERSHIP/OFFICES:

_____

_____

_____

AWARDS/SCHOLARSHIPS:

_____

_____

_____

EXTRACURRICULAR ACTIVITIES:

_____

_____

_____

PUBLISHED WORK:

_____

_____

_____

VOLUNTEER/COMMUNITY WORK:

_____

_____

_____

If you have devoted a substantial amount of time to volunteer or community work that is related to your objective, you may want to include it under your experience component instead. Remember that no matter how committed you may be to a cause, you may scare off an employer who has a great job opening if you broadcast your political or social position in your resume. Be careful! Keep the focus on your skills and ability to do the job.

APPEARANCE, FORMAT, AND ELECTRONIC DISTRIBUTION

This section considers the overall appearance of your resume. Most important, the resume must be readable. Your resume should be not only informative but also attractive and pleasing to the eye. Frame your resume with margins wide enough to present the document as if it were a picture to be admired. Although it is best to use only one or at most two of the more traditional typefaces, the use of uppercase, underlining, italics, and boldface can add to a resume's appeal. Use these functions conservatively and consistently. If you capitalize job titles then don't capitalize the names of the companies. If you underline job titles then don't capitalize them. Experiment with different highlights and choose an attractive final format that emphasizes your marketability. Include enough white space—bunched-up information is difficult to read and unappealing to employers. Have you ever turned a page in one of your textbooks and groaned upon seeing that the entire page is one long paragraph? Employers feel the same way. Keep them interested by dividing up the information in a lively style.

Generally, a resume should be confined to one page, but you may need two pages to include all the relevant information. Don't hesitate to use a two-page format if your details fill both pages in a balanced way. Details lend credibility to your resume and this may be especially appropriate if you have a strong experiential background. Don't worry if you only come up with enough for one page, though. One strong page is better than two pages of "fluff."

Any word processing software can be used to create your resume. Additionally, there are resume software packages available, like *Resumail*, that allow you to use formatting tools to create a resume and distribute it on the Internet. The final product can then be printed on a high-quality laser printer, e-mailed, or downloaded to a Web site database for distribution to possible employers.

Have your resume reproduced at a reputable quick-copy shop on their high-quality photocopiers. If the copier works correctly, the originals and the copies should be indistinguishable. Most of these shops also sell paper and matching envelopes suitable for resumes and cover letters. Choose conservative, basic colors such as white, ivory, buff, or light gray, and high-quality bond paper.

Store your resume on diskette. Most colleges and quick-print shops now offer resume services or personal computers with which you can update your stored resume. This allows you to distribute your resume electronically and makes revision an easy process. You can then tailor your resume to specific positions as they become available. Some colleges now offer an electronic resume database from which employers can access, scan, and select resumes. If this is true of your school, find out from the career services professional who administers the database what you need to do to effectively showcase your resume on that system.

Formatting your resume for Internet distribution may take a little more planning, but it's worth the effort, particularly if you are open to seeking employment outside of your community or region. Electronic format requires that the font you choose for your resume be readable when scanned electronically. The best fonts for this purpose are "nonproportional" fonts, which allocate the same amount of space to each letter. Examples are Courier and Prestige, the traditional "typewriter" fonts. However, because scanning equipment is much more sophisticated today, you are probably safe using a conservative "proportional" font such as Times or Helvetica. You will also have to remove those features that make the paper resume visually pleasing: italics, underlining, boldface, tabs, brackets, and hard returns. These enhancements may distort your copy when transmitted electronically. As with the hard copy, keep the text open between sections and use wide margins.

Your resume is a living document that should change as you grow and acquire new skills. Some people get lazy and assume that now that they have a resume they'll never again have to bother writing another. This may be your first resume but it won't be your last.

THE STEPS IN FINDING A JOB

Finding a job using traditional means is a step-by-step process, as depicted in Figure 7.5. (This process may vary slightly if you use nontraditional job-search methods, such as being referred by a friend.)

The first step is crafting a well-written resume. After that, you are ready to start using it as your introduction to employers. The cover letter is the next step: It acts as your resume's escort in your presentation to an employer. The cover letter is just as important as the resume because you want to convince the employer to read your resume. Once an employer reads and is impressed by a resume, he will invite the applicant for an interview. From the interview comes the job offer.

Once you begin sending out your resume and cover letter, you can begin to determine the weaknesses in your job campaign. If your resume is reaching employers and yet you are not being invited to interview, then you may need to fine-tune your letter or your resume. If you are getting interviews but no offers, then you may want to evaluate your interview style and make the necessary adjustments. You will be able to see exactly where you need to focus your attention based on the real-world results of your efforts.

You have already met the first challenge of job seeking: writing your resume. The next step is to write a persuasive cover letter.

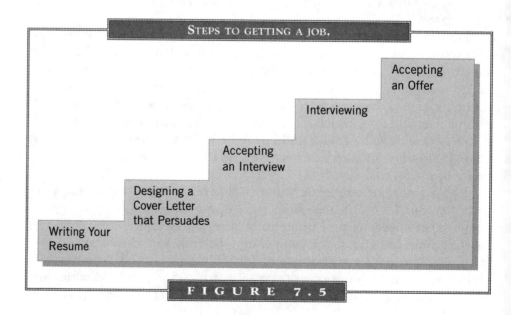

STEPS TO GETTING A JOB.

Accepting
an Offer

Interviewing

Accepting
an Interview

Designing a
Cover Letter
that Persuades

Writing Your
Resume

FIGURE 7.5

THE COVER LETTER

Your cover letter is a crucial step toward getting a job. You must write a letter that convinces the employer to review your resume, interview you, and then discuss employment with you. A well-written cover letter follows a logical progression in each of its paragraphs:

Paragraph 1: This is why I am writing to you. (newspaper ad, referral)

Paragraph 2: This is who I am.

Paragraph 3: This is what we have in common.

Paragraph 4: Conclusion: We should get together.

If you follow this format and back it up with solid reasoning, you will increase your chance that the employer will clearly see your value as a serious candidate for the position. The cover letter in Figure 7.6 uses this traditional but effective approach. Each of the paragraphs in this letter contributes to the writer's goal of making a logical, persuasive presentation. In addition, the candidate takes every opportunity to refer to the attached resume, further encouraging the employer to read on and consider him as a serious candidate.

Tailoring a cover letter to the specifics of each job for which you apply is one way to ensure that you are doing everything you can to market yourself effectively. Each employer wants to feel that her job is the only one in which you are interested. Take advantage of this fact by paying careful attention to any job description. Address your letter to a specific person within the organization, rather than writing to "Human Resources Director." If you must send your letter to a blind address, then use the salutation "Dear Sir or Madam:" rather than "To Whom It May Concern." (Never use just "Dear Sir:"—it would rightly be interpreted as sexist.)

Again, your cover letter is crucial. As with your resume, consider having one or more people read/edit/proofread your cover letter. You may miss errors or awkward statements that others may catch.

You will need a cover letter every time you send out your resume, so take the time now to come up with a format that you can fine-tune for specific jobs. Use the form provided in Exercise 7.6 to write your own persuasive cover letter.

TAKE A CLOSER LOOK 7.6

Writing a Persuasive Cover Letter

Complete the form letter using the logical approach just described. Refer to Appendix 1 for another example of a persuasive cover letter.

_____ Your Address

_____ City, State, Zip

_____ Date

1463 49th Avenue North
St. Petersburg, Florida 33703
June 18, 2001

Ms. Rita Huss
The Vaughan Group, Inc.
45 North Banks Street
St. Petersburg, Florida 33705

Dear Ms. Huss:

I am writing in response to your ad for the position of entry-level account assistant, which appeared in the St. Petersburg *Times* on June 15.

I am currently attending the University of Southern Florida and will be graduating at the end of this month. My degree is in business administration, with an emphasis in marketing. My recently completed internship with Affiliated Accounts has been an important part of my education and that is why I am very interested in an opportunity to work with you and your staff at The Vaughan Group.

I am confident that I possess the combination of skills and training necessary to become a valuable asset to The Vaughan Group. As you can see from my attached resume, I have dedicated myself to academic excellence with the long-term goal of working as an advertising professional. I feel that my background is ideally suited to the needs of your firm and that this position will offer me the challenges I am seeking.

I am eager to learn more about the position you advertise at The Vaughan Group. I am available for an interview at your convenience and look forward to hearing from you in the near future.

Sincerely,

William R. Gooding

Enclosure

FIGURE 7.6

_____ Name of Contact Person

_____ Organization Name

_____ Address

_____ City, State, Zip

Dear Mr./Ms. _____ :(Salutation)

Paragraph 1: Why

_____

_____

Paragraph 2: Who you are

_____

_____

_____

Paragraph 3: What organization and you have in common

_____

_____

_____

Closing paragraph: Logical conclusion—We should get together!

_____

_____

Sincerely,

_____

(Signature here)

Typed name

Enclosure

If it is a little awkward at first to write about yourself, that's okay. You'll get used to it. You aren't expected to be original or creative in cover letters. So feel free to get ideas from books or manuals with phrases that you think capture what you are trying to say. Just be sure that your letters don't sound "canned." If you use ideas from manuals, alter the language.

Discuss your reactions to all of the exercises with your group or with the class.

JOB APPLICATIONS

Many organizations may ask you to complete an application as part of your candidacy for a position. Your resume allows you the freedom to decide what aspects of your background to highlight and what to exclude, but the application process doesn't give you quite as much latitude. Applications are usually straightforward, fill-in-the-blank documents that would appear to dictate your responses. You may have little choice about revealing your prior positions, but you may consider it prudent to keep certain aspects of your life private. "Dilbert" needs to think through his responses more carefully.

Your name, address, and social security and telephone numbers are standard requirements on any application. You will be asked to list prior positions, the organizations in which you have worked, the inclusive dates, and the responsibilities you held. Carry an index card with you that recaps this information so you can be sure of the dates of your former employment. If you are asked to state your reason for leaving a job, always relate your departure to an opportunity for growth or improvement. Avoid mentioning that you couldn't get along with an employer or supervisor. If you are not a U. S. citizen but have applied for citizenship or have a green card, note that on the form. Some positions require that you be bondable, a term that refers to a type of insurance policy on employees that vouches for their performance. Unless you have had a criminal conviction, you should not have any trouble being bonded. Answer these questions simply and honestly.

It is possible that the application may ask questions that are illegal and probe areas of your life that are private in most states. Information related to your race, color, religion, sex, national origin, disability, age, or ancestry is protected by law. Attempts to elicit private information to exclude you from a job are illegal. Despite laws that prohibit these types of questions, you may find that employers continue to include these questions as part of the application process. Your answers may make the difference between an opportunity for an interview and no response. If full candor is going to jeopardize your chance at the job, then you must make a decision. If you feel that being straightforward with an employer will decrease your chance for a job, then leave that question blank. Never answer dishonestly. Leaving the answer open may not be the answer that the employer wants to see, but if your background makes you a strong candidate for the job, there is still a good chance that you will get an interview. Once you are in the interview, you always have an opportunity to overcome the interviewer's objections and sell yourself around negatives that come from those gray areas.

The application Jenny is filling out asks her (illegally) if she has children and their ages. Jenny has two children but knows that this fact does not compromise her ability to do the job for which she is applying. She can respond in two ways. She can answer that she does have kids and that they are well provided for through her child care arrangements or she can leave the question blank. There are risks with either approach. It is up to you to decide which one works best for you.

The most difficult judgments concern people with disabilities and those who have had encounters with the criminal justice system. Despite laws that

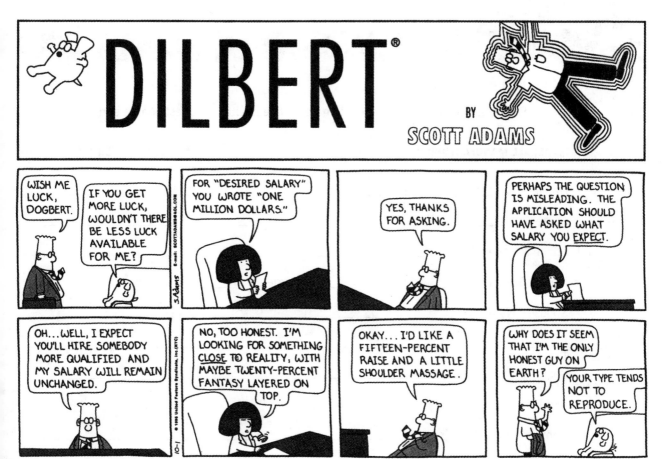

DILBERT reprinted by permission of Universal Feature Syndicate, Inc.

protect people with disabilities, most people are still not ready to leave their biases behind when evaluating people for employment. Any physical or mental impairment can incorrectly be assumed to represent increased costs to most employers. For this reason, if you have a disability but it is not apparent, do not indicate your disability on the application. You are being hired for your *ability* to do the job. Anything else is irrelevant. If your disability is apparent, then when you get to the interview, emphasize your skills, accomplishments, and ability to do the job.

Having a criminal record can pose another obstacle to employment. Most applications ask if you have ever been convicted. If you have, leave the spot blank on the application. The worst thing that can happen is that you won't get an interview. If you do get an interview and the subject comes up, you can then sell yourself by emphasizing that you have paid your dues and are now on the straight and narrow. You may be surprised to know how many people are hired who have made mistakes and are working to turn their life around.

Some applications ask for references. Make sure that the people whose names and numbers you provide know you are using them as a reference and will speak favorably of you. Again, carrying an index card with their names and contact information will help you.

Exercise 7.7, on the following pages, addresses how to answer certain questions on an application.

7.7 TAKE A CLOSER LOOK

A Practice Application

Complete this sample application, deciding how to deal with any questionable entries.

MARSHALL MANUFACTURING   **APPLICATION FOR EMPLOYMENT**

Name _____

Address _____

Phone Number(s) _____

Marital Status _____ Single _____ Married _____ Divorced

Spouse's Name _____

Spouse's Employment _____

Spouse's Salary _____

Children _____ Yes _____ No

Names/Ages _____

Date of Birth _____   U. S. citizen? _____

Sex _____   Height _____   Weight _____   Disabilities _____

Recent Hospitalizations _____

Person to Contact in an Emergency _____

Have You Ever Received or Applied for Unemployment Compensation? _____

If so, when? _____

Have You Ever Been Convicted of a Felony? _____

Do You Have a History of Mental Illness? _____

EDUCATION

High School _____

College/Vocational Training _____

Other Training _____

_____

(continued)

EMPLOYMENT HISTORY

Employer _____

Job Title/Dates of Employment _____

Job Duties _____

_____

Reason for Leaving _____

Employer _____

Job Title/Dates of Employment _____

Job Duties _____

_____

Reason for Leaving _____

Employer _____

Job Title/Dates of Employment _____

Job Duties _____

_____

Reason for Leaving _____

REFERENCES

Name _____   Phone _____

Address _____

Name _____   Phone _____

Address _____

Name _____   Phone _____

Address _____

I, the undersigned, submit this application for employment. If at any time the information included in this application is found to be false or untrue, it shall be considered grounds for immediate dismissal with no recourse.

Signed _____   Date _____

How did you respond to the questionable inquiries on this application? Discuss your responses with your group or with the class.

RUSSELL'S STORY

Russell had been looking for a job for over four months and was getting discouraged. He had been on a few interviews but was disappointed that he wasn't getting the same positive results as his classmates. Even when considering other factors like experience and grades, he knew something wasn't working.

Russell took his resume to the college services center and met with an advisor, Yolanda, who was happy to review his resume. After a quick scan of his resume, Yolanda saw what might have been causing Russell difficulty.

Russell's resume was completely factual and honest yet it did little to convey the real talent and

---

Russell Banks
542 Cherry Street
Bryan, New Hampshire 03255
Phone: 632-6639

Objective
Seeking a position in which I can use my skills to benefit myself and the organization.

Education
Adrian College, Bryan, New Hampshire
Business administration major, Graduated 2001

Experience
Tool Room Monitor, 6–99 to present
Heritage Tools, Inc., Bryan, New Hampshire
    Monitor use of tools by employees, maintain orderly system for
    tool use, keep running inventory of tools and location.

Retail Selector, 6–95 to 9–98 (Part-time/summer)
Sears Distribution Center, Columbus, Ohio
    Took catalog orders and pulled items from inventory for delivery
    to customer.

Personal

Birth date:	May 23, 1978	Marital Status:	Single
Birthplace:	Columbus, Ohio	Health:	Excellent
Hobbies:	Softball, jogging, fitness, car shows		

References
Available upon request.

hard work that Russell had demonstrated in the past or was capable of in the future. Russell didn't see why he had to "fancy up" the facts. Like Popeye, he was who he was and he had little patience with what he considered the "cosmetics" of job seeking. Only his growing frustration with the puzzle of finding employment was driving him to seek advice.

Yolanda asked Russell a few questions that allowed him to think about his goals for the first time.

What did he see himself doing for an employer? Describe the setting in which the work would take place. Are there other people around or is he alone in a room? Is the room an office or another setting? What kinds of activities is he engaged in? What kind of business would the employer be conducting? What specific classes in his major had he enjoyed the most?

After some deliberation, Russell began to articulate images of himself that fit into the con-

---

Russell J. Banks

rjayb@hotmail.com

542 Cherry Street Bryan, New Hampshire 03255   (603) 632-6639

PROFILE

Strong experience in inventory control and purchasing; reliable team player able to take initiative

SKILLS AND ABILITIES

- Knowledgeable in all aspects of purchasing, including make-or-buy decision making and cost/price analysis
- Experienced in logistics and inventory control, including MRP II
- Familiar with ISO 9000 standards
- Capable of operating the following software: Microsoft Excel, Microsoft Word

EDUCATION

Adrian College, Bryan, New Hampshire
Graduated 2001, Bachelor of Science
Major: Business Administration/Purchasing
GPA: 3.1
Other Training: MRP II Workshop, 9/1999
Automated Inventory Management, 1/2000

RELATED EXPERIENCE

Heritage Tools, Inc., Bryan, New Hampshire
Tool Room Monitor, 6/1999 to present
Manage and control distribution and retrieval of tools used in manufacturing company with annual sales over $5M

Major Accomplishment:

- Developed and implemented improved system for cataloging tool usage resulting in approximate annual savings of $2,500

OTHER FACTS

- Organized and coordinated college fund-raiser to benefit Children's Medical Center—net contribution $6,580
- Member, National Purchasing Management Association, 2000

text of a work environment. He saw himself involved in a variety of situations, not just one single activity. He liked working with a team but didn't want to work with the public. He was interested in working with data and things more than with people. While he couldn't remember feeling passionate about any of his classes, he recalled clearly that a series of courses in purchasing and business communication had been more interesting than his other classes.

On the basis of this discussion, Yolanda suggested that he might focus his goal a bit and consider the possibility of working in purchasing and supply with a small company. The opportunity of working with a small company had never occurred to Russell but it made sense now. A small company would give him the chance to be involved in a variety of tasks, rather than being limited to doing just one thing with a big organization. Purchasing sounded good, too. He could work with a team to determine com-

pany needs and then develop the data for purchasing on his own. Additionally, his background in supply would help him interface effectively with the consumers.

With a focused goal, Russell was able to design his resume more effectively to bring out the skills and achievements that he and his advisor thought would be most marketable. He chose to highlight his degree differently and left out those things that didn't relate directly to his profile. His new resume made him feel more competitive, and just writing it helped him focus his thoughts for interviews.

Russell resumed his job search. He continued to fine-tune and improve his new resume as he received feedback and became more comfortable with the process of developing the right words and phrases. After six weeks of looking and several more interviews, Russell landed a job as a purchasing/inventory control assistant with a small manufacturing firm.

7.8 TAKE A CLOSER LOOK

Pulling It All Together

Now that you have had a chance to work on the individual components that compose a resume, try pulling the components together to develop a solid integrated document.

IDENTIFIERS _____

_____

_____

_____

SUMMARY/PROFILE

_____

_____

_____

SKILLS

_____

_____

_____

_____

EXPERIENCE

Company/City _____

Title/Dates _____

Duties _____

_____

_____

Accomplishments _____

_____

Company/City _____

Title/Dates _____

Duties _____

_____

_____

Accomplishments _____

_____

Education _____

College/University _____

Date of Graduation/Degree Awarded _____

Major Area of Study/Emphasis _____ GPA [if over 3.0] _____

Other Training _____

_____

_____

Related Information _____

Memberships/Awards/Scholarships/Licenses/Volunteer Work, and so on

_____

_____

_____

Based on your career goal and the unique combination of skills and abilities that you possess, decide whether a chronological, functional, or achievement resume will work best for you.

Chronological: Showcases work experience and continued growth in one field

Functional: Showcases skills; ideal for career changers, new job seekers

Achievement: Aggressively showcases accomplishments as they relate to expected job skills

You may already have a good idea of how to lay out your resume. If not, use scissors to cut out the different components of the resume you have developed. Shuffle the components around, remove those that don't work, and see how different combinations sound and flow. This should help you decide which format and layout will work best for you. Buy a diskette and start writing!

Discuss the results of your "shuffling" with your group or with the class.

To review, you have found out that the resume is a unique document in which you determine what information to provide and how to present it. You can conform to the conventions of typical hiring practices and still present an image of competence and self-assurance.

You should now be able to decide which resume style will work best for you in different job-seeking situations and how to present the information you include. You also should be comfortable designing a document that will change and evolve as you mature, a document that is as appealing as it is informative. You also are able to take advantage of a variety of conventional and electronic means to circulate your resume.

You are now ready to write cover letters that do more than "cover" your resume. Your letters should be developed using facts that persuade the employer to act on your resume and offer you an interview. You are now prepared to distribute your resume online, as well as respond to inquiries on applications that could be awkward or ambiguous.

A LOOK BACK

Finally, go over this checklist before you send out your resume:

_____ Is my resume completely free of errors in spelling, punctuation, usage, and grammar?

_____ Does my resume have enough attractive white space?

_____ Is my use of type styles simple, conforming to the requirements of electronic scanning?

_____ Is my resume one solid page of information?

_____ If I have two pages, is the information meaningful or "filler"?

_____ Does my resume flow and have a logical layout?

_____ Do I use short phrases and action words?

_____ Is the information focused only on the skills needed for the job, excluding irrelevant or meaningless facts?

Other Sources and Suggested Reading

The Damn Good Resume Guide by Yana Parker

This classic resume-writing manual published by the same company that produces *What Color Is Your Parachute?* has been rewritten and is now easier to follow. Still a useful, all-around guide to writing your resume.

Dynamite Cover Letters and *Dynamite Resumes* by Ronald L. Krannich and Caryl Rae Krannich

These authors offer their philosophy on writing job-seeking documents that get employers' attention.

Effective Phrases for Performance Appraisals by James E. Neal, Jr.

Although this book is really designed to assist managers in writing performance appraisals, it is equally helpful if you are looking for phrases that express your abilities.

Electronic Resumes & Online Networking by Rebecca Smith

This is an outstanding tool to use the Internet to develop and distribute your resume.

National Business Employment Weekly Cover Letters by Taunee Besson

The national newspaper devoted to job seeking and careers publishes this book on cover letters.

The New Perfect Resume by Tom Jackson

A recognized authority on career development, Jackson updates a comprehensive look at resumes and resume writing.

Resumail designed by Resumail Network

This is a software package that makes electronic resume distribution as simple as the click of a mouse.

Web Sites and Internet Resources

www.eresumes.com/

A very well-developed site for electronic resume information.

www.jobweb.org/catapult/guenov/restips.html

This site offered by the National Association of Colleges and Employers is a great place to stay up-to-date on what employers have to say about resumes.

www.quintcareers.com/resres.html

This site, part of a full-service career Web page, covers everything from resume writing and electronic distribution to books and links to other resume sites.

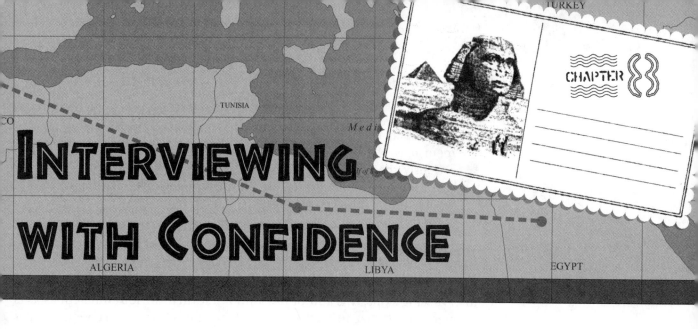

INTERVIEWING WITH CONFIDENCE

Probably the most intimidating aspect of anyone's career development is the prospect of interviewing for jobs. Job interviews present a unique challenge to job hunters. You are offering yourself as a candidate for employment and, as such, may have limited control over the circumstances of the interview. You may feel that you have to win the approval of the all-powerful interviewer and thereby influence him to offer you the job.

Your challenge is not to please the interviewer, however. A positive dialogue with the interviewer is only one of the goals in interviewing. The real challenge is in preparing yourself and performing during the interview so that your capabilities are clear to the interviewer. All of your preparation is about to pay off. You know about the prospective job through your library research and network interviews. You are familiar with the field. You have gained the technical and academic background you need to compete effectively. The only thing remaining is preparing yourself for the scrutiny that comes with the job interview.

Preparing for a job interview involves a rather complex set of dynamics, which can be broken down into specific parts.

PREPARING YOURSELF TO INTERVIEW

Getting ready for an interview can be divided into specific tasks:

- *developing and sharpening your style*—A significant part of interviewing well is projecting a sense of personal power and confidence. This is accomplished through carefully assessing your appearance, poise, and presentation, everything from what you wear to the way you speak and move.

- *knowing your field and your skills*—All the poise in the world will not make up for a lack of substance and competence. To be credible, you must convey the knowledge you have gained about the field and the job through education, experience, company research, and so on. Operate from a solid base of information.

139

■ *understanding the rituals of the interview*—Everything about you is magnified and amplified during the interview process. You will be expected to respond in certain ways to the process of interviewing. If you display a lack of understanding of what is expected, your judgment may be called into question. It is important for you to take seriously the behaviors you exhibit at the interview and realize that they take on a much greater significance in an interview than they would in any other business situation.

THE DYNAMICS OF INTERVIEWING

After working with hundreds of students and professionals in developing interviewing skills, this author has found that there are four different aspects of interviewing that influence how well an interview goes. These dynamics include: exchange of information, sales presentation, social occasion, and theatrical performance. The dynamics are flexible and change throughout the interview. We will examine each of these dynamics separately.

An Exchange of Information

The first and most important dynamic of the interview is that it is an *exchange of information*. The era of going into an interview and being willing to accept anything offered is gone. Interviewing for a job is more like dating than it is getting married. You certainly wouldn't want to marry every person you date and you definitely wouldn't want every job for which you interview. Your task is to learn as much as you can about the job, the organization, the people, and the work. That means using your powers of observation and sensitivity during the interview. The interview is also the time to ask any questions that you need answered to make the decision about whether to accept the job if it is offered. Everything you learn about the interviewer and the organization will help you determine whether the job will be a good fit for you.

A Sales Presentation

This is the dynamic of interviewing with which you are probably most familiar. Part of interviewing well is selling yourself and your skills to the interviewer. An interview is, in some respects, a *sales presentation*. As in any sales presentation, you will be showcasing information about yourself that makes you a strong candidate for the position and de-emphasizing those aspects of your background that conflict with the employer's assumptions. It is important to be "fast on your feet," reinforcing your strengths and enthusiasm to encourage the employer to offer you the job. To do that, you have to know what the employer needs and draw attention to the ways you can meet those needs.

A Social Occasion

Even though an interview is usually businesslike, sometimes even formal, it is also a *social occasion*. People who are likable get job offers. People who are not don't. Interviewers need to assess whether you will "fit in" with their present team; you can make them feel comfortable by being friendly and warm during the interview. This is not easy for everyone. Some of us are naturally open and friendly; others of us struggle to smile. Take advantage of your assets when you interview and, without question, the ability to smile and respond warmly is a key factor.

A Theatrical Performance

The fourth dynamic in the interview is that it is indeed a *theatrical performance*. You are being observed by an audience of one, the interviewer. Think about how you will answer the interviewer's probable first question, "How are you today?" In all likelihood, you will answer with the expected response, "Fine, thanks." If you have a headache or nervous stomach, you will probably keep that to yourself and *act* as though you feel fine. Most often, job seekers work at appearing confident. It helps to look confident and comfortable during an interview, but nervousness is actually not the worst trait you can display. Nervousness can even be interpreted favorably. It shows the employer that you care about the outcome of the interview and that your behavior is authentic and genuine. Above all, you will be trying your best to act the role of competent professional.

Interviewing well and taking into consideration these four dynamics is a complex and difficult task. You may make friends with the employer but feel that you did not *sell* yourself well. You may convey the attitude of a professional but be unable to connect with the interviewer. Since you have limited control over most of the externals that dominate an interview—the time, the location, the person interviewing you, or the tone of the interview—interviewing is always a challenge. (It may help to remember that others interviewing for the job face these same challenges and may be less prepared!)

Remember, you do have control over some very important variables. What do you control and how can you use these variables to your advantage? We'll start with the things over which you have the most control and proceed from there.

ASPECTS OF THE INTERVIEW YOU CONTROL

Many of the factors that affect the circumstances of the interview may be outside your control, but that doesn't necessarily determine the outcome. The variables you control have a much greater influence on the outcome than any of the externals. Knowing what you can do to influence the interview will help you feel more comfortable with interviewing as a whole and help you focus your energy productively.

Variable 1: Your Appearance

Your appearance is one variable over which you have great control. Your dress, haircut or style, makeup, and accessories all contribute—or detract—from the image you project. The image you want to confirm in the employer's mind is that of a competent, credible professional. To do that, you need to dress the part. Dressing the part can also influence how you behave.

If you *look* the part, you will find it easier to convey a professional demeanor. If you doubt that the way you dress has an impact on your behavior, just think of teenagers in their prom formals and tuxedos. Notice any differences in their behavior?

Conventional wisdom has emphasized that the first 30 seconds of the interview are the most critical to success. The first impression created by the image you project can have a substantial effect on everything that follows.

Although some organizations have adopted casual dress in the workplace, interviewing still requires your most polished appearance. Traditionally, the standard uniform for interviewees has been the business suit both for men and women. Men are typically expected to wear dark suits, white cotton shirts, and dark ties. Women are to be similarly attired in dark-skirted suits and light blouses. But it doesn't mean that a woman wearing a red suit is immediately disqualified from consideration. It may mean that she has to work a bit harder to convince the employer that she respects all of their conventions. If you are interviewing in the ultra-conservative professions of accounting or banking, these rules are especially true.

The remaining details of your appearance should also be considered carefully and reflect the nature and attitudes prevalent in the profession you wish to enter. Shoes should reflect the same traditional look as the suit you wear. Dress shoes are the preferred choice for both men and women. Sandals or athletic wear are not appropriate and will project a negative impression. Don't let the trend in casual office dress fool you. For interviews, casual dress does not apply.

Accessories for both men and women should be kept to a minimum and, again, very traditional. Avoid frilly blouses, jangly bracelets, or athletic watches. Women should use makeup sparingly and avoid cologne. You also may wish to leave your purse at home or bring a leather portfolio instead.

DOONESBURY   **BY GARRY TRUDEAU**

Hairstyle is an important part of your image and should reflect the same classic look. Be sure your hairstyle is neat and businesslike. Men with mustaches or beards may want to trim them before an interview.

Although the above advice is meant to set guidelines, you may find that some professions are more flexible than others. Art, advertising, construction, and information technology professions are less focused on appearance and image than are the fields of banking or finance. Conventional wisdom suggests dressing two levels above the job that you want. That means if you are seeking a carpenter's position, you would apply wearing clean denim jeans, a work shirt, and steel-toed shoes. If you were to show up in a suit, you might convey the image that you didn't know what was expected of you on the job.

Knowing the culture of the occupation you are entering will give you insight into the expectations of your interviewer. Will you be working independently, expected to take initiative and produce on your own? Or will you be working closely with other team members, expected to take direction from a manager or team leader? The more autonomous your role, the more latitude you may be given in the way you present yourself.

TAKE A CLOSER LOOK 8.1

Mirror, Mirror on the Wall . . .

Before your interview appraise yourself in the mirror, from head to toe. Remember, you are trying to convey confidence and professional poise. Go through the following checklist and assess how you look.

_____ Is my clothing appropriate for a professional business meeting?

_____ Is it in keeping with the typical business dress of the profession that I am seeking to enter?

_____ Are my accessories (jewelry, footwear, makeup, fragrance) minimal and appropriate?

_____ Is my hairstyle conventional and neat?

_____ Does my appearance fit the culture of the job for which I am interviewing?

Some of you may be wondering how you can afford to wear clothes just to accommodate the employer's expectations. From my experience, it is worth the investment to buy one good wool/wool-blend suit for interviews. Dressing well for an interview boosts your confidence and creates a favorable impression.

Variable 2: Questions and Answers

Every interview includes questions you will be expected to answer specifically. You can't control what you're asked, but you can control your answers. Part of your preparation must include anticipating the different types of questions you might be asked and thinking in advance about how you will answer them.

Many of the questions will be _skills questions_. For example, "What can you do?" questions relate to technical or academic knowledge. These questions can cause you unnecessary anxiety. Because they tend to deal with how much you know, you might feel that the interviewer will find a weakness in your knowledge, thereby eliminating you from the competition.

In reality, skills questions are a great way for you to showcase what you can do and, for the most part, the easiest. Most employers would not be interviewing you if you didn't have the background they were seeking, so the chances are good that you will know how to answer these questions. If you don't know the answer, don't try to cover up by saying just anything. Instead, say "I'm not familiar with that particular issue but I have had some experience with _____." Let the employer know that even if you don't know the answer to a particular question, you do feel secure about your background. The *Chicago Tribune* reports that studies of American managers have found that skills questions are a secondary determinant in candidate acceptability. The more important factor is attitude.

Attitude questions are another type of question that you can expect. These are the "What will you do?" questions that employers might ask to see how you feel about overtime, weekend work, night work, working with women or men, minority group members, disabled coworkers, and so on. Try to answer the questions in a straightforward, sincere manner that accommodates the employer's needs. Sometimes questions like these can alert you to an employer's hidden agenda, or an issue with which the company might be struggling. Questions about overtime might mean that the company is chronically understaffed and covers their employee shortage by expecting people to pick up the extra workload. Listen carefully and see if you can detect what is implied by the question. In most cases, you should respond positively to the interviewer. Signs of lack of commitment or bias will be viewed negatively. Most employers are looking for "can-do" employees.

Some interviewers will use *scenario questions*. These questions typically describe a situation and then ask you to provide your ideas on how you would handle it. Sometimes employers might be looking for specific answers and sometimes they might simply be looking at how you make decisions and solve problems. These are difficult questions to prepare for, so use your best judgment and be thoughtful and creative. You will probably do better than your competition given your knowledge of the field and your preparation.

Occasionally, just as with applications, employers may ask questions that would be considered illegal, usually relating to private information protected by law. Unfortunately, if you point out the impropriety, you will do little to endear yourself to the interviewer. These questions must be handled delicately. You have a right to privacy so disclose only information you believe to be pertinent to the job. Try to answer with a "non-answer" if possible. For instance, if an interviewer asks how many children you have, you might ask how that relates to the job. If you are asked if you plan on having any more children, you might simply state that you are happy with the size of your family. These types of questions tell you a lot about the employer you would be working for; that alone might be a warning about whether you would be comfortable working in that organization.

A new type of interviewing that is becoming more popular is called *behavior based interviewing*. This approach focuses on the skills required by the position and asks you to respond very specifically to events from your experience that reflect those skills. The circumstances of the event, how the skills were used, and the resolution are all part of exploring how you have actually performed in similar situations. The approach for this type of interview is based in the belief that past behavior is the best predictor of future behavior. Preparing for this type of interview offers distinct advantages, even if your interviewer doesn't use this approach. Being able to showcase situations from your experience in which you have demonstrated a high level of skill is a powerful way of responding to an employer's questions. Exercise 8.2 is designed to prepare you to respond to an interviewer in a meaningful and substantive way.

Telling, Not Bragging

Identify 5 to 10 experiences or events in which you feel you demonstrated exceptional skill with good results. These should be accomplishments that required you to use skills related to the position for which you are applying—a valuable way to "show off" your expertise.

Describe the events using a model that divides the experience into four components:

Event: Describe the challenge you or your team (in work or school) faced in factual terms. Make sure the event was one that showcased a skill relevant to the position.

Skill: Use details to create a picture for the employer that allows them to "see" you using the skill that they are seeking.

Solution: Relate the resolution of the situation, highlighting your role.

Results: Make sure you include the results of your highlighted event. Nothing is as impressive as getting concrete, positive results.

Event 1:

_____

_____

_____

Event 2:

_____

_____

_____

Event 3:

_____

_____

_____

Event 4:

_____

_____

_____

Event 5:

_____

_____

_____

Use additional sheets if you have more than five events to describe.

After completing this exercise, you will be able to use the information about these events to respond factually to questions about specific skills and abilities. You needn't wait for the interviewer to ask; look for opportunities to introduce the kind of information that "sells" you. When you sense an opening, you might start with a question related to your relevant skill such as, "Do you use Microsoft Word as your word processing software?" Regardless of the interviewer's answer, you can continue your dialogue by citing your mastery of that particular package (and others if applicable) and the situation in which you used it to meet a need successfully.

Be yourself in an interview, answering questions genuinely and authentically. Ask a friend to critique your grammar and usage so that you can practice your communication skills. A complaint that employers have related to me as a career services professional is that young people as a group don't possess strong communication skills, especially in terms of speaking standard English. Your ability to articulate your thoughts in an understandable way gives you a competitive edge that will reach far beyond the interview.

Aside from being prepared for specific skills and attitude questions, there is a standard group of questions that most interviewers use as a way to establish baseline information about you. Exercise 8.3 is a way to prepare yourself for these typical questions.

 TAKE A CLOSER LOOK

Sample Interview Questions

Look over the following list of questions. Think of how you might respond, and be conscious of any hidden agenda in the questions. Have a partner from your group or your class ask you the questions in a role-playing dialogue to see how your answers sound.

Tell me about yourself.

Keep your answer focused on the skills and your interest in the field. Stay away from family and personal information.

What are your strengths and weaknesses?

You can take advantage of the strengths question to reinforce your suitability for the job, especially in the skill area, but be careful of the weakness part. Don't tell anything that is damaging to your image as a dedicated worker. My favorite is "I find that sometimes I can't say 'no' to an opportunity to do something if it needs to be done." Avoid answers such as "I don't get along with people" or "Sometimes I'm late." The interview may continue but you will probably be out of the running. Also, try to avoid "Dilbert's" dilemma by thinking through the answer ahead of time.

What brings out your best?

The single best answer to this is "A challenge." Go on to describe what that means to you.

How do you work under pressure?

You know what to say here.

Why should I hire you?

Again, there is only one answer: "Because I know I can be an asset to this organization." Tell how.

Why do you want to work here?
Try to say something that indicates you are looking for a place where you can use your skills to good advantage.

What was your favorite class in college?
Name one that was related to the job.

What was your least favorite class in college?
Name one that was unrelated to the job.

What did you like the best in your last job?
Focus on the similarities to the job you're seeking.

What did you like the least in your last job?
Come up with an answer that reinforces your interest in facing challenges that might have been absent in your last job.

Where do you see yourself in five years? Ten years?
This is a goals question, so project forward a few years and emphasize your commitment to growth and becoming a better employee. Be careful though. You don't want to sound as if you have your sights set on taking over the company or the interviewer's job.

Discuss your experience in the role-playing dialogue with your group or the class.

DILBERT reprinted by permission of Universal Feature Syndicate, Inc.

Variable 3: Nonverbal Cues

Surprising as it may seem, one variable that you may have difficulty controlling is your nonverbal communication. While you might be very conscious of what you tell an employer verbally, you might find it a challenge to monitor the information you communicate nonverbally. Nonverbal cues are habits and behaviors that we all use unconsciously. An employer can learn a lot about you—positive and negative—by observing your nonverbal communication.

You may be sitting in the lobby of a company waiting to be called to your interview and thinking about what you will say to the interviewer. You may be completely unaware that you are tapping your foot, jiggling your leg, and picking lint off your suit. These relatively innocuous behaviors may communicate to others your anxiety about the interview. Your nonverbal behavior can tell the employer more than you might want her to know.

Your goal should be to control and modify your nonverbal communication to support the overall positive impression you are striving to convey. Convince the interviewer that you are confident and at ease, eager to respond openly and sincerely. The best way to create this image is to focus on the ways you can connect with the person interviewing you. As the interviewer greets you, step forward with your hand extended, a warm smile on your face. Shake hands firmly, make eye contact, and greet the interviewer with a pleasant "Happy to meet you, Ms. Payne." Make sure you say the interviewer's name. It establishes the appropriate tone of a business meeting. Don't call the interviewer by her first name unless invited to.

When you get to the interviewer's office, wait to sit until after the interviewer takes her seat. Maintain your warm demeanor while you get comfortable. Try to relax and observe the room. You might chat about the weather or perhaps an item in the interviewer's office that sparks your interest, but keep small talk to a minimum. Casual conversation is a good way to start off, but the interviewer will want to move along.

When seated, keep both feet on the floor or crossed at the ankles. Sit up straight and relax your hands in your lap. Try not to appear rigid or stiff. Continue making good eye contact—this is the best way to connect. When you are talking, be expressive and enthusiastic. Have a pleasant look on your face, smile easily, and use gestures that are appropriate to what you are saying.

Vary your tone of voice when you convey your ideas. Try to avoid saying "ums" to fill in silences. Vocalized pauses and habitual behaviors such as twirling your hair or bouncing your leg can be extremely distracting and conflict with the image of a professional you are trying to confirm in the employer's eyes.

Variable 4: The Interview's Tone

If you begin to feel more comfortable, you will better be able to communicate your enthusiasm about the job opportunity. Stay businesslike even if your interviewer behaves quite informally. Exercise 8.4 will help you assess how your nonverbal cues support you in the interview.

TAKE A CLOSER LOOK **8.4**

How Am I Acting?

Ask yourself these questions as a way of becoming sensitive to how you are communicating nonverbally.

_____ Do I look comfortable and friendly when smiling?

_____ Is my handshake firm without being too strong?

_____ When seated, are my feet crossed at the ankles or next to each other flat on the floor?

_____ Is my posture correct without being stiff?

_____ Are my hands folded in a relaxed manner in my lap?

_____ Am I comfortable gesturing appropriately when my remarks call for it?

_____ Can I refrain from fidgeting?

_____ Can I look at my interviewer in a confident manner, making eye contact without "staring" him down?

_____ Is my diction clear and verbal tone pleasant?

Discuss the challenge of monitoring your nonverbal cues with your group or with the class.

My experience has led me to believe that formal, high-stress interviews are less common today. Interviewers have found that putting candidates under stress can intimidate interviewees. The goal of the interviewer is to help you feel comfortable so you will reveal as much of yourself as she needs to know to determine whether you are a viable candidate for the position. That most often translates into friendly behavior. Be careful to distinguish friendliness from friendship. The interviewer is *not* your friend. While he may not wish you any ill, the interviewer is paid to qualify people for further consideration. Anything that might make you a risk could disqualify you. The recruiter or interviewer is the organization's gatekeeper. Stay focused on your goals, your skills, and what you can do for the organization.

Variable 5: It's Your Turn to Ask

Gathering information about a job also requires you to formulate questions to ask your interviewer. Many of your questions about a position and the organization may already be addressed during the interview. If not, be prepared to bring them up at an appropriate point.

Typically, the questions you might like to ask are the very ones to avoid in a first interview. I'm referring to questions about salary and benefits. The interviewer is focused on how you meet the organization's needs and wants to believe that is your focus as well, although you are both aware that this is a job for which you will be paid. Save the money and benefits questions for a later date. If you are offered the job, a salary will then be discussed. If not, you may be better off not knowing what might have been.

Most often questions should focus on the nature of the work to be performed, the work team, the company, the industry, and future growth.

Sometimes you might find that your interviewer is not giving you a chance to tell what you can do. In that case, use the questions you have prepared to highlight the skills you think make you the ideal choice for the position.

The best questions tell the employer that you have done your homework on the company and the industry. If you don't already know about a company, check with your college career center to see if there is company information available to you. If not, try the library. *Standard & Poor's*, *Thomas's Register of American Manufacturers*, and *Dun & Bradstreet Reference Book* are a few resources that might offer information about a company. An Internet search may also yield an organization's Web site. Web sites might go well beyond the products and services offered to philosophy or policy. The Better Business Bureau and the local chamber of commerce also offer information about member organizations.

You might want to call the company with which you will be interviewing and ask the receptionist if you can drop by and pick up a brochure or an annual report. Most companies are happy to accommodate such requests. An added benefit is that you get the opportunity to "dry run" your visit to the company. Being well prepared for the interview is a strong statement of your willingness to go the extra mile to reach your goals, a definite plus with any employer.

Always leave an interview with a clear understanding of the next steps in the process. Follow up by sending a thank-you note to her. A brief, positive note shows your appreciation, reinforces your candidacy, and brings the interview to an appropriate close. A thank-you note is a necessary courtesy. If you have not heard from the interviewer in a reasonable amount of time, be sure to follow up with a phone call.

Use Exercise 8.5 to think about the questions you might ask your interviewer.

8.5   TAKE A CLOSER LOOK

Prepare Your Questions

The best candidates are ready with questions, so take advantage of this opportunity to practice asking some of the more typical ones.

What is the career path for this position?

What is the person who performed this job doing now?

Are there opportunities for professional growth in this position?

Are there training opportunities in this position?

For whom would I be working?

Could you tell me about the team of people with whom I would be working?

What skill would you say is critical to the performance of this job?

How could I best prepare myself were I to be selected for the position?

What is the next step in the process? May I follow up with you?

Come up with questions of your own. Remember: Save your questions about salary, vacation, or benefits until a later time.

ELECTRONIC INTERVIEWING

Given the impact of technology on the landscape of career planning, it is no surprise that it is even now changing the boundaries of interviewing and job screening. Two trends, video interviewing and interviewing by computer, while relatively new, signal how far technology continues to find its way into every aspect of our lives.

Video interviewing allows the candidate and the interviewer to speak face to face for the initial screening interview without incurring the inconvenience and expense of travel. It does not take the place of selection interviews but it does speed the interview process by eliminating unsuitable candidates. If you find that the first interview is to be conducted by video, don't panic. Here are a few recommendations that will help you prepare for this new form of interviewing.

1. *Request a brief telephone conversation prior to the interview.* Use this telephone call to establish rapport with the interviewer and to determine what the technical requirements are for the interview.

2. *Arrive at the interview site early and familiarize yourself with the computer/camera set-up.* Most video interviews are conducted at third-party settings such as career services offices or agencies. See if you can spend a few minutes looking over the equipment and getting some training, if necessary. That will allow you to feel comfortable and keep distractions to a minimum during the interview.

3. *Interviewing on video is the same as interviewing in person . . . but different.* The camera tends to mute our behaviors, so communicating enthusiasm through tone of voice and nonverbal communication is tricky. Speak slowly and clearly but don't overdo it. Look at the camera and try to appear animated but don't go overboard. You are not actually on TV so there's no need to put on a show. With some systems, there may be a gap between transmission so wait until the interviewer is finished speaking before you respond.

Computer interviewing may be conducted by e-mail or through online real-time interviewing. The e-mail option allows you to review questions and respond with prepared, thoughtful responses. The computer interview process resembles the video interview in that it allows the video to be transmitted over telephone lines in the manner similar to the process that takes place when information is faxed. Your picture appears on the computer screen with accompanying audio, though not synchronized. Use the same approach in preparing for these interviews as you would for the video conferencing based interview.

KEEP YOUR FOCUS

Keeping your focus can be a challenge. You may understand the individual dynamics of interviewing well but juggling all the different variables can be overwhelming. Set your goals before you go into the interview and stay focused on them. Try not to be consumed by anxiety or nerves. Say to yourself "I'm so excited." You must be an attractive candidate to have gone this far, so be proud of yourself. You are exactly where you want to be—one step away from your goal.

One way to keep your focus is by visualizing beforehand how you would like to see yourself perform in the interview. World-class athletes use visualization to inspire performances that win them the championship or the gold medal. You can do the same. Try Exercise 8.6 to see how visualizing helps you feel ready for the interview. Then simply imitate the images of yourself doing well.

 TAKE A CLOSER LOOK

Visualize Your Success

Take 30 minutes daily for a week before your interview and imagine yourself going through the entire interview experience. Close your eyes and see yourself driving to the interview. You are the model of professional dress and personal power. You are calm and have been preparing for this meeting for a long time. You are obviously better prepared than any other candidate for this job.

You are in the office now, shaking hands with the interviewer. You are smiling, happy to be there. Your handshake confirms your confident, open approach to the world. The interviewer likes you and wants you to do well. You answer questions thoughtfully, taking whatever time you need to feel comfortable. Your interviewer thinks your answers are excellent. You are poised and comfortable and ask questions that impress the interviewer. Your interviewer closes the session, expressing regret that there isn't more time to explore your views on the position and the company. You are also disappointed that there isn't more time to share your thoughts but are pleased to have had the chance to meet your interviewer regardless of the outcome.

You leave the interview and return home to write immediately a warm thank-you note, reinforcing the ideas discussed in the interview and expressing appreciation for the opportunity to meet the interviewer.

If you have worked through the exercise diligently, you should feel relaxed, uplifted, and totally prepared for your interview.

Discuss with your group or the class how the visualization exercise worked for you.

YOUR INTERVIEW GOALS

As you prepare for the interview, you may feel like a programmed robot. "Sit straight. Feet flat. Smile. Shake. Answer. Question. Leave." You may feel that trying to integrate all the suggestions here is going to have you spinning like a top. The intent of this chapter is to offer you methods of communicating that have been proven to be successful. Ultimately, to be genuine and sincere, you must be yourself. If you want to strengthen your interview skills, set some goals that you want to achieve for each interview you schedule. Assess the variables and choose one or two areas in which you want to improve your performance. Integrate these improvements into your presentation until they become a part of you and you no longer have to think about them.

Keep in mind that your primary goal is to get the job offer. In the past, students may have been agonizing over an interview for a job they're not sure they want. My advice is always the same. If you go into an interview with any doubts, you will convey them to the employer. If you find out halfway through the interview that it is your dream job, your doubts may have already eliminated you from consideration. So go into the interview with the goal of getting the offer and let the employer tell you about the job.

It's important to recognize that for every question the interviewer asks you, there are two answers . . . the one you want to give and the one he wants to hear. If the job is a good fit for you, the distance between the two answers may be small to negligible. If you find, however, that the answers are far away from one another on the continuum, then it is a strong sign that the job may not be the right one for you. Don't be disappointed—be glad you found out now. It will save you time and a hundred heartaches if you simply withdraw your candidacy or turn the job down.

Finally, be prepared to respond quickly to an offer. The shortage of skilled employees has quickened the pace of hiring. You may find yourself being asked to make a decision with little time to reflect. Go into the interview prepared. Set your goals, understand the issues that are most important to you, and use the interview to answer the questions you have about the job and the organization. If everything looks good, you can say "yes" knowing that you've done your homework and you're making an informed choice.

JAIME'S STORY

Jaime was a highly competent graduate student in math. He had graduated with honors and decided to stay on as a graduate assistant at the university to earn his master's. Most of his friends thought he was continuing on as a student because of his interest in computers. While that was part of his motivation, the truth was that Jaime had failed miserably in his job interviews. The final humiliation had come when a job recruiter had stopped an interview because Jaime had begun hyperventilating in the interview room.

Jaime was close to graduating again and wasn't really interested in getting a Ph.D. Somehow he had to get a handle on his fear of interviewing and begin on his real life away from the university.

Jaime went to the career services center and chatted with Consuelo, a staff advisor. Consuelo recommended a few books for Jaime to read to understand better how interviews work. She also suggested that Jaime view a videotape about interviewing so he could develop a model to emulate. Jaime read through one of the books on interviewing and watched the tape but felt overwhelmed by what he was expected to do. How could he possibly display the kind of behavior shown in the tape and described in the book? It might be easy for some people but he knew he couldn't do it and didn't even want to try. He decided he would take the books and tape back to the center and not even bother the advisor anymore. He was hopeless.

When Jaime got to the center, he tried just to drop the materials off, but Consuelo was at the front desk when he walked in. She was glad to see Jaime and commented on how quickly he had returned. Consuelo was eager to know what Jaime thought of the information he had reviewed. At first, Jaime said that he thought it was great, really helpful, but as he continued he started to feel angry. Why was it so important to act a certain way in interviews? Couldn't they see he was smart and hard-working just from his academic record and resume?

Consuelo sensed Jaime's frustration and suggested they talk a bit more. After a long discussion of the whys and hows of recruiters' behaviors, Jaime relaxed a bit. Consuelo knew he was trying but was having a hard time finding a way to approach his problem. She suggested two things to Jaime for managing his anxiety. "First," she said, "set one goal before you go to the interview. Maybe it's something as simple as wearing a good suit and polished shoes and trimming your hair. Don't worry about getting a job offer just yet. Work on one thing at a time. Then, after you have set your goal, go to the interview and 'act as if' you are the guy in the videotape. Even if you are nervous or worried on the inside, pretend that you are comfortable and at ease. Whatever else happens, never admit to your interviewer that you are nervous—just get through the interview."

Jaime listened to Consuelo skeptically. He was still unhappy that he would have to go through the same gauntlet as everyone else, but he was starting to accept the fact that it was the only path to the goal—a job doing what he loved. He told her he would try.

Jaime signed up for an on-campus interview and borrowed his roommate's suit. He got a good haircut, shined his shoes, and smiled at himself in the mirror so much that his roommate yelled at him for hogging the bathroom. The day of the interview was no different from the ones that Jaime had experienced before. He woke up groggy from a worried sleep and found himself sweating at breakfast. He wondered how everyone else in the cafeteria could be so calm when he was so frightened.

Then it dawned on him. No one knew how he felt about the interview. No one could tell from looking at him how much he was tied up in knots. No one, not even the interviewer, would recognize his anxiety unless he let them know. For some reason, this was encouraging to Jaime. He felt a little more in control. He looked at the interview differently now. Even if he didn't get the job, he would determine what he would show the interviewer and today he would *not* show his fear.

Jaime arrived at the interview and began sweating in the lobby. He saw Consuelo and she gave him a "thumbs up" and told him how great he looked. Jaime was grateful, even though he felt she was only saying it to make him feel better. At the exact moment that Jaime had decided he couldn't go through with it, he noticed a tall African-American man in a double-breasted suit moving toward him who introduced himself as his recruiter. Jaime swallowed hard, rubbed his palm on his jacket, and shook hands. He followed the recruiter back to the interview room and closed the door.

Most of the interview was a blur to Jaime. He got through it though and signed up for another the next day. Four more interviews followed in the next three weeks. Each one was difficult, calling on Jaime to reach down into himself and find his courage. But he did it and he did more than that. He tried what Consuelo had suggested. For each interview he worked on one thing. One time it was his eye contact, the next, his answers to questions, another his facial expression, and so on. Each time he confronted a new issue, the ones he had worked on before were already behind him and he felt confident in his new-found skills.

By the end of on-campus interviewing, Jaime had a second interview scheduled with two different companies. He wasn't sure whether either one would produce a job offer, but he felt good enough about his prospects that he threw the Ph.D. applications away.

Pulling It All Together

Before you go to your first interview, check this list to make sure you are prepared.

_____ Does my appearance (dress, shoes, hair, accessories) present the image that is appropriate for a business meeting for the field in which I seek employment?

_____ Have I thought through the answers to the typical questions encountered in an interview?

_____ Have I sat down and written about my skills and accomplishments that are related to the position for which I am interviewing?

_____ Have I thought about how I will respond to attitude questions?

_____ Have I assessed my nonverbal behavior or asked someone to observe and critique my nonverbal cues so that they convey a professional image?

_____ Do I have a list of relevant questions for my interviewer?

_____ Have I practiced my interview visualization exercise?

_____ Am I excited and happy to be meeting my interviewer?

_____ Have I set my goals and know what I want to accomplish in the interview?

A LOOK BACK

This chapter has introduced you to the complex ritual of interviewing and your role in making it a productive and positive experience. It is part meeting to exchange information, part sales presentation, part friendly visit, part performance.

The interview can seem at times like a mystery over which you have no control. In fact, the variables over which you have control are those that have the greatest influence on the outcome. Your appearance is a variable over which you exert complete control and which you can use to your advantage. The answers to questions, whether about skills, attitude, or scenarios, are also under your control. Your nonverbal cues can be an important part of communicating with the employer and demonstrating a positive image. The tone of the interview, though generally set by the interviewer, can offer you the opportunity to establish yourself as a businesslike and friendly individual. Finally, you can use the questions you ask the interviewer to support your image as a strong candidate for the position and lead the interviewer to your most important skills.

You should be able to set goals when approaching the interview, with the primary goal of getting the job offer. Then prepare yourself fully by visualizing the kind of interview in which you achieve every goal and receive the recognition you deserve.

Other Sources and Suggested Reading

Adams Job Interview Almanac & CD-ROM published by Adams Publishing

This interactive resource lets you respond to interview questions, view responses, watch interviews, and test your interview skills.

Can You Start Monday? by Cheryl A. Cage, Scott Hareland, and Pam Ryan

One of my favorite aspects of this book is the authors' emphasis on telling "stories" that characterize your skills during the interview.

Creative Visualization by Shakti Gawain

This book focuses on tapping the power of the mind to energize growth and achievement. Regardless of your philosophical perspective, the techniques and exercises described here are useful and effective.

Interview for Success: A Practical Guide to Increasing Job Interviews, Offers, and Salaries by Caryl Rae Krannich and Ronald L. Krannich

Preparation, etiquette, and effective listening are covered as well as negotiating salary.

Job Interviews for Dummies by Joyce Lain Kennedy

Comparing the interview to a performance, Kennedy provides an upbeat take on interviewing successfully.

Manager's Tough Questions Answer Book by Al Guyant and Shirley Fulton

This book offers job seekers answers to the questions that create the most anxiety.

Web Sites and Internet Resources

www.careerbuilder.com/gh_int_htg.html

This is a full-service site from which you can gather the latest information on interviewing techniques.

www.collegegrad.com

This is a great site with information about interviewing in all its forms. This is especially useful to recent college grads.

www.dac.neu.edu/coop.careerservices/interview.html

This site from Northeastern University offers detailed advice on interview preparation.

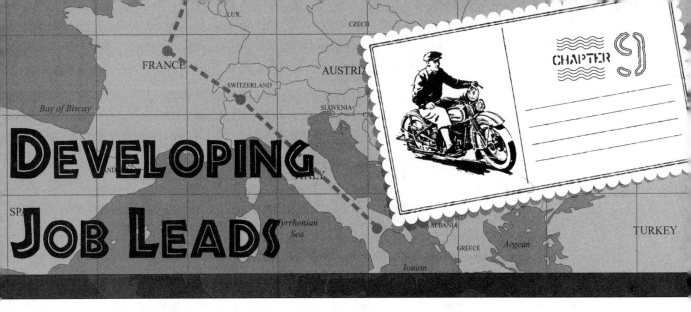

DEVELOPING JOB LEADS

For most of us, the prospect of finding a job feels like a mystery in which we play the clueless detective, more like Inspector Clousseau than Sherlock Holmes. Gamely we follow leads, most of which are dead ends of rejection and frustration. Finally, our persistence and preparation pay off, and we're the right person in the right place at the right time.

Too often, job seekers using traditional search methods end up feeling as helpless as a clueless detective. And too often, job seekers experience frustration and rejection as a result of traditional job-search methods. Over the years we have begun to question these traditions and come up with new approaches to achieving our employment goals.

Part of the overall philosophy of your career adventure is the expectation that *you* have the greatest influence over the goals and outcomes that you choose to pursue. You have acted on this belief in each different portion of this book. The same philosophy is reflected in the final part of your adventure—finding the right job.

In this chapter, we explore the methods and approaches that will give you control over your job search. The process won't remain a mystery. It is more like a guidebook that shows you how to move toward your goals. This is hard work, so be prepared to throw out any fixed notions of what success means when looking for a job.

THE HIDDEN JOB MARKET

The most frustrating part of finding a job when using traditional methods is *waiting*. You see an ad, you write a letter, you send a resume, you wait . . . and wait . . . and wait. Without question, waiting is more discouraging to job seekers than any other single aspect of job seeking.

But you don't *have* to wait for someone to offer you a job. You can be actively engaged in developing new leads and pursuing new possibilities. If you want a job, *you* must find the employer, not the other way around. Too often, job seekers think that employers should look for them, either through newspaper ads or placement agencies. Those methods may work at times, but not often.

By now, you have probably heard of the mythical "hidden job market." Perhaps it isn't as well hidden as it has been in the past. The hidden job market refers to the process by which thousands of jobs are filled. The primary method used to fill jobs in the hidden job market is networking. You are already familiar with networking from the material in Chapter 5. The networking that employers use when filling a position is only slightly different.

Imagine you are Matt, the manager of accounting in a small company. Everything is going well until your ace accounting associate, Shelley, comes in and tells you that she is going back to school full-time and is giving you two weeks' notice. It's February and the April 15 tax deadline is looming. You try to talk Shelley into postponing her departure. She's firm, however, so you accept the decision. Shelley is telling you about her college schedule, which begins at the end of March, but you aren't hearing a word. You are mentally scanning your current staff to determine who might be able to pick up her workload. With difficulty, you acknowledge that the staff isn't up to absorbing her work and you will have to hire someone new. Experienced accounting people are scarce this time of year. Slowly, you mentally return to the office, and you ask her if she knows of anyone who might be able to take her place.

Bingo! That is how the hidden job market works. Now imagine that you are a good friend of Shelley's—someone with comparable ability and dedication but unhappy in your current position. Shelley knows you are available and just happens to have your resume with her. It would be difficult to find a better way to be introduced to an employer. The trick is becoming "Shelley's friend."

You may be surprised to know that you already are "Shelley's friend." Somewhere in your existing network, there may be a Shelley who is in a position to recommend you to her boss the next time a vacancy occurs. Your responsibility is to let Shelley and everyone else in your network know that you are available for a job and that you have particular skills that their organization can use.

The process of alerting your network to your goals and availability is a great way to start your job campaign. It is an opportunity to practice your sales skills before you get to the interview. Here are some ways to get started.

ALERTING YOUR NETWORK

In Chapter 5, you spent some time making contact with people whom you know and some you didn't to discuss careers and jobs. Those people are bona fide members of your network now. You are a member of *their* network as well and, as such, you can rely on one another for information or assistance when necessary.

At this point in your job search, it is important that all the people in your existing network are aware that you are seeking employment. Not just any job, though. Uncle John down at the automotive plant might know about an opening that is coming up in maintenance. That doesn't mean that you are qualified or interested in it. Uncle John also may know someone in design at the same plant. If design is an area in which you have an interest, it is up to you to let Uncle John know that he can help you.

Contacting Uncle John will probably be easy. Friends and family members are accessible and often happy to assist you. All you need to do is give them a call. That call is important, though. Don't take for granted that Uncle John will automatically understand what you want from him. Make your intentions clear to everyone you contact.

When calling someone in your network, have a statement prepared that capsulizes your request in a straightforward manner. First let them know you are looking for a job and you need their assistance. Describe your skills and the job you are seeking. Most important, let them know what they could do for you that would help. It might not always be obvious, so be as specific as you can.

Just as you did in Chapter 5, compile a comprehensive list of people who could help you. Then get on the phone and let them know you need them to be your eyes and ears in your job hunt. Not everyone will be able to channel your resume. The most valuable help you can receive is information about a possible opening and whom you might contact. Any help at all can be a welcome advantage over your competition.

Exercise 9.1 will help prepare you to ask the people in your network for assistance.

TAKE A CLOSER LOOK 9.1

Enlist Your Network's Support

During your initial contact with those in your network, let them know in exact terms what you believe their role is. Choose your words thoughtfully. Your statement should cover four issues:

1. The fact that you are looking for a job:

   "I'll be graduating in June and I'm starting to look for a job."

   "I've decided to make some changes and my career is one of the things I'm thinking of changing."

   "I'm eager for a chance to do something that's related to my major so I'm looking for a new job."

2. Why the person might be in a position to help:

   "You work in the field I'm interested in and probably hear about things before anyone else."

   "I enjoyed working with you at the plant and thought you might know what's happening in the field."

   "You were a big help to me before and I am hoping that you might be in a position to help me out again."

3. What skills you bring to the job:

   "I have a good background in engineering with special skills in the use of AutoCAD."

   "I've written ad copy for a number of local firms and have had some experience in public relations."

4. What the person can do for you:

   "Can I use your name as a reference?"

"Have you heard of any jobs that might be available at your company? Do you know someone specific I could contact about a job? Could I use your name when I contact that person?"

Use the following space to develop your own statement that tells the person in your network what he could do to give you a boost into your career.

NETWORKING STATEMENT

_____

_____

This statement will change depending on the person with whom you are talking and what that person might be able to do for you. Work on perfecting your delivery in a calm, self-assured manner. Remember, your current network of friends, family, college acquaintances, and work associates will be the easy ones. Take advantage of this type of networking contact to see what it feels like to "sell yourself" both in person and over the phone.

Try the dialogue out with a partner in your group or the class and then discuss how it might feel to ask for someone's assistance.

ACCEPTING SUPPORT

For some job seekers, asking for help from the people in their network causes great anxiety and discomfort. Sometimes asking someone you know for assistance is more difficult than asking a stranger.

Based on what you learned in Chapter 5, you know that using the telephone to contact people can result in obtaining valuable information about careers and organizations. The process of networking for a job is similar. You are not asking for a job. You are recruiting the people in your network to provide you with support through information and referrals. None of us would mind helping someone if we could. It is a win-win situation. It solidifies and reaffirms our relationships with one another and offers us a chance to do something worthwhile with minimal effort. When the time comes, you will provide the same support to someone else, whether it is the person who helped you or someone new. Anyone who provides information to someone that results in a job offer will likely have a favor returned to them at some time in the future. The network continually renews itself through everyone's efforts. Now it's your opportunity to become a part of a network that could be a continuing asset in your career for many years.

MARKETING YOURSELF

You are ready to start your all-out, full-court-press marketing campaign. You have informed all your initial contacts and may have been able to generate some leads from that effort. In what other ways can you market yourself?

The most important aspect of marketing yourself is constantly being on the lookout for an opportunity to sell your skills. Every person you encounter during this time is a potential resource of information and referral. Let everyone you meet, even through a chance encounter, know what you are looking for and ask them to help. One of the simplest ways to do this is to carry index cards with your name, address, phone numbers, and a brief statement of your skills and the job you want. Bring them with you wherever you go, and if you do happen to run into someone you haven't contacted yet, just pull out a card. Every time you leave your home is an opportunity to extend your network a bit further.

If you intend to use the newspaper to seek employment, go beyond the want ads. Read the paper from front to back looking for any information that could lead you to your future employer. An article that mentions a company's new contract, the expansion of an organization, or a promotion can mean that the company will soon need to hire a new person. There is no reason why it shouldn't be you.

Now is also the time to go back to the resources you accessed in Chapter 4. Look at the directories in the library that detail information about companies in your field of interest. *The Harris Industrial Directory*, *Thomas' Register*, and *Standard & Poor's* offer job seekers information about companies that provide a host of employment opportunities. Local resources such as the chamber of commerce and the yellow pages can be valuable in your exploration of the job market. Specialized publications such as Gale's *Job Seeker's Guide to Private and Public Companies*, or the *Job Hunter's Sourcebook* focus on a wide range of information about companies and sources for leads.

Using the traditional methods of finding employment is a good start—you also want to include any other avenues you can. The conventional approaches represent only 20 percent of the jobs that need to be filled and are usually found in the want ads. At first glance, the ads can seem to offer a wealth of possibilities. However, you have no way of knowing who will read your resume or with whom you are competing. Sometimes ads that seem to describe you to a T will be the ones you enthusiastically write to but never hear from. Did they have a candidate in mind already? Did someone better qualified than you apply? You will never know.

Other times, jobs that seem like a long shot will be the ones for which the employers are dying to interview you. Essentially, there is no logic to the process so don't even try to understand it. Do try everything.

Job banks may be useful if they are available where you live. Hospitals, government agencies, public utilities, and colleges frequently offer recorded message lines that relay to callers what positions are available and how you might go about applying for the jobs.

A more recent development in job seeking is the increase of the *career fair* as a job-seeking tool. These events are typically focused on a particular career emphasis such as health careers or information technology careers. A career fair is essentially a sales pitch from employers with immediate openings seeking potential employees with hard-to-find skills. During the career fair, organization representatives meet and greet job seekers and present the organization's opportunities. They prequalify candidates for possible further examination and, in some cases, may schedule interviews on the spot. If you are planning to attend a career fair, dress as you would for an interview. Bring several copies of your resume for distribution and be prepared to answer a few cursory questions as part of the screening process. Smile warmly, shake hands firmly, and try to stay fresh through the repetitious ritual of meeting lots of human resource professionals.

Using the career services office at your college should also be part of your search strategy. There are companies that rely heavily on college career services offices for referrals and resumes. Register for services and discuss the particulars of your search with the professionals there. Become familiar with the referral system and take full advantage of whatever information is available. The advisors are not in a position to "place" you on a job. Take their advice and support seriously, but remember that you are responsible for your own success.

At some point you may want to consider working with a placement agency. If you decide to pursue this avenue, do so with your eyes wide open. The people with placement agencies generally work on a contingency basis. That is, they find people for jobs, not jobs for people, and they are paid only if they deliver. Your value to them is related to how much money they can make placing you in a job. An interview with an agency person will probably be congenial since the person never knows when an employer might call and need exactly the skills you have. Don't be disappointed if you don't hear from agencies. They will call you only if an employer has called them first. If they make the placement and charge their fee, your worth could be as much as 30 percent more than if you had called the employer yourself. You are better off foregoing the services of a placement agency and marketing yourself directly to the employer.

USING THE INTERNET

Today it may be easier than ever to market yourself directly to employers, thanks to the networks that link computer users around the world. It is now possible to accomplish the following (and much more!) using a personal computer (PC). More information about each of these topics is presented on the following pages.

1. Research organizations and potential employers through electronic employer databases.
2. Access online job ads from around the nation and world.
3. Distribute your resume to potential employers via computer.

Depending on the career you wish to establish, the type of job you are seeking, and the geographical parameters you set for your job search, the following resources will be of greater or lesser significance to you. If you wish to stay in your current location, the local newspaper may be your most important printed information source, while others may find they need to broaden their job search to include electronic methods. Should you decide that an electronic job search will benefit you, the first step is to investigate resources that may be appropriate to your search.

The key issue that may determine the extent of your use of electronic resources is access. Most colleges and universities now offer access to the Internet. If you do not have a home computer, check out what access services your college or university offers students. Residential colleges with the best services offer a port-to-pillow ratio of 1 : 1. Community colleges and commuter universities should offer various locations, including the classroom, where you can hook up.

Free internet access is now available from a variety of freenet internet service providers (ISP), like *Juno* or *Accessmicro.com*. (A list of free ISPs is available at **www.lights.com/freenet/.**) Signing up for freenet access to the internet requires only a personal computer, modem, and internet browser software such as *Netscape* or *Microsoft Internet Explorer*. Once you have completed a brief registration process, you can hook up.

Without question, however, most people access the Internet through the numerous online services available at both a local and national level. There are trade-offs to consider when determining whether to sign on with a local or national server. Although some local servers might offer access for lower cost, their support and services may be "bare bones," which could translate to busy signals and recorded messages when you want to sign-on or get technical support. National services might cost more but might offer a much wider range of information and usage plans. The question of whether you need all that the nationals offer is based on your own individual needs. The names of the more widely used national online services available to users are offered below. These and local servers offer access to many of the more specialized databases and resources discussed in the rest of this section. You will need the online service software to get started but information about monthly rates and usage can be found on the service Web site or from the address or phone number below.

America Online 8619 Westwood Center Drive Vienna, VA 22182	**www.aol.com** 800-827-6364
Juno 1540 Broadway, 27th Floor New York, NY 10036	*www.juno.com* 800-879-5866
Microsoft Network One Microsoft Way Redmond, WA 98052	**www.msn.com** 800-386-5550
Prodigy 445 Hamilton Avenue White Plains, NY 10601	**www.prodigy.com** 800-PRODIGY

The best value, by far, that any server offers is the access to the Internet. Even if you never need the extras offered by some servers, you will benefit from the ability to search the Web for sources and information. If however, you are unable to "hook up" with any of these servers, don't worry. Accessing the Internet is as simple as operating your TV remote. Both Sony and Phillips/Magnavox offer a set-top device that converts your TV into a Web browser and e-mail terminal. You simply connect the box to the TV, plug it into a phone line, and subscribe to WebTV service. For a monthly fee, you get unlimited access to the Web. As technology continues to advance, we will increasingly find access to interactive electronic sources becoming cheaper and more readily available. That's the great thing about technology. If you don't like it now, just hang around awhile. Something new and better is coming right up.

Researching Employers and Jobs Electronically

With the number of career and employment Web sites currently available for review, you will probably have no trouble finding Internet sources. The real problem will be conducting your search wisely so that you avoid hours waiting for documents to transfer and then wading through information that is only marginally useful. As described in Chapter 4, using Internet search engines and directories is the cheapest and quickest way to find Web sites that can provide you with almost any type of information you need. While there may be technical differences in what the various search engines cover, the process is similar for each. The key factor is narrowing your search to yield productive information. There are two approaches that can serve your needs.

1. *Search for specific sites:*   Whether you are researching employers or seeking job postings, you can find specific sites that are dedicated to single subject areas. This requires that you choose key words that adequately narrow your search. The best approach is to take a few minutes and review the suggestions offered by the search engines to help you narrow your search. Sometimes something as simple as phrasing ("all X not XY") will limit your search to more useful sources.

2. *Search for vertical portals ("vertals"), sites with links:*   There are sites that offer links to other sources that can be equally valuable that your original search might not have grabbed. This allows you to go to one site and then skip back and forth between your original site and the related sites offered by links. The downside of this type of search is, again, you end up with much more than you need or can use.

Many organizations have their own Web site and can easily be accessed by searching under the company name. If you wish to avoid the one-by-one process of researching employers, try one of the following sites that offers either information at the Web site or a link to the employer Web pages.

www.careermosaic.com/cm/

Employer profiles, jobs, even online job fairs make this one of the most visited Web sites on the Internet.

www.jobweb.com/

The National Association of Colleges and Employers Web site is a great place for all types of career information, including "Employer Profiles."

www.luc.edu

Loyola University/Chicago has information, links, even a quick tutorial on how to maximize your time on the Internet. Under "Student and Campus Life," click "Career Center," then click "Index" for additional links.

www.skidmore.edu

This site, available from Skidmore University, offers an extensive database of links to employer Web pages. Click "Life at Skidmore," "Career Services" and then click "Exploring Careers" for the links to other career sites.

One resource available to you through the Internet is access to electronic "help wanted" ads. Several valuable Web sites have evolved that can give you the ability to access thousands of job ads quickly and conveniently. Using conventional methods, you would need to search through dozens of newspapers from all over the country to achieve this. You may be able to download your resume either to companies or to resume distribution services as a way of advertising your availability and responding to advertised openings. The number of ways to distribute your resume electronically multiplies every day. If you feel this service may be of use to you, you must do some research. There may be resume distribution networks and resources available specifically for individuals in your field. A good source of reference for electronic distribution will be the professional organization affiliated with the discipline to which you belong.

Many companies provide job seekers the service of classifying, storing, retrieving, and sending resumes to prospective employers. Resume information may be scanned into the database and retained either in its original form or as a standardized form produced by the computer. Sometimes the resume is synopsized into the database. The stored information is then provided to employers using the system. Job seekers can use the service by delivering a hard copy of their resume, but most often downloading directly to the service speeds the process and allows you to demonstrate your ability to use computer resources. Software like *Resumail* offers you assistance in designing, formatting, and downloading your resume to the network that will make it available 24 hours a day to employers.

While distributing your resume electronically is not a complete substitute for a conventional job search, it offers you as a job seeker access to a far greater number of employers than you would be able to reach using conventional methods. A list of some of the services in operation follows. Some may require a fee for access and distribution, but most are free.

www.ajb.dni.us/

America's Job Bank matches employers' job listings with resumes as well as tips for getting the most out of this site.

www.fedworld.gov

The FedWorld Information Network allows you to browse 20 different FedWorld databases.

www.joboptions.com

Job Options is one of the original services linking employers and job seekers.

www.jobsite.co.uk

Jobsite UK (Worldwide) provides a sampling of jobs available in Great Britain. Check the exchange rate between British £ (pounds) and U. S. $ (dollars) before you surf this site.

www.monster.com

One of the first interactive databases with current job openings, The Monster Board is also one of the most frequently visited on the Web.

Perhaps the ultimate in "posting" your resume is having your own home page. If you choose to go this route, be prepared for plenty of "spam," the e-mail equivalent of junk mail. If you that doesn't bother you, free home page support is available through *Geocities* as well as *America Online*. If all you want is an e-mail service, this is available from *Hotmail*. All the information necessary to take advantage of these services, including how to design your Web page, is available at these sites. The Internet addresses are:

Geocities   **www.geocities.com**
Hotmail   **www.hotmail.com**

Staying Aware of the Electronic World

New ways of applying the world of computer information systems to the field of job search are constantly and quickly evolving. Some college career services offices now offer employers interactive online services that allow human resource professionals to access the resumes of registered students based on the company's hiring needs. As mentioned earlier, computer interviewing as well as computer-assisted interviewing, focused on measuring attitudes and integrity, is becoming more common. The potential for the development of new systems to assist both employers and job seekers seems unlimited. Your challenge is to keep informed about the latest in information technology innovations so you can take advantage of every tool available to you.

ENLARGING YOUR NETWORK

Now that you have activated your network, you can begin to enlarge it to include those organizations and people that might be in a position to hire you. Some of the people you contact might have been leads you obtained through others in your network. Others might be people of whom you are aware from newspaper articles, directories, chamber of commerce publications, or the yellow pages. All leads have two things in common: They are all in a position to assist you, and none of them knows you.

Your challenge is to reach out to each of these people to enlist them into your network. There are two basic ways to accomplish this. The first is the conventional method of launching a letter-writing campaign. Develop a standard cover letter that attempts to persuade the person to contact you to discuss possible employment opportunities. This method can be productive, but you typically get responses from only 1 to 2 percent of those contacted. That means you must send out 100 letters to get one or two calls. To boost the possibility of results, you can include a line at the end of the letter letting the person know that *you* will be contacting *her* on a particular date at a particular time to follow up. You might get a few more interviews so be sure to follow up with the phone call and not squander that lead.

A more productive method is the telephone campaign. Think back to Matt, the desperate accounting supervisor. Suppose Shelley tells him that she doesn't know anyone who can help him. Just as she leaves his office the phone rings. You are calling to tell him that you are graduating soon. You are skilled in corporate accounting and tax work and would like to schedule an appointment with him. Not only will Matt clear his calendar to accommodate your schedule, but he'll also consider you an exceptional candidate based on your skills, initiative, and self-confidence.

Landing a job is, of course, the ideal telephone campaign result. You might be surprised to know that it happens regularly to people who employ these methods. Why is this approach so successful? Because people know the right people to call and what to say.

It is usually counterproductive to contact the human resources department. The people there may not necessarily know about relevant job vacancies and can be very skeptical about people applying for employment. Just as you did in Chapter 5, contact the person who works in the field that you wish to enter. If it is accounting, call and ask for the name of the person who manages accounting. Managers are more willing to meet with and talk to potential employees than are human resource professionals. If a manager has an opening, he will be eager to meet you. If you do well in the interview, you will meet the human resources personnel when they help you fill out the paperwork necessary to hire you.

Just as in the networking process, approach potential leads and employers with caution. A large percentage of these people may not have an immediate opening. They might have an interest in you, so convey your enthusiasm without being too aggressive.

Try not to scare them off. Attract their interest by telling them immediately what you can do for them. Then ask if you could drop by for a brief chat about opportunities at their organization. Many of the people you contact by phone will tell you right away that they don't have anything. That's okay. Then you can ask if they are aware of anyone who is looking. Even a telephone call that doesn't result in an interview can offer you useful information.

The most difficult part of a telephone campaign is picking up the phone the first time. With each successive call it becomes easier. You save a great deal of time and money by calling instead of writing, and the results are much better as well.

That brings us to the second reason for your success. You must know what to say. We mentioned briefly some of the points to touch on. Exercise 9.2 details the information you need to include in your phone conversations.

TAKE A CLOSER LOOK 9.2

Generating Interviews

The most important part of contacting people for job leads is to mention your specific skills related to the field. If the people you contact have an opening, they will begin to probe your background and ask questions. That is when you will know there is a potential opportunity. Grab it and start your heavy-duty marketing right there. It should result in an interview. Fill in the blanks in the following dialogue to practice your telephone campaign:

Operator: Good morning. Wayne Industries.

You: Good morning. Could you please give me the name of your (public relations, engineering, accounting) _____ manager?

Operator: Yes, that would be _____ .

You: May I speak with _____ ?

Manager: _____ speaking.

You:	Good morning, Mr./Ms. _____ . My name is _____ . I am highly skilled in the areas of _____ , _____ , and _____ . I am wondering if I might drop by at your convenience and chat with you concerning opportunities available at Wayne Industries.
Manager:	I'm sorry but we don't have anything right now.
You:	Do you know of any company that might be interested in someone with my background?
Manager:	Yes, I think there is an opening with Hale Environmental right now. Jean Cook is the manager there, I think.
You:	May I say that you referred me?
Manager:	Sure.
You:	Thank you for your help. Goodbye.

Try out your telephone role play with your partner in your group or in the class. Practice it until you are sure of what you are going to say and then discuss the results with your group or the class.

BE ORGANIZED AND PERSISTENT

Employers will frequently put you off during your search by requesting your resume or by telling you to call back at another time. They may be sincerely interested but otherwise preoccupied. Staying organized is essential to follow-up. You need to know when and where your interviews are, and who is awaiting your resume, a follow-up call, or a thank-you letter. Use your index cards to keep your campaign organized and to record each contact you have made and the results of your calls. To market yourself effectively try to make at least 10 calls each day to people who might be in a position to hire you or give you useful information.

Ten calls may sound like you will spend a lot of time on the phone. In reality, if you apply yourself to the task, it should take no more than 45 minutes to an hour. One especially effective way to ensure that you actually make the calls is to work with a partner in job seeking. Make a commitment to meet with your partner every morning in a private place where you won't be interrupted. Take turns making calls until each of you has completed your 10 calls for the day. Monitor each other's calls, encouraging your partner when the calls are not going well and celebrating when you get results. By the end of the first week, you should be booked with interviews that will keep you busy. Don't stop making calls, however: Continue until you have a firm job offer in hand.

Anyone who is in sales will tell you that persistence is the greatest predictor of success. Your willingness to keep calling will have a greater impact on your success than any amount of luck. Make the 10 calls. There is an old saying: "If breaking a rock takes hitting it 10 times, you don't want to stop on the ninth time." Don't give up on the ninth call or the second or the fifth. Keep calling. There are bound to be disappointments. Don't dwell on the calls that end quickly. You're well prepared and will be successful as long as you keep trying.

Exercise 9.3 provides you with a way of organizing your campaign and gives you a taste of what marketing yourself is like.

The Mini-Campaign

Using the following information categories, make up a form or spreadsheet to track your job campaign.

Company

Address

Phone

E-mail

Contact person

Outcome

Follow-up

Using the resources mentioned throughout this book—yellow pages, directories, professional journals, computer databases, newspapers—develop a list of 10 new contacts. From the prior role-play exercise, develop the list and try to arrange interviews. Work with partners and conduct a mini-campaign using all the techniques available to sell yourself. Keep track of your results. If people request a resume, forward one and then follow up for their response. Even if the person doesn't offer you an interview or a job, see if you can get feedback about your resume or a referral to another source. Be polite, persistent, and flexible, and you will be gratified with the results. If you are engaged in a serious job search and not just completing a class assignment, extend your mini-campaign, making 10 contacts per day until you find the position that will get you started on your career path.

Discuss with your group or the class the responses you received when you conducted your mini-campaign.

BEING A RESOURCE TO SOMEONE ELSE

Now that you have experienced what it feels like to pick up the phone and persuade someone to give you their time and consideration, you can hardly go back to the old assumptions about seeking employment. The techniques described here are becoming more accepted as part of an overall employment strategy. The chances are very good that at some time in the future you may get a call very much like the ones that you placed. If you are looking for someone to fill a spot in your organization, you might welcome the call. If not, please remember your own experience and greet your job seeker graciously and with encouragement. Making calls requires a high level of confidence and courage for job hunters. Your support will help them continue to pursue their goals.

SCOTT'S STORY

Scott was nearing the end of his rope. He had been looking for a job ever since he graduated in June but had been unsuccessful. It was almost February now and he was still working at a tablecloth factory, hoping for something to break. His parents were trying to be supportive but he dreaded even telling them that he was sending out another resume. The look of hope on their faces was almost worse than the disappointment that typically followed.

Scott paid regular visits to the career services office at the college from which he had graduated. He decided maybe it was time to talk with an advisor at the college to find out what else he could do to get something going. He was beginning to feel like a failure.

The career services office set up an appointment for Scott with LaDon, an advisor who was in charge of on-campus recruiting. Scott was encouraged. Surely this guy, LaDon, would know somebody who would offer him a job, a job that nobody else knew about so he would have a good shot at it.

LaDon was understanding about Scott's frustration but he wasn't aware of any "secret" jobs. He reassured Scott that he was not the only person who was having a hard time. Many graduates were struggling to get their careers started. Then he asked, "What have you done to find a job, Scott?"

"The usual," Scott replied. "You know, read the ads, filled out some applications, gone on a few interviews. Same as everybody else."

LaDon felt that Scott had some excellent skills to market but was having a hard time distinguishing himself from the mass of available candidates. His primary obstacle was not that he didn't have anything to offer but that he wasn't marketing his skills effectively. LaDon encouraged Scott to focus on one or two primary skills that set him apart from the competition. With LaDon's help, Scott revised his resume to highlight those skills better.

LaDon also pushed Scott to take a more active role in finding a job. He suggested that Scott register for a job-seeking partner, someone like Scott, who was facing the same challenges and would act as a support person. In return, Scott would do the same for his partner.

Later in the week, Scott attended an orientation session that explained how to develop contacts using the Internet, what to say when calling, and how to organize a job campaign. He also met Ray, who had graduated in December and was just starting his search. Even though Ray was looking in a different field, they decided to work together on finding jobs. Ray thought he could learn from Scott's experiences and Scott thought Ray's energy would keep him motivated.

Scott and Ray decided to meet every other day at Ray's place to make their phone calls. On the days that they didn't make calls, they went to the library on their own or checked other resources to develop new contacts. They practiced their role playing and monitored each other's calls. By the end of their second session, Ray had an interview and a referral set up. Scott reworked his opening statement, this time emphasizing the special skills the employer might want. By the end of the second week, Scott had two interviews scheduled.

Scott didn't stop there, though. He continued to monitor jobs through the placement center, called friends, neighbors, and relatives, and followed the want ads. By April, Scott had made countless telephone calls, followed up numerous leads, posted his resume on the Internet, interviewed with a dozen employers, and had finally accepted a position as a human resources trainee with a company in a city 40 miles away. His experience in taking charge of his search had made him more a confident, self-assured young man. Scott and all the people who had supported him were happy to see him move on to the first step in his career and the next step in his adult life.

TAKE A CLOSER LOOK 9.4

Pulling It All Together

This exercise looks at your overall job-search strategy.

What are your top three skills that an employer would find most useful in the work setting?

1. _____

2. _____

3. _____

Does your statement to the people in your network highlight these skills? Are you clear about what you need from your contact?

_____ Yes   _____ No

Does your statement to a potential employer focus on these top three skills?

_____ Yes   _____ No

A referral can be valuable in your job search. Does your telephone inquiry mention your interest in other opportunities that might be available?

_____ Yes   _____ No

What resources have proven to be most valuable in providing you with contacts?

_____ Current network   _____ Job banks   _____ Computer databases

_____ Directories   _____ Placement office   _____ Other

_____ Newspaper   _____ Telephone book

What system of organization works best for you?

_____ Index cards   _____ Organizing calendars

_____ Forms   _____ Electronic organizer

Have your calls generated any interviews? If not, what part of your approach needs work?

A LOOK BACK

The responsibility you assume for your success is the most important aspect of your career development. The methods described in this chapter are your key to open any door—for referrals, networking support, internet links, or interviews. The critical factor in successfully using these methods is knowing the people or resources to contact and knowing what to say or e-mail. Emphasizing your skills and probing for referrals will create opportunities that result in job offers. Persistence in pursuing leads will have more impact on your future than relying on outside agencies and newspaper ads. This chapter has described ways to make your job search a comprehensive, all-out marketing campaign that will take you where you want to go.

Other Sources and Suggested Reading

The Adams Electronic Job Search Almanac 1997 by Emily E. Ehrenstein

A solid resource for anyone who is job hunting on the Web for the first time.

College Grad Job Hunter: Insider Techniques and Tactics for Finding a Top-Paying Entry Level Job by Brian D. Krueger

This perennial favorite of college grads comes with a money-back guarantee from the author, a hiring manager.

The Complete Job-Search Handbook by Howard Figler

Figler covers every aspect of the job search. His section on "The Prospect List" is especially noteworthy.

Cyberspace Job Search Kit by Mary B. Nemnich and Fred E. Jandt

This book is a great resource for your Internet job search.

Get That Interview! The Indispensable Guide for College Grads by R. Theodore Moock, Jr.

A good resource if you are interested in getting the most out of every resource available: direct mail, Internet, networking, and college career centers.

Real Life Guide to Life After College by Margot Lester Carmichael, Michael Verne, and Nicky Rousseau

A great all-purpose book for the post-graduation job search.

Web Sites and Internet Resources

www.careermag.com/

This Web site from Career Magazine offers job listings, a resume bank, and current articles on career issues.

www.dnaco.net/~dantassi/jobhome.html

This site is ideal for recent college grads who are looking for that first job out of college.

www.thingamajob.com

More than a resume posting site, this site offers a variety of services for job hunters.

TRYING OUT A CAREER

B uying a car is a decision that you have to live with for a long time. We all use various methods to come to a final decision on what car to buy. Some consumers trust the auto advertisements. Others might read consumer ratings or automotive magazines to find out more. They might talk to people who own the kind of car they're interested in. Almost everyone looks over the cars at a showroom, checking stickers just to see what the prices are. Usually, whether the car is new or used, they discuss with the salesperson the car's price. Finally, after they've decided, signed the papers, and paid the money, the transaction is concluded.

"But wait," you say. "What about the test drive?" You're right. Few of us would be willing to purchase an automobile without first sitting in the driver's seat and driving the car ourselves. The test drive doesn't always guarantee that we will love the car, but it gives us a feel for the automobile that we cannot obtain from reading books and talking with people. Getting the feel of the car is one part of the information-gathering process we undertake before the final decision.

"IS THIS RIGHT FOR ME?"

The process of career decision making is not unlike the process of selecting a car to purchase—with one important difference: Most career decision makers don't bother to "test drive" their career choice before they decide. Most of us are in too big a rush to jump into our professional lives and start building a career to stop and take the time to try one out.

The value of trying out a career cannot be overstated. Although no one would deny that the training and knowledge you experience in the classroom is important, most of us would agree that there is a huge difference between classroom work and on-the-job experience. Having the chance to experience your prior learning in a new setting tells you a great deal about the nature of work in your new field and about your "fit" for the career you have chosen.

There are several ways to try out a career. In this chapter, we examine a number of avenues to "test drive" your career before you actually make a choice. The possible ways of trying out a career that we cover are classroom study, community resources, part-time employment, and cooperative education/internship opportunities.

Classroom Study

Classroom study has already played a major role in getting you this far in your career adventure. During high school, you were probably beginning to understand how different academic disciplines related to the world of work and how much or how little you enjoyed work in different areas. Your response to the demands you encountered may have influenced you in determining what areas you wanted to pursue or avoid in your post–high school training.

Now you are ready to use your classroom experiences to determine further what career might be a good fit for you. This is particularly true if the field that you are considering is highly technical. Engineering, accounting, information systems, and health care are all fields that require classroom experiences in which you are immersed in the data and language of the discipline. If you are considering a career in systems analysis, then your study in the field of information systems will quickly tell you whether you would enjoy working in the field. If you are bored with the class's subject matter and alienated from the people who enjoy the class, you would probably be better off looking someplace else for your career.

Of course, if you have a deep interest in a particular field, don't be put off if one or two classes are difficult. Many people hated their academic work but love their career, so anything is possible.

Using classroom study as a barometer of interest works best when you think you may be more attracted by the *image* of a certain career than by the work itself. This author once asked a young woman what she thought she might like to do and she answered, "You know, all those women downtown who carry briefcases and go into the office buildings? That's what I want to do." She didn't need training to adopt that image. She did need to learn more about herself and how to figure out if that image and the work that went with it would translate into a specific, satisfying career. Taking a few classes in business or accounting might have been enough to confirm her interest or to set her on a different path.

10.1 TAKE A CLOSER LOOK

Sampling Careers

Check through the college catalog and see if there are introductory classes with few prerequisites—you then have a chance to see what a particular discipline is like. Identify any classes that you think could help you learn more about a particular field.

CLASSES

_____

_____

_____

_____

If you haven't done so already and you are interested in liberal arts as a major, you may wish to schedule an appointment with an advisor to learn about the kinds of careers in which graduates from that academic area eventually find jobs. Some networking with graduates will also help you focus your direction academically.

Discuss the results of your catalog scan with your group or with the class.

TAKE A CLOSER LOOK 10.2

Learning from Your Community

Check with your local United Way agency or with the local department of human services to find out which organizations in your area would have opportunities for you to volunteer your time and talents. The information and insight you would gain from such an experience could help you make the right career decision now, rather than making a mistake later that could be costly in time and investment. Note the agencies that would be interested in your contribution.

AGENCIES INTERESTED IN VOLUNTEERS

_____

_____

_____

_____

Discuss the different types of organizations that offer opportunities with your group or with the class.

Community Resources

Opportunities to try out careers are available through a number of community agencies and organizations. United Way agencies, hospitals, government agencies, and service organizations all are possible sites where you might offer your energy and abilities in exchange for an introduction to the career field of your interest.

If you have an interest in health care, hospitals and long-term care facilities are eager for volunteers to interact with patients and health care professionals in providing service. While you wouldn't be involved with the patients in the same way as a nurse or doctor would, you would be in the same setting and have a first-hand opportunity to witness the pace and atmosphere associated with the work.

If your skills or interests are in business areas, many agencies welcome accounting, marketing, and business majors who would like to try out their skills. You might even be able to take on more responsibility as a volunteer or intern than you would in the more formal hierarchical setting of the business world.

Another community resource that is dedicated to assisting young people in finding out about careers is the Boy Scouts of America's Exploring

Program. Exploring is a program open to young women and men ages 14 to 20 who are interested in learning more about particular career fields. Under the guidance of professionals from designated careers, young people have the opportunity to develop leadership skills and provide service to their community while they learn about those careers. The career sponsors who act as mentors for each chapter reflect the careers that are represented in the community. Information about Exploring Programs in your area is available from the local Boy Scouts of America office.

Part-Time Employment

A part-time job that brings you into the setting related to your career choice is one of the best ways to try out a career. Many aspects of part-time work parallel volunteer experience. In both situations you are working in the setting in which your career work would take place and observing the type of work there. Part-time work also offers you the added benefit of income, which can be particularly important for enhancing your resume. One negative aspect of part-time work is the lack of flexibility typical of entry-level positions. If you have been hired to file and deliver mail, then you will have little opportunity to experience aspects of your career outside of those duties. You are employed not on your terms but on the terms of the employer, which are not geared to accommodate your individual need to understand a particular field or discipline on a broad level.

Still, if your objective is to work someday in management for a Fortune 500 company, getting in anywhere, even the mail room, is a great way to start your career and learn more about how a large organization functions.

10.3 TAKE A CLOSER LOOK

Acquiring Hands-On Experience

Check with the student services division of your college to see if there is an office on campus that arranges part-time employment for students. If so, look over their postings of available jobs. Note any that are related to your area of interest, even those that may not be an exact match but are perhaps in a related field.

JOBS IN AREA OF INTEREST

_____

_____

_____

_____

If no office on campus offers part-time job support, scan the want ads in the newspaper. See if part-time jobs are available in the area you hope to enter.

Discuss the results of your scan of the part-time market with your group or with the class.

Cooperative Education/Internship Opportunities

The opportunity to participate in a cooperative education experience or internship is one of the best ways to try out a career. Since the first co-op program was instituted in 1906 at the University of Cincinnati, students have been using co-op as a way of applying the theory they have learned in the classroom to the world of work and finding out at the same time if their career choice is the right one for them.

"Co-op job" refers to a job in a field related to your major that allows you to obtain academic credit that will be applied toward your degree. While such credit may not be necessary to graduate, it does provide you with a work/learning experience that is otherwise unavailable. This differs from an "internship," which is usually required by the school conferring the degree to qualify the student for graduation and does not include a salary.

The benefits associated with co-op education and internships can be summarized in three statements:

- You learn how the academic learning to which you have been exposed relates to the world of work.
- You get a head start on your career by being exposed to the standards and expectations of the professional world. It also establishes a platform from which to launch your own career.
- You have an opportunity to begin visualizing yourself as a professional by working as an associate and colleague with others who are established in the field.

In a co-op job, you are in the work environment as an extension of the learning environment. You earn credit toward your degree that is approved by the degree-granting institution. Your work must meet certain standards related to your major field of study or it will not be recognized by the college or university. That requirement ensures that your co-op job will offer you the opportunity to be involved in tasks and responsibilities that are substantial and integral to the work environment. Your time will be spent on meaningful work and you won't be exploited by the employer.

To further encourage that real learning takes place, a work/learning contract is usually developed with the guidance of the co-op student's job mentor and the approval of the faculty coordinator. This contract sets forth the goals and objectives that the student must achieve during the work assignment term. Its primary value is to guide the student in her conduct and effort and to act as a device for feedback between student and faculty for future improvement.

The easiest way to become involved in co-operative education is to find out if your college or university offers co-op and internship opportunities. Most institutions have some provision for granting credit for experiential learning. Requirements for participation in co-op may vary based on the degree and the school. Anything from minimum number of credit hours to mandatory classes in career planning or resume writing and interviewing workshops could be part of the qualifying prerequisites. These requirements have been established to assist you in preparing yourself for the challenges and competition of the workplace. Once you have met them, the professionals involved in administering co-op programs may arrange a co-op job with an organization that provides you with the right co-op experience or may show you how you can use the employer database to arrange your own co-op opportunity. Faculty members act as guides, advocates, and evaluators as you begin to adapt to the new role of employee and professional.

It is easy to understand the value of co-op experience from a student perspective. The full appreciation of the value of co-op to the American economy and our human resource planning tasks is still ahead of us. Our most challenging foreign competitors have long since adopted comprehensive training programs that include a substantial commitment to the idea of workplace training. In Germany, the Dual System developed from the old apprenticeship training model is a significant asset in providing a steady stream of trained workers for a variety of industries. The Japanese model has successfully placed 100 percent of high school graduates in either college or a training school affiliated with a major employer who will subsequently hire almost all of its graduates.

To date, the element lacking in the U. S. model is the commitment of significant resources by the private sector in the training of our young people. Forward-thinking organizations like Microsoft have recently initiated programs that provide for training combined with hands-on experience for careers, such as information technology, that are experiencing shortages of new hires. These programs are still a novelty, however. Until business understands the obstacles it faces by not ensuring the career growth of our work force's youngest members, the U. S. economy will play catch-up, continually understaffed in key areas and stealing talent away from each other.

10.4 TAKE A CLOSER LOOK

Finding a Setting to Hone Your Skills

In order to learn more about how co-op education and internships work, find out if your school offers these programs. Make an appointment with an advisor to the co-op office and discuss the opportunities available through co-op. Request assistance in talking with a typical co-op employer or co-op student. Using the referrals from the co-op advisor as well as the resources available to you through the library (directories, newspapers, professional journals, and so on), make a list of agencies, organizations, or companies that offer co-op jobs or intern opportunities.

ORGANIZATION	CONTACT	PHONE NUMBER
_____	_____	_____
_____	_____	_____
_____	_____	_____
_____	_____	_____

After compiling the list, choose one organization and contact the person responsible for co-op or intern positions. Discuss the types of opportunities the organization offers and the reasons for the organization's commitment to co-op education. Find out from your college co-op office what requirements you would have to meet to become a co-op student.

Define Work/Learning Contract

Part of the co-op experience is having the opportunity to develop and achieve learning goals that assist your growth as a professional. These goals may be synonymous with the goals of the organization with which you are placed or they may be related to learning objectives that closely parallel your classroom work. It is up to you, with the guidance of your supervisor and the approval of your faculty coordinator, to develop goals that will guide your learning in the work setting.

In formulating your learning goals, first describe the broad overall goal you wish to achieve. Then identify a more specific activity related to the achievement of the overall goal. Look at the following example for a better understanding of how to approach the establishment of work goals. In each example, the goal articulates the broad perspective of your work while the activity focuses on the details.

If you are currently placed in a co-op job, ask your supervisor to assist you in focusing on the key skill areas of the job. Ensure that the goals are related to the learning associated with your major. Develop four goals and complete the work/learning contract.

Examples:

GOAL	ACTIVITY
Become more familiar with and proficient in the use of AutoCAD for production of machine tool components	Provide engineering support through the production of drawings and blueprints using AutoCAD software
Develop improved understanding of wholesale distribution management techniques and their application	Participate in team meetings to discuss application of enterprise resource planning (ERP) in wholesale distribution

At the end of your co-op assignment, evaluate your performance on your work assignment as it relates to the goals you have set for yourself. Review the past term and rate yourself on a scale of 1 to 10 (1 = little progress toward goal, 10 = complete achievement of goal) to measure your progress. Ask your supervisor to evaluate your performance as well, ensuring that his evaluation is based on the goals and related learning activities, not on the organization's goals.

LONG-TERM SURVIVAL

One of the most valuable lessons to be gained from the co-op/internship experience is exposure to the workplace. Firsthand knowledge of the behaviors that can serve your long-term growth is a strong base on which you can build your career. In the workplace you will be able to observe how people in different disciplines interact together to achieve group goals, defuse tension, and resolve conflict.

Your first exposure to the world of work may make you feel anxious and awkward, which are completely natural responses. You are transitioning to a new role and a new realization of who you are becoming. All of this ideally takes place under the watchful eye of your workplace mentor, who is actively seeking to promote your learning and transition. There is no better introduction to your new career.

Use this opportunity wisely. Compare the styles of people in your work team. Note which behaviors contribute to the group's progress and which detract from the ability of the group to work effectively. Listen closely to the ideas and feelings expressed by the people with whom you are working. Ask questions that help you understand the relationships within the work environment.

It is easy to dismiss issues of style, work relationships, and group cohesiveness as irrelevant to the learning that co-op was designed to promote. The demands of the work environment go far beyond the mechanics of production and output. Your ability to identify and adapt to the complexities of interacting in a work setting will be at least as important as any theoretical knowledge you bring to your career. It is your chance to become "work wise" about the environment you are about to enter.

Your co-op job can take you far beyond the obvious objectives you have set for yourself. It can be the foundation for your growth as a professional and the beginning of a new type of learning: learning that promotes understanding, creativity, communication, patience, prudence, courage, wisdom, caution, planning, decisiveness, tolerance, trust, enthusiasm, autonomy, confidence, vision, and leadership. Taken as a whole, it constitutes learning how to make your life and your career a success, and that lasts well beyond the workplace experience.

Co-op–Internship Work/Learning Contract

This contract represents the acknowledgment and agreement of all parties that the student will, with the guidance of the work supervisor and the faculty member, conscientiously strive to achieve the goals set forth below.

Goal 1 _____

Activity 1 _____

Evaluation—Goal 1 _____ / _____
                              Student   Supervisor

Goal 2 _____

Activity 2 _____

Evaluation—Goal 2 _____ / _____
                              Student   Supervisor

Goal 3 _____

Activity 3 _____

Evaluation—Goal 3 _____ / _____
                              Student   Supervisor

Goal 4 _____

Activity 4 _____

Evaluation—Goal 4 _____ / _____
                              Student   Supervisor

(Evaluation scale: 1 to 10. Maximum total = 40)

   As supervisor, I agree to provide guidance, encouragement, and feedback to _____ during the term of the co-op assignment.

Comments _____

_____

_____

_____

_____   _____
Co-op Supervisor   Co-op Student

_____   _____
Faculty Coordinator/Co-op Advisor   Date

10.5 TAKE A CLOSER LOOK

Pulling It All Together

List below one or two classes, volunteer settings, part-time jobs, or co-op/internship opportunities that might offer you the chance to try out a career.

CLASSES

_____

_____

VOLUNTEER SETTINGS

_____

_____

PART-TIME JOBS

_____

_____

CO-OP JOBS/INTERNSHIPS

_____

_____

If you have considered a co-op/internship arrangement, list one or two goals and corresponding activities that might be a focus of your work/learning experience.

Goals   Activities

_____

_____

_____

Discuss the results of your survey of learning opportunities with your group or with the class.

TERI'S STORY

Teri was excited to be nearing graduation. She had completed most of her requirements toward her two-year degree in business and was ready now for her co-op assignment, a mere formality before leaving college for good.

Teri stopped by to meet with her co-op advisor, Meredith, to discuss the possibilities she might consider. Meredith looked over Teri's resume, which highlighted her clerical and administrative skills. Teri had been working in a veterinarian's office for the past two years on a part-time basis and was ready to move on. Meredith was curious, however. Just what did Teri plan on doing after her co-op assignment?

Teri just smiled. "I'm getting married in February, so I'm not really thinking about anything else right now. Just finishing and getting a better job."

"What about transferring to a four-year school and getting a bachelor's?" Meredith wanted to know. "You've got a solid 3.3 GPA here, Teri. That tells me something about your abilities."

Teri gave a perky little shrug and shook her head. "Not me," she said. "I was totally bored with school. Besides, I can't imagine anything I would want to do. I just want a better job than working in a vet's office. That's why I'm here."

Meredith encouraged Teri to consider seriously a four-year degree but Teri wasn't interested. She knew what she wanted and what she didn't and, at this point, she couldn't see the value of a four-year degree.

Meredith discussed two possible co-op jobs that were currently available. One was with a small graphics firm that needed an administrative assistant. The other was with a large company at their world headquarters. The division with the co-op job was devoted to operations in Latin America. Teri had taken Spanish, so her choice was easy. She hoped the job at the large company might offer her the opportunity to use her language skills.

Teri was a great success in the interview. She started her co-op job the following week, completed her paperwork to get credit toward her degree, and thanked Meredith for all her help.

Six months later, Meredith was asked to make a presentation to an undergraduate business class about co-op. She was surprised to see Teri sitting in the second row. After class Meredith and Teri stayed behind to talk.

"I thought you graduated last term," Meredith said. "What are you doing here?"

"My life is completely different," Teri said. She explained how her co-op job had changed her outlook. Prior to accepting the job, Teri had no real understanding of what the world of work could offer her. Her experience had been limited to the small-business environment of a one-person office and she had had little opportunity beyond that setting. Her co-op job had opened the door to a whole range of possibilities.

Now she was working in a support position for men and women involved in a variety of business activities. Marketing, product development, engineering, purchasing, and accounting were just a few of the professional disciplines represented in her office. More importantly, she was seeing women perform meaningful work and enjoying the rewards that went along with that. Her contribution was valued and she was made to feel like a full team member. Her co-op supervisor had asked her many of the same questions that Meredith had and had encouraged her to rethink her decision to complete her education. She was still getting married, but she had returned this term to pick up classes whose credits would transfer to the four-year college that she would be attending in the fall.

Best of all, Teri was ready to go after a career that would offer her fulfillment and satisfaction. She could see her future self in the people whom she had met in her co-op job. Teri had gained more than knowledge from her co-op job—she now had a vision of what she could become in her career and her life. She was on her way to becoming someone she hadn't even known existed six months before.

Teri said goodbye to Meredith and thanked her for giving her the chance to see what was out there in the world of work.

This chapter explored ways to find out if a career will offer you what you are seeking. "Test driving" a career might not guarantee you long-term satisfaction, but it will give you a feel for the nature of the work, the work setting, and the people with whom you would interact.

We examined different ways of trying out a career.

■ Classroom study: a chance to check out subject matter and find out what other people are like who enjoy that subject

■ Community resources: places to learn more about jobs and careers first-hand and perhaps even perform work related to your major

■ Part-time employment: earn a salary while you learn more about a work environment and related tasks; a good addition to any resume

■ Co-op jobs/internships: a superior way to transition to the world of work while learning more about your chosen field and earning college credit

A LOOK BACK

One final advantage to trying out a career is the opportunity to learn more about the behaviors and traits that might enhance your chances for survival in the workplace. These are behaviors that can mean the difference between success and failure and are often not addressed in school.

Other Sources and Suggested Reading

Boy Scouts of America Exploring Program

> Contact your local chapter of the Boy Scouts of America to learn more about what Exploring programs may be available in your area.

Internship Success by Marianne Ehrlich Green

> This book is a great source for advice on developing internship opportunities and getting the most from your internship experience.

Peterson's 2000 Internships by Peterson's Guides

> If you are able to relocate for a short time, this book gives you all the information you need to get an internship in almost any career.

The Successful Internship: Transformation and Empowerment by H. Frederick Sweitzer and Mary A. King

> This is an excellent resource for getting the most out of your internship experience.

Web Sites and Internet Resources

www.acm.org/crossroads/resources/internships.html

> This "vertal" is an outstanding site for links to a variety of co-op sites.

www.collegegrad.com/internships

> A good place to scan available internship positions.

www.usajobs.opm.gov/co-op.htm

> This is the co-op job site for the Federal Government.

CHAPTER 11

CONTINUING YOUR ADVENTURE

We act as though comfort and luxury were the chief requirements of life, when all that we need to make us really happy is something to be enthusiastic about.

CHARLES KINGSLEY

Your career adventure has led you to many places but it is far from over. You have only begun to explore the surface of what your career will mean in your life. You will continue to learn and grow, going beyond the superficial aspects of work and success toward a deep understanding of what is meaningful and important to you.

Now is a good time to prepare yourself for any obstacles and frustrations you may encounter. And you can be sure that there will be many, whatever path you choose to take. It is important to prepare yourself consciously for what might lie ahead.

UNDERSTANDING YOUR EMPLOYER'S EXPECTATIONS

"And now, ladies and gentlemen, straight from his last management assignment as the safety monitor for your third-grade class, it's *your new boss!*"

Thankfully most of us will spend our entire careers without encountering anyone who acts like the third-grade safety monitor. Even so, all employers have expectations.

What *do* employers expect from us on the job? As with almost every other aspect of our society, we have seen employers' expectations affected by the increasingly competitive global economy. Employees are now expected to become "partners" with their employers in learning how to do business better and how to respond to changes in the economy.

One of my students lamented to me that he was disgusted with his coworkers at a local plant. He was on assignment for a temp agency but he was appalled to see the employees retire to the back room to play cards after they had finished the work required by their contract. He wondered if the workers at their competitors' plants were playing cards during their shift.

Companies that have to carry workers such as the card players won't be able to absorb the economic losses that are sure to result. The company in which this incident took place has shifted manufacture of some product lines to other countries. The global economic reality has fostered a new understanding of employers' expectations.

The New Rules for Workplace Survival

1. Self-starters will survive. Take responsibility for your career and what you accomplish each day. Don't wait for your boss to come over and tell you what to do next.

2. Be a contributor. If your company is a winner, then you will be, too. If you cheat your company, arrive late, steal office supplies, or "goof off," you hurt the company and, in the long run, yourself.

3. Don't become too comfortable. If you get in a rut and find yourself playing it safe, push yourself by taking on a new project or new idea. Employers are listening intently today to their best assets, their employees.

4. If you become frustrated and do not find the opportunities to grow that you seek, don't whine and assign blame. Look for something that is a better fit for you.

The new rules are actually an update of some old rules that still hold true. Here's a quick review of guidelines that will help you keep your job.

Tried but True Rules for Keeping Your Job

1. Arrive on time!
2. Stay focused on your task and don't distract your coworkers.
3. Accept change willingly and work hard at learning new things.
4. Watch the details. Avoid repeating the same errors.
5. Demonstrate that you can work without supervision.
6. Make sure your work is done on time and is complete.
7. Don't procrastinate. Plan your work and stick to your plan.
8. Work hard at communicating effectively.
9. Seek opportunities for growth.

There are indications that most workers now accept responsibility for their own success. They've internalized the reality of the workplace of the future and taken steps to secure their future on their own. That usually translates to moving on when salary or opportunity no longer appeal. Companies are now trying to instill loyalty in their most valued employees through bonuses for longevity, profit sharing, and more autonomy in their positions. As our culture becomes more information focused, relying on the "brain power" of its workers, employees with the right skills will become the value centers of their organizations.

THE REAL WORLD: BEYOND 2000

As a whole, our culture often chooses to define success rather narrowly. If you have a job that provides you with regular promotions, salary increases, good fringe benefits, and greater and greater responsibility, then you are considered successful.

The growth that the economy experienced during the 1990s surprised everyone by remaining strong for an unprecedented period of time. The effect of this boom on job availability and salaries has varied from career to career. Professional positions are available but in selected fields, not across the board. More "second-tier" positions, those not requiring a college degree, are being filled by people with degrees. More companies are hiring contract and temporary employees to cover gaps in their human resources needs. Salaries and benefits may reflect the state of flux that some fields experience as companies find new ways to cut overhead.

All of this indicates a pattern of career growth emphasizing selected skills. Prior to the 1990s, the typical career path of a college graduate required finding an entry-level job and working one's way up. The 1990s afforded some people shortcuts, but we still need to do our "homework" on careers. Today, graduates should take nothing for granted.

Students in some fields will find competition to find a job, any job. Others will have trouble deciding which offer to accept. Companies that do everything right will struggle to compete with foreign companies, particularly if the work they specialize in is low skill/low pay. Technology will provide new ways to distribute workload, making it possible for employees to perform as well at home as they might in a corporate facility. It will also make it possible to send work that might have taken place here in the U. S. overseas by satellite to workers that can provide the same support for one-half or even one-tenth the cost of an American worker.

Careers are no longer straightforward choices, and you must know what's ahead before you venture down a career path. Yet, predicting the future has always been a tricky endeavor. It can be frustrating or exciting depending on how you approach the task.

The best way to plan for career success is to experience growth one step at a time. Use the research techniques you've learned. Actively seek the information you need to make a decision. Plan your steps to your goal. Have faith in your ability to handle the obstacles. And then work, work, work to make your goal a reality.

See the value in any job you do, regardless of the visibility or recognition associated with the job. Pay attention to the details of your job and perform to the best of your abilities. You may have many more capabilities than the job gives you a chance to use; accept the fact that you will have to earn the right to move into a more rewarding position. Keep your mind and your eyes open, and eventually you will see a job that represents the next step in your career growth. It may be one that you've always wanted or it could be something brand new. Then plan for how you will get to that next step.

WIGGLING AROUND

Building your career step-by-step is what I call "wiggling around." It is impossible for you to anticipate what you may encounter as your career progresses. It is almost as difficult to project the ways in which you will grow and change over the years. Locking yourself into a career path or goal that doesn't let you breathe and blossom could be a mistake. Give yourself room to grow, stay flexible, and wiggle your way into the career that offers you what you need to have a happy and meaningful life.

Does this mean that you will automatically take any promotion offered? Or that your path will always be straight up—with no excursions on interesting side streets? Who knows? You will make those decisions when you get there. What you must do is stay in touch with the voice that guides you today, the one you have been in touch with throughout your career adventure. That inner voice will tell you which path is best when the time comes. If you are fortunate you may find a career that offers you the opportunity to consistently challenge yourself, build your skill, and continually grow. This state, called "flow," when everything seems to fit and fall in place, is the path to lasting career satisfaction. As one of my students put it, "If I can find the right career, one that makes me consistently try to do my best, and helps me develop to meet the challenges, then I'll never work again."

YOUR CAREER: A WORK "IN PROCESS"

I believe I can do three things: I can cook. I can write. And I can drive. Given an assignment in any of those three areas, I believe I will carry out the assignment with grace and maybe even some flashes of brilliance.

MAYA ANGELOU

A remarkable woman, Maya Angelou, has been tested in her lifetime and has found the things that she knows about herself and what they mean to her. She is far from finished with creating the person she is, however. She refers to herself as a work "in process."

If you listen closely to the voice within, you will find, as has Maya Angelou, that you cannot only do some things with grace but also that within you are flashes of brilliance—perhaps even a brilliance that will light the world for those around you.

Your career adventure will be one of self-discovery and evolution. Always follow where it leads. Your career is a work "in process" that will mirror your growth and change, a vehicle to give you profound knowledge of yourself and the world. If you value your talents and the way you use them, your career will offer you satisfaction and meaning. Most important, pay attention to the brilliance that lies at your core. Finding a way to reveal that quality is part of the challenge of the career adventure. I hope, as a result of this process, you are ready for the adventure to continue. If you are fortunate, it will never end!

SAMPLE RESUMES AND COVER LETTERS

Cynthia Cook

587 Sandalwood Road   (805) 567-2433
Santa Barbara, California 93107   ccook18@netzone.net

PROFILE   Experienced nursing professional; specialized training in an acute
                     care setting

EDUCATION   The University of California at Los Angeles
                     Bachelor of Science/Nursing
                     Graduated 2001, magna cum laude. GPA: 3.6

EXPERIENCE   UCLA Medical Center, Los Angeles, California
                     Med-Surg Nurse, June 2001 to present
                     Responsible for full range of patient care for five to seven patients;
                     focus on primary care

CLINICAL   UCLA Medical Center, Los Angeles, California
EXPERIENCE   Student Nurse, September 2000 to June 2001
                     Provided nursing services through clinical training in variety of
                     departments

COMMUNITY   South Central Free Clinic, Los Angeles, California
EXPERIENCE   Volunteered on weekends through special program in conjunction
                     with UCLA Medical Center

LICENSURES   California Licensure, June 2001
                     Southern California Regional Board, June 2001
                     National Board Certification, May 2001

Functional/Achievement

Bruce Anderson

banderson96@aol.com

2367 Golden Lane
Cincinnati, Ohio 45204

(513) 473-5898

CAREER PROFILE

Strong analytical, financial, and interpersonal skills; acknowledged performer and team member

SUMMARY OF ACCOMPLISHMENTS

Analytical and Financial

Proven analytical and financial skills as indicated by the following accomplishments:

- Researched and initiated the use of cost accounting software that increased assignment efficiency by approximately 35 percent over the prior year
- Prepared financial statements for various corporations, including multinationals
- As treasurer of a social collegiate organization, undertook management and accounting of all financial transactions

Interpersonal

Exceptional interpersonal and communications skills:

- Organized and monitored a successful United Appeal Executive Prospector Program at Ernst & Young, which resulted in pledges in excess of $27,000 during the 2001 campaign
- Received highly favorable commendation based on client comments regarding work on a particular auditing assignment

Work Experience

Ernst & Young, Internship, August 2000 to December 2000

Education

Bachelor of Science degree, 2001, Accounting (cum laude),
The Ohio State University

Honors

Who's Who in American Colleges and Universities
National Dean's List
Dean's Honor List

Theresa Kelner

502 Indiana Avenue
Clintonville, Wisconsin 54929

(715) 457-9045
TKELNER@HOTMAIL.COM

SUMMARY

Recognized specialist in assessing and responding to customer needs; aggressive self-starter

WORK EXPERIENCE

1994–1998   Policyholder Services Representative (PSR)
Metropolitan Life/Casualty Insurance Companies

Provided support to policyholders, sales representatives, and other interested parties primarily through telephone communications; furnished information and answered inquiries on billing, coverage, and rating criteria

Major Achievement:

Revised PSR response form to facilitate communication between customer and PSR, resulting in annual savings of approximately $560

EDUCATION/TRAINING

2000–Present   University of Wisconsin—Green Bay
Currently majoring in Business Administration
GPA: 3.2

Other Training: Policyholder Services Representative Training, 1995
Customer Service Seminar, 1996

2242 Springmill Road
Helena, Montana 59601
September 23, 2001

Mr. Ben Jackson
Mark-It Labeling Company
635 Courtney Road
Helena, Montana 59605

Dear Mr. Jackson:

Ted Rose, an associate of yours at Mark-It, suggested I contact you concerning the possible expansion of your design engineering department.

As a recent graduate of Northwestern University, I am currently exploring opportunities in which my training can be utilized most fully. My college degree is in design engineering with a special emphasis in mechanical design. In addition, my internship with Monarch Marking in Dayton, Ohio, gave me an excellent chance to gain hands-on experience in this field.

My conversation with Ted confirmed my favorable impressions of your company. Mark-It's leadership in the areas of design and cost control has set a recognized standard for excellence. My ability to work hard and earn my place on a team have always been my strongest attributes. I am convinced I could become a valued member of your design team and would welcome the opportunity to discuss further how we might work together.

My resume is enclosed for your consideration. I am available at your convenience for a personal interview and look forward to hearing from you.

Sincerely,

Deon Neal

Deon Neal

Enclosure

Cover letter, parallel format

34 Narrows Trace
Wilberforce, OH 45384
July 17, 2001

Mr. Brian Meisinger
Advertising Fresh
59 Arundel Drive
Spring Valley, OH 45370

Subject: Account Representative (*Dayton Daily News;* July 16, 2001)

Dear Mr. Meisinger:

YOUR REQUIREMENTS	MY BACKGROUND
■ Strong communication skills	B. A. in Communications, *Summa cum laude*
■ Full service client orientation	Sales account manager, *Clarion* Student Newspaper
■ Detail-oriented, well-organized	Worked full-time while carrying full-time class load
■ Good interpersonal skills	On good terms with all coworkers and clients

As you can see from my resume, my background is ideally suited for the account representative position you are seeking to fill. My current work setting is fast-paced and deadline oriented. It requires the skills of a juggler with the nerves and balance of a high-wire artist. I've been "walking the wire" for two years now and have loved every minute of it!

I'm ready to raise the wire to a new level. I believe I have the combination of dedication and aggressive creativity your organization seeks. I've enclosed my resume for your consideration and look forward to hearing from you. Please don't hesitate to call if you have any questions.

Sincerely,

Linda Jay

Linda Jay

Enclosure

ADDITIONAL RESOURCES

The unprecedented change brought about by electronic technology has had an enormous impact on career development. As technology continues to evolve it will bring new ways of connecting with people and organizations. Here are some resources that will help you take maximum advantage of this dynamic approach to career development. See Chapter 9, "Developing Job Leads," for further information.

ONLINE SERVICES*

These services allow you to connect with Web sites on the Internet for self-assessment and career exploration, post your resume, and scan job ads electronically.

America Online	8619 Westwood Center Drive Vienna, VA 22182	**www.aol.com** 800-827-6364
Juno	1540 Broadway, 27th Floor New York, NY 10036	**www.juno.com** 800-879-5866
Microsoft Network	One Microsoft Way Redmond, WA 98052	**www.msn.com** 800-386-5550
Prodigy	445 Hamilton Avenue White Plains, NY 10601	**www.prodigy.com** 800-PRODIGY

Free internet access is available from a number of Internet service providers (ISPs). Visit **www.lights.com/freenet,** click on "Looking for a Free ISP?" and you will be able to choose from hundreds of ISPs worldwide.

*These are national servers. Check your local yellow pages for local organizations offering Internet access and support. These servers will charge access fees and will require you to have net browsing software (Netscape, Microsoft Explorer) to access Internet sites.

SEARCH ENGINES

Search engines sort Web sites and Internet resources and provide listings that correspond to your search request. Web browsing software will offer a point-and-click site that automatically connects your search engine with the option to access several others. If you wish to go directly to a search engine home-page, simply go to "www.(insert search engine name).com". Each search engine's home page offers a full range of information on the best way to conduct your search and how best to set parameters so your search yields relevant information. The following is a list of most-frequently used search engines.

Excite	LookSmart	Yahoo
Infoseek	HotBot	Google
WebCrawler	Lycos	Snap

Each search engine offers a window in which you will input your search code words. Use just two or three specific search terms. That will help you locate resources more precisely.

WEB SITES AND INTERNET RESOURCES

While your own search will reveal thousands of career Web sites, here is a list of some of the most useful to get you started.

www.acinet.org

America's Career InfoNet is a complete career exploration site.

www.ajb.dni.us/

Job openings nationwide with opportunities to post your resume and contact employers.

www.alx.org

One of a triad of sites, along with *America's Career InfoNet* and *America's Job Bank*, which provide information about careers, education, and jobs. This site, *America's Learning Exchange*, addresses education.

www.bls.gov/blshome.html

The site for Department of Labor information, including the *Occupational Outlook Handbook*.

www.careermag.com

An online magazine offering articles, employer profiles, a resume bank, and links to other sites.

www.careermosaic.com/

This site offers job information by geographic region.

www.dbm.com/jobguide

The Riley Guide is one of the best sites on the Web for career information and links to other useful sites.

www.doleta.gov

This site, provided by the Employment and Training Administration, is continually updated through employer links and labor market sources.

www.fedworld.gov

Federal database links are posted at this site.

www.jobtrak.com

Internships for students and jobs for recent college graduates.

www.jobweb.org

The National Association of Colleges and Employers (NACE) provides a full range of career support information services.

www.monster.com

The Monster Board is more than a job posting Web site. Learn about careers, network, find a job overseas. It's all on this site.

www.online/onetcenter.org

The O*NET is the Department of Labor's best source for updated occupational information and career development data.

www.salary.com

The ultimate site to find out how much you might get paid.

REFERENCES

Chapter 1

Goleman, Daniel. 1997. *Emotional Intelligence.* New York: Bantam.

Chapter 2

Bengis, Ingrid. "Sunbeams," in *The Sun*, April 1993. Chapel Hill, NC.

Bolles, Richard Nelson. 2001 Edition. *What Color Is Your Parachute?* Berkeley, CA: Ten Speed Press.

Brown, D., and L. Brooks. 1991. *Career Counseling Techniques.* Boston: Allyn & Bacon.

Combs, Patrick. 2000. *Major in Success: Make College Easier, Fire Up Your Dreams, and Get a Very Cool Job.* Berkeley, CA: Ten Speed Press.

Dictionary of Occupational Titles. 1991. Washington, DC.: U. S. Department of Labor.

Gordon, L. V. 1975. *The Measurement of Interpersonal Values.* Chicago: Science Research Associates.

Hall, Brian P. 1976. *The Development of Consciousness: A Confluent Theory of Values.* New York: Paulist Press.

Hart, Gordon M. 1978. *Values Clarification for Counselors.* Springfield, IL: Charles C Thomas.

Maslow, Abraham. 1954. *Motivation and Personality.* New York: Harper & Row.

Maslow, Abraham. 1968. *Toward a Psychology of Being.* New York: Van Nostrand Reinhold.

McNeil, Elton B., and Zick Rubin. 1977. *The Psychology of Being Human.* New York: Harper & Row.

McWilliams, John-Roger, and Peter McWilliams. 1991. *Do It!* Los Angeles: Prelude Press.

Rokeach, M. 1973. *The Nature of Human Values.* New York: The Free Press.

Rokeach, M. 1979. *Understanding Human Values: Individual and Societal.* New York: The Free Press.

Ryckman, Richard M. 1978. *Theories of Personality.* New York: Van Nostrand Reinhold.

Sher, Barbara. 1996. *Live the Life You Love.* New York: Delacorte Press.

Zunker, Vernon G. 1986. *Using Assessment Results in Career Counseling.* Monterey, CA: Brooks/Cole.

Chapter 3

Black, Sandra, and Lisa M. Lynch. 1996. *How to Compete: The Impact of Workplace Practices and Information Technology on Productivity.* Washington, DC: U. S. Department of Labor.

Brown, Duane, and Linda Brooks. 1991. *Career Counseling Techniques.* Boston: Allyn & Bacon.

Drapela, Victor J. 1987. *A Review of Personality Theories.* Springfield, IL: Charles C Thomas.

Holland, John L. 1973. *Making Vocational Choices: A Theory of Careers.* Upper Saddle River, NJ: Prentice Hall.

Jeffries, William C. 1991. *True to Type.* Norfolk, VA: Hampton Roads Publishing.

Jung, C. G. 1971. *Psychological Types.* Princeton, NJ: Princeton University Press.

Keirsey, David, and Marilyn Bates. 1984. *Please Understand Me.* Del Mar, CA: Prometheus.

Kroeger, Otto, with Janet M. Thuesen. 1988. *Type Talk.* New York: Dell Publishing.

Kroeger, Otto, with Janet M. Thuesen. 1992. *Type Talk at Work.* New York: Delacorte Press.

Learning a Living: A Blueprint for High Performance. A SCANS Report for America 2000, Part I. 1992. Washington, DC: U. S. Department of Labor.

Levy, Frank, and Richard J. Murnane. 1996. *Teaching the New Basic Skills: Principles for*

Educating Children to Thrive in a Changing Economy. New York: The Free Press.

Maze, Marilyn, and Donald Mayall, with Michael J. Farr. 1991. *The Enhanced Guide for Occupational Exploration.* Indianapolis: JIST Works.

Moore, Roberta, Barbara A. Baker, and Arnold Packer. 1996. *College Success.* Upper Saddle River, NJ: Prentice Hall.

Sharp, Daryl. 1987. *Personality Types: Jung's Model of Typology.* Toronto: Inner City Books.

Tieger, Paul D., and Barbara Barron-Tieger. 1995. *Do What You Are: Discover the Perfect Career for You Through the Secrets of Personality Type.* New York: Little, Brown & Co.

Chapter 4

Berkman, Robert. "Internet Searching Is Not Always What it Seems," *The Chronicle of Higher Education,* July 28, 2000.

Calvert, Robert, Jr., Editor. "Ready for Work in 2025? What to Anticipate," *Career Opportunities News,* October 2000.

Coates, Joseph F., Jennifer Jarrett, and John B. Mahaffie. 1990. *Future Work.* San Francisco: Jossey-Bass.

Cosgrove, Holli R., Editor-In-Chief. 2000. (11th ed.) *Encyclopedia of Careers and Vocational Guidance.* Chicago, IL: Ferguson Publishing.

Dictionary of Occupational Titles. 1991. (4th ed.) Washington, DC: U. S. Department of Labor.

Dohm, Arlene. "Gauging the Labor Force Effects of Retiring Baby-Boomers," *Monthly Labor Review,* July 2000.

Field, Shelly. 2000. *100 Best Careers for the 21st Century.* New York: Arco Publishing.

Fisher, Helen S. 1999. (5th ed.) *American Salaries and Wages Survey.* Detroit, MI: The Gale Group.

Fleetwood, Chad, and Kristina Shelley. "The Outlook for College Graduates, 1998–2008: A Balancing Act," *Occupational Outlook Quarterly,* Fall 2000.

"Futurework: Trends and Challenges for Work in the 21st Century," *Occupational Outlook Quarterly,* Summer 2000.

Giangrande, Gregory. 1998. *Liberal Arts Advantage: How to Turn Your Degree Into a Great Job.* New York: Avon Books.

Hafner, Katie, and Michael Meyer. "Help Really Wanted," *Newsweek,* December 8, 1997.

Kennedy, Shirley Duglin. 1998. *Best Bet Internet: Reference and Research When You Don't Have Time to Mess Around.* Chicago: American Library Association.

Kleiman, Carol. "Employers Make Office A Great Place," *The Chicago Tribune,* September 21, 1997.

Korry, Elaine. "Regaining Employee Loyalty," *National Public Radio,* December 11, 1997.

Kunde, Diana. "Job Sharing Gives Clients, Employers Double Benefits," *Dallas Morning News,* September 21, 1997.

Lenox, Richard A., and Linda Mezydio Subich. "The Relationship Between Self-Efficacy Beliefs and Inventoried Vocational Interests," *The Career Development Quarterly,* June 1994.

Lewis, Diane E. "Unwritten Pact Gets '90s Rewrite," *Boston Globe,* September 21, 1997.

Lieta, Carole. "Evaluating Internet Resources: A Checklist," *InFoPeople Project,* Institute of Museum and Library Services, 1999, www.infopeople.org.

Luzzo, Darrell Anthony, Dylan P. Funk, and Jason Strang. "Attributional Retraining Increases Career Decision-Making Self-Efficacy," *The Career Development Quarterly,* June 1996.

Maze, Marilyn, and Donald Mayall, with Michael J. Farr. 1995. (2nd ed.) *The Enhanced Guide for Occupational Exploration.* Indianapolis: JIST Works.

Naisbitt, John. 1994. *Global Paradox.* New York: Morrow.

Naisbitt, John, and Patricia Aburdene. 1990. *Megatrends 2000: Ten New Directions for the 1990s.* New York: Morrow.

Occupational Outlook Handbook. 2000–2001 Edition. Washington, DC: U. S. Department of Labor.

Peterson's 2001 Internships. 2000. (21st ed.) Princeton, NJ: Peterson.

Pottruck, David S., and Terry Pearce. 2000. *Clicks and Mortar: Passion Driven Growth in an Internet Driven World.* San Francisco: Jossey-Bass.

Rayman, Jack R. 1990. "Computers and Career Counseling," in *Career Counseling: Contemporary Topics in Vocational Psychology.* W. Bruce Walsh and Samuel Osipow, eds. Hillsdale, NJ: Lawrence Erlbaum Associates.

Resnick, R. Linda, with Kerry H. Pechter. 1994. *A Big Splash In A Small Pond: Finding A Great Job In A Small Company*. New York: Fireside.

Samuelson, Robert J. "The Value of College," *Newsweek*, August 31, 1992.

Thurow, Lester C. 1996. *The Future of Capitalism: How Today's Economic Forces Shape Tomorrow's World*. New York: Morrow.

Weise, Elizabeth. "One Click Starts the Avalanche," *USA Today*, August 8, 2000.

Winefordner, David W. 1978. *Worker Trait Group Guide*. Charleston, WV: Appalachia Educational Laboratory.

Working for Your Uncle: The Complete Guide to Finding a Job with the Federal Government. 1997. Ossining, NY: Breakthrough Publications.

Wright, John W. 2000. *The American Almanac of Jobs and Salaries*. New York: Avon Books.

Chapter 5

Azrin, Nathan H., and Victoria A. Besalel. 1980. *Job Club Counselor's Manual*. Austin, Tex.: PRO-ED.

Bolles, Richard Nelson. 2001 Edition. *What Color Is Your Parachute?* Berkeley, CA: Ten Speed Press.

The Career Guide 2000: D&B® Employment Opportunities Directory. 1999. Bethlehem, PA: Dun & Bradstreet.

Hansen, Katharine. 2000. *A Foot in the Door: Networking Your Way into the Hidden Job Market*. Berkeley, CA: Ten Speed Press.

Mandell, Terri. 1996. *Power Schmoozing: The New Etiquette for Social and Business Success*. New York: McGraw-Hill.

Stoodley, Martha. 1997. (2nd ed.) *Information Interviewing: How to Tap Your Hidden Job Market*. Garrett Park, MD: Garrett Park Press.

Chapter 6

Arnold, John D. 1978. *Make Up Your Mind!* New York: AMACOM.

Barinov, Zelma. 1998. *How to Make Instant Decisions and Remain Happy & Sane*. Bala Cynwyd, PA: Access Press.

Carroll, John S., and Eric J. Johnson. 1990. *Decision Research*. Newbury Park, CA: Sage.

Dawson, Roger. 1995. *The Confident Decision Maker: How To Make the Right Business and Personal Decisions Every Time*. New York: William Morrow/Quill.

Dickerman, Alexandra Collins. 1992. *Following Your Path*. Los Angeles: Jeremy P. Tarcher.

Goza, Barbara K. February 1993. "Graffiti Needs Assessment," in *Journal of Management Education*, vol. 17, no. 1, pp. 99–106.

Hammond, John S., Ralph L. Keeney, and Howard Raiffa. 1998. *Smart Choices: A Practical Guide to Making Better Decisions*. Cambridge, MA: Harvard Business School Press.

Harris, Mark. 1956. *Bang the Drum Slowly*. Lincoln: University of Nebraska Press.

Kanchier, Carole. February 1997. "Using Intuition For Career Decision Making," in *Counseling Today*, vol. 39, no. 8, pp. 14–16.

Kaye, Harvey. 1992. *Decision Power*. Englewood Cliffs, NJ: Prentice Hall.

Lenox, Richard A., and Linda Mezydio Subich. June 1994. "The Relationship Between Self-Efficacy Beliefs and Inventoried Vocational Interests," in *The Career Development Quarterly*, vol. 42, no. 4, pp. 302–313.

Luzzo, Darrell Anthony, Dylan P. Funk, and Jason Strang. June 1996. "Attributional Retraining Increases Career Decision-Making Self-Efficacy," in *The Career Development Quarterly*, vol. 44, no. 4, pp. 378–386.

Martino, R. L., and Elinor Svendson Stein. 1969. *Decision Patterns*. Wayne, PA: MDI Publications.

McKowen, Clark. 1986. *Thinking About Thinking*. Los Altos, CA: William Kaufmann.

Miller-Tiedeman, Anna. 1988. *Lifecareer: The Quantum Leap into a Process Theory of Career*. Vista, CA: LIFECAREER Foundation.

Chapter 7

Besson, Taunee. 1999. (3rd ed.) *National Business Employment Weekly Cover Letters*. New York: John Wiley & Sons, Inc.

Bolles, Richard Nelson. 2001 Edition. *What Color Is Your Parachute?* Berkeley, CA: Ten Speed Press.

Jackson, Tom. 1996. *The New Perfect Resume*. New York: Doubleday/Main Street Books.

Kennedy, Joyce Lain, and Thomas J. Morrow. 1994. *Electronic Job Search Revolution.* New York: John Wiley & Sons, Inc.

Krannich, Ronald L., et al. 1999. (4th ed.) *Dynamite Cover Letters: And Other Great Job Search Letters.* Woodbridge, VA: Impact Publications.

Krannich, Ronald L., and Caryl Rae Krannich. 1999. (4th ed.) *Dynamite Resumes: 101 Great Examples and Tips for Success.* Woodbridge, VA: Impact Publications.

Levine, Donald, and Blythe Cozza. 1996. *Resume Magic: Master Resume Writer's Secrets Revealed.* Westbury, New York: Sharp Placement Professionals, Inc. www.liglobal.com/b_c/career/res.shtml.

Neal, James E. 1998. (8th ed.) *Effective Phrases for Performance Appraisals.* Perrysburg, OH: Neal Publications.

Parker, Yana. 1996. (3rd ed.) *The Damn Good Resume Guide: A Crash Course In Resume Writing.* Berkeley, CA: Ten Speed Press.

Resumail Network. 1996. *Resumail: Real People, Real Jobs, Real Fast.* (Software.) Irving, TX: Resumail Network.

Smith, Rebecca. 2000. *Electronic Resumes & Online Networking.* Hawthorne, NJ: Career Press.

Stromp, Steve. "E-mail Resumes Require Special Format, Content." *The Dayton Daily News.* March 16, 1997.

Guyant, Al, and Shirley Fulton. 1999. *Manager's Touch Questions Answer Book: Word for Word Responses for the Most Difficult Questions Managers Face.* Englewood Cliffs, NJ: Prentice Hall Trade.

Jackson, Tom. 1978. *Guerrilla Tactics in the Job Market.* New York: Bantam.

Kennedy, Joyce Lain. 2000. (2nd ed.) *Job Interviews for Dummies.* Foster City, CA: IDG Books Worldwide.

Krannich, Caryl Rae, and Ronald L. Krannich. 1998. (7th ed.) *Interview for Success: A Practical Guide to Increasing Job Interviews, Offers, and Salaries.* Manassas Park, VA: Impact Publications.

Levenson, Lisa. "High-Tech Job Searching," *The Chronicle of Higher Education,* July 14, 1995.

Madigan, Charles M. "Attitudes of Bosses Hold America Back, Study of Work Finds," *Chicago Tribune,* July 15, 1990.

Questioning Applicants for Employment. Brochure. June 1985. Columbus, OH: Ohio Civil Rights Commission.

Stucker, Hal. "Rethinking the Interview," *Impress,* 2000.

Thomas Register of American Manufacturers: 2000. 2000. New York: Thomas Publishing Company.

Zielinski, Jennifer, Editor. 2000. *Dun and Bradstreet and Gale Industry Handbook.* Detroit, MI: The Gale Group.

Chapter 8

Adams Job Interview Almanac & CD-ROM. 1997. Boston: Adams Publishing.

Bolles, Richard Nelson. 1994 Edition. *What Color Is Your Parachute?* Berkeley, CA: Ten Speed Press.

Cage, Cheryl A., Scott Hareland, and Pam Ryan. 1998. *Can You Start Monday? A 9-Step Job Search Guide.* Englewood, CO: Cage Consulting.

Calvert, Robert, Jr. "Video Interviews Coming, So Get Ready For Them," *Career Opportunities News,* September 1997. Chicago: Ferguson Publishing.

Gawain, Shakti. 1995. *Creative Visualization.* Mill Valley, CA: Whatever Publishing.

Chapter 9

Azrin, Nathan, and Victoria A. Besalel. 1980. *Job Club Counselor's Manual.* Austin, Tex.: PRO-ED.

Bolles, Richard Nelson. 2001. *What Color Is Your Parachute?* Berkeley, CA: Ten Speed Press.

Branscum, Deborah. "Life at High-Tech U," *Newsweek,* October 27, 1997.

Calvert, Robert, Jr. "Why Pay for Something That's Free?" *Career Opportunities News.* October 1997. Chicago: Ferguson Publishing.

Carmichael, Margot Lester, Michael Verne, and Nicky Rousseau. 1998. *Real Life Guide to Life After College: How to Hit the Ground Running After Graduation.* Chapel Hill, NC: Pipeline Press.

Consumer Reports Editors. "That's Entertainment: WebTV," *Consumer Reports.* November 1997.

Coxford, Lola M. 1995. *Resume Writing Made Easy.* Upper Saddle River, NJ: Prentice Hall.

Ehrenstein, Emily E. 2000. *The Adams Electronic Job Search Almanac 2001.* Boston: Adams Publishing.

Figler, Howard E. 1999. (3rd ed.) *The Complete Job-Search Handbook: All the Skills You Need to Get Any Job and Have a Good Time Doing It.* New York: Henry Holt.

Gonyea, James C. 1995. *The On-Line Job Search Companion.* New York: McGraw-Hill.

Iwata, Edward. 1994. "1994 Job Hunters, Take Heart with Tips," *Orange County Register.* Santa Ana, CA: Orange County Register.

Job Hunter's Sourcebook. 1991. Detroit: Gale Research.

Job Seeker's Guide to Private and Public Companies. 1992. Detroit: Gale Research.

Kennedy, Joyce Lain, and Thomas J. Morrow. 1994. *Electronic Job Search Revolution.* New York: John Wiley & Sons, Inc.

Kennedy, Joyce Lain, and Thomas J. Morrow. 1995. *Hook Up, Get Hired! The Internet Job Search Revolution.* New York: John Wiley & Sons.

Kramer, Marc. 1997. *Power Networking: Using the Contacts You Don't Even Know You Have to Succeed in the Job You Want.* Lincolnwood, IL: VGM Career Horizons.

Krueger, Brian D. 1998. (4th ed.) *College Grad Job Hunter: Insider Techniques and Tactics for Finding a Top-Paying Entry Level Job.* Milwaukee: Quantum Leap Publishing.

Moock, R. Theodore, Jr. 1996. *Get That Interview! The Indispensable Guide for College Grads.* New York: Barrons.

Mossberg, Walter S. "Computers Are Still Too Complicated, But Changes Are Coming," *Wall Street Journal,* October 23, 1997.

Nemnich, Mary B., and Fred E. Jandt. 2000. (3rd ed.) *Cyberspace Job Search Kit.* Indianapolis, IN: JIST Works.

Riley, Margaret, Frances Roehm, and Steve Oserman. 1996. *The Guide to Internet Job Searching.* Lincolnwood, IL: VGM Career Horizons.

Ringo, Tad and Editors. 1996. *World Wide Web Top 1000.* Indianapolis, IN: New Riders Publishing.

Chapter 10

"Exploring." Brochure #34627. 1993. Boy Scouts of America.

Green, Marianne Ehrlich. 1998. *Internship Success.* Lincolnwood, IL: VGM Career Horizons.

Nothdurft, William E. 1989. *SchoolWorks.* Washington, DC: The Brookings Institution.

Peterson's 2000 Internships. 2000. (21st ed.) Princeton, NJ: Peterson.

Sweitzer, H. Frederick, and Mary A. King. 1998. *The Successful Internship: Transformation and Empowerment.* Pacific Grove, CA: Brooks/Cole Publishing.

Chapter 11

Csikszentmihalyi, Mihaly. 1990. *Flow: The Psychology of Optimal Experience.* New York: Harper & Row.

Hafner, Katie, and Michael Meyer. "Help Really Wanted," *Newsweek,* December 8, 1997.

Holmstrom, David. "The Voice of a Writer 'In Process,'" *The Christian Science Monitor,* October 20, 1993.

Kingsley, Charles. "Sunbeams," in *The Sun,* February 1994. Chapel Hill, NC.

Kleiman, Carol. "College Grads Get a Dose of Reality," *The Chicago Tribune,* January 24, 1994.

Kleiman, Carol. "New Rules Key to Survival in the Workplace," *The Chicago Tribune,* March 21, 1994.

Korry, Elaine. "Regaining Employee Loyalty," *National Public Radio,* December 11, 1997.

Romac & Associates. "Survey: Employers Versus Employees: What the Other Half Thinks." Undated. Romac & Associates.Index.

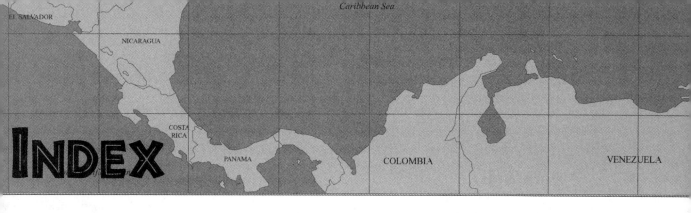

INDEX